A Prophetic Voice—David Smith Cairns (1862–1946)

A Prophetic Voice—
David Smith Cairns
(1862–1946)

An Intellectual Biography of One of Scotland's
Leading Theologians and Ecclesiastical Figures
in the Early 20th Century

Marlene Elizabeth Finlayson

PICKWICK *Publications* · Eugene, Oregon

A PROPHETIC VOICE—DAVID SMITH CAIRNS (1862–1946)
An Intellectual Biography of One of Scotland's Leading Theologians and Ecclesiastical Figures in the Early Twentieth Century

Pickwick Publications
An Imprint of Wipf and Stock Publishers
199 W. 8th Ave., Suite 3
Eugene, OR 97401

www.wipfandstock.com

PAPERBACK ISBN: 978-1-5326-0007-4
HARDCOVER ISBN: 978-1-5326-0009-8
EBOOK ISBN: 978-1-5326-0008-1

Cataloguing-in-Publication data:

Names: Finlayson, Marlene Elizabeth.

Title: A prophetic voice—David Smith Cairns (1862–1946) : an intellectual biography of one of Scotland's leading theologians and ecclesiastical figures in the early twentieth century / Marlene Elizabeth Finlayson.

Description: Eugene, OR : Pickwick Publications, 2018 | Includes bibliographical references.

Identifiers: ISBN 978-1-5326-0007-4 (paperback) | ISBN 978-1-5326-0009-8 (hardcover) | ISBN 978-1-5326-0008-1 (ebook)

Subjects: LCSH: Cairns, D. S.—(David Smith),—1862–1946.

Classification: BX9225.C23 A3 2018 (print) | BX9225.C23 A3 (ebook)

12/04/18

Contents

Introduction

David Smith Cairns (1862–1946)

WHEN, IN THE AUTUMN of 1937, in his seventy-fifth year, David Smith Cairns retired from the chair of Christian Dogmatics in the University of Aberdeen, many felt that a permanent memorial should be made to honor his thirty-year connection with the university. During the discussions about the form which the memorial should take, the professor of biblical criticism, James A. Robertson, remarked, "Stone, perhaps, rather than canvas, might be chosen to represent David Cairns. No medium less massive could so well convey his nobility, his profundity, his calm."[1] For most of his time in Aberdeen, Cairns had taught in Christ's College, in Alford Place, where the United Free Church trained its clergy, and it was decided that a refurbishment of the college would be a fitting tribute to him as its former principal, and that a portrait of him might be placed in the college hall.[2] A letter appealing for funds to implement the scheme included the following tribute to Cairns.

> Few teachers in our generation have had so wide and lasting an influence on youth as our honoured friend. He was beloved by the students who sat at his feet, and far and wide on every continent he is known and revered for his work in connection with the Student Christian Movement. As a writer of many books in his own special field of Theology, he has an international reputation; as a Church-man, his eminence was recognized by his elevation to the Moderator's Chair of the United Free Church of Scotland in 1923; as a citizen of Aberdeen, he took a prominent part in every movement which made for righteousness; and as

1. Simpson, *Fusion of 1860*, 236

2. This portrait, painted in 1940 by Gordon D. Shields (1888–1943), is stored in the Marischal Museum of the University of Aberdeen.

a Christian thinker, he has been in close contact with men in many lands, by whom he is held in honour for his fine humanity and wisdom. All who have the privilege of his friendship have found in him a wise counsellor, a great-hearted comrade, and a man of charity and humble faith.[3]

An impressive list of eminent figures, described as "friends of Principal Cairns," commended the appeal, including civic, ecclesiastic, and academic dignitaries from Scotland, England, India, and America, as well as representatives of the Student Christian Movement, the World Student Christian Federation, and the International Missionary Council.

Cairns was born into the United Presbyterian Church tradition, in which an emphasis on personal experience and a strong sense of mission combined with concern for the rights of the individual to enjoy civil and religious liberty. As a result it was a dynamic and more liberal part of the church in Scotland, with an ecumenical spirit and a tendency to inclusiveness. His immediate family was characterized by evangelical piety, an ethos of hard work, liberal politics, and serious scholarship, and his forebears were among those Scottish theologians who contributed to the move away from rigid Calvinism to a more flexible application of subscription to the Westminster Confession of faith. Such was the inheritance which Cairns brought to his own theological quest. He was among a number of academics, for example, George Adam Smith (1856–1942), Alexander Balmain Bruce (1831–99), Andrew Bruce Davidson (1831–1902), Thomas Martin Lindsay (1843–1914), and Hugh Ross Mackintosh (1870–1936), whose academic work helped the church maintain intellectual credibility at a time of ferment caused by scientific theory and biblical criticism. Cairns's significance is most clearly seen in his major contributions to three areas of church life in the first half of the twentieth century: in the debate between science and religion; in the struggle to redefine the missiological task as the church began to distance itself from Western imperialism; and in the churches' response to the cataclysmic events of the First World War.

First, between 1906 and 1937, he published four major texts, which earned him an international reputation as a theologian and apologist, challenging the prevailing assumption of the day that science provided the only intellectually legitimate means of exploring the world. Respectful of science and its achievements, and continuing to keep informed about its developments, he was nonetheless prepared to challenge some of its claims. In the

3. "Retirement of Principal D. S. Cairns, O.B.E., D.D., L.L.D. Proposed Commemoration of his work." Appeal for funding, Aberdeen, December 1938, issued by Adam Fyfe Findlay (master of Christ's College) and G. D. Henderson (secretary of the college).

language of quantum theory he found challenges to the rigid causality and determinism that had developed out of the Newtonian view of the universe. His apologetics earned him academic accolades, and led to him being in demand as a speaker and lecturer on the international circuit, where he appealed particularly to young people. Through his apologetics he also came to the attention of John R. Mott, perhaps the leading evangelist of the day, who encouraged his involvement with the World Student Christian Federation, in which Cairns became a leading and influential figure.

Second, his international reputation as a theologian was matched by the esteem with which he was held within the ecclesiastical world in Scotland and throughout the United Kingdom. At a crucial time of rethinking the missionary role for a new century, Cairns was invited to chair Commission IV of the World Missionary Conference in Edinburgh in 1910. There he was instrumental in leading the way for the adoption of a more inclusive approach to the different world religions and the subsequent report of the commission provided the church with the opportunity to redefine its role in relation to them. Its basis was a fulfillment theology, which called for a respectful and dialogical approach to people of different faiths, a sea change, in contrast to the traditional confrontational model of mission.

Third, when the disaster of the First World War struck, Cairns was chosen to lead an interdenominational enquiry into the effects of the war and the implications for the future life of the church. In his role as chair of *The Army and Religion Inquiry* into the effects of the First World War on the religious life of the nation, Cairns was able to amass and analyze information collected among the men who were fighting in France and Belgium. Based on their responses, the report, published in 1919 under the title *The Army and Religion*, offered reasons for their disaffection from the churches, developing the men's criticisms into a rallying call for church reform and renewal. In his call to action in this widely read report, Cairns emphasized the significance of Christian social witness, alongside the need to articulate more clearly the Christian vision.

The period in which Cairns developed his theology, the first four decades of the twentieth century, has been relatively neglected by historians of Scottish religion. While there has been considerable attention given to the Presbyterian reunion of 1929, there has been much less attention to developments in popular belief or nonbelief, or in historical theology. Cairns was a highly respected and influential figure in the life of the church, both nationally and internationally, and in describing and reflecting on his pivotal role in these three areas, I will examine some of the central issues facing the churches of that time, and the various reactions to them.

In spite of his prominence as a theologian and apologist, no biography of Cairns has been written, although later in life he began an informal autobiographical account, intended mainly for his children. Ill health denied him the opportunity to finish it, and his account ended around the year 1907, although it did include some letters from a later date. The autobiographical fragment also included a brief memoir of Cairns by Donald Baillie, and was published in 1950. Nearly thirty years later, in 1979, the Saint Andrew Press published *A System of Doctrine*, in which Cairns's theology was presented in systematic form. Based on drafts that Cairns had prepared shortly before his death, it was edited by his son, who pointed out that the book contained much that was scattered throughout his other published works, but with some fresh emphases.

Only one particular area of Cairns's work has been the subject of scholarly investigation—the work of Commission IV of the World Missionary Conference in 1910. The historian Brian Stanley has observed that it has received more intensive scholarly attention than any other of the conference reports, and that it is the only commission whose questionnaire responses have been analyzed in published work. Among the scholars who have studied the report, Stanley lists the Anglo-Australian scholar of religious studies Eric J. Sharpe, the Dutch scholar J. J. E. van Lin, the prominent scholar of religious studies James L Cox (in a PhD thesis at Aberdeen), and the Sri Lankan ecumenist Wesley Ariarajah; but according to Stanley, the most comprehensive studies were undertaken by British theologians Kenneth Cracknell and Paul Hedges.[4]

This study will provide an intellectual biography of Cairns, one that sets his major works in the context of his life and times: it will locate his thinking at the high point of British imperial expansion, amid the social tensions of a highly industrialized society, in the cataclysmic events of the First World War, and in the light of rapidly expanding scientific knowledge. The thesis takes a chronological approach, in order to demonstrate how his thinking developed through interactions with the intellectual, social, and religious currents of his day. As one observer described his theology, it was a search for "a liveable truth . . . grown on the robust stem of living experience."[5] The material has been organized to show the progression of Cairns's thinking in relation to his personal, academic, and spiritual development within the cultural, social, and religious milieu described above.

4. Stanley, *World Missionary Conference, Edinburgh 1910*, 205, 208. Stanley's own examination of the commission is found at 205–47.

5. Archie A. Craig, foreword to David Cairns, *System of Christian Doctrine* (this foreword is a lecture that was delivered in Aberdeen on the Centenary of Principal D. S. Cairns's birth).

The main sources are Cairns's published works and writings, his extensive personal correspondence, and journals and newspapers of the time.

Chapter 1 (1862–1880) describes his family and United Presbyterian Church heritage, and a brief period of spiritual crisis, which was resolved through reading a work by Baptist theologian William Landels, on the unconditional love of God. This work became the foundation for all of Cairns's later thinking. Chapter 2 (1880–92) covers the period of Cairns's university and theological training. It reveals how he recovered slowly from a complete collapse of faith, by setting himself the task of developing a coherent worldview, which he could share with others who had struggled to overcome doubt. This task included a rigorous study of the Synoptic Gospels, which, accompanied by a term under the influence of the Ritschlian theologian Wilhelm Herrmann, led him to focus on the concept of the kingdom of God. In chapter 3 (1892–1906) we see Cairns embark on his ministerial work, first in a variety of probationer posts and then in a twelve-year ministry in Ayton in Berwickshire, where he married Helen Craw Wilson. With the publication of his first book, *Christianity in the Modern World*, he gained international recognition for his original approach to apologetics, and it was in this period that he began his lifelong relationship with the Student Christian Movement. Chapter 4 (1907–15) describes his move into academic life in Aberdeen, having been appointed to the chair of Dogmatics and Apologetics. Helen's illness and death proved a pivotal point in his life, adding a sense of personal urgency to his search for a theodicy. His growing reputation as a theologian resulted in an invitation to chair Commission IV at the World Missionary Conference in Edinburgh, and contacts made there led him into an evangelical network in which he developed friendships with people in a variety of religious denominations, but particularly within Anglican clerical circles, where he was highly regarded and sought after as an inspiring speaker. Chapter 5 (1916–23) traces the development of his apologetics, and includes his major role in producing a significant report on the effects of World War I as they related to religious belief and attitudes to the churches. Chapter 6 (1924–46) describes his continuing theological quest and its flowering in his most distinctive work, *The Faith That Rebels*, and in his most mature apologetics, *The Riddle of the World*. The chapter reveals how to the very end of his life, Cairns engaged passionately with the theological task, and with its application to the life of the church, the individual, and the larger society.

Chapter 1

Religious Inheritance and Spiritual Crisis, 1862–1880

> In every Church there are names that for more than one gen-
> eration have been household words. In the Scottish Church the
> name Cairns is such a name.[1]

The Early Years at Home

IT WAS INTO THIS ecclesiastical family, that David Smith Cairns was born in the United Presbyterian manse in Stitchel, near Kelso, in the Scottish Borders, on 8 November 1862. The manse was large enough to accommodate a family of six and a maid (the defining characteristic of the middle class in the mid-Victorian period). Cairns had three siblings: John (1857–1922), Jessie Brown Cairns (1859–1938), and William Thomas (1868–1944). The house stood on an elevated site, and from its secluded garden could be glimpsed not only green meadows, forests, and cornfields, and low wooded ridges with the Cheviot Hills in the distance, but the sites of historic battles between the English and the Scots. Hume Castle, to the north of Stitchel, was just one of the many grim reminders of four centuries of border warfare that had brought so much tragedy and suffering to the area. The traditional songs and ballads ensured that historical events remained in the conscious-ness of the Borders people.[2] It is unsurprising that this region, steeped in history, should produce in Cairns a thinker for whom the historical per-spective in theology was of the utmost importance.

---

1. Barclay, review of *Alison Cairns and Her Family*, 288.

2. Cairns, *Autobiography*, 39–40, and Carlaw and Ogston, *Stitchill Parish*, 19–20. In appendix 1 of the same work, Carlaw and Ogston list twenty-three variations in spelling of Stitchel. Throughout this thesis, I use Cairns's preferred spelling.

1

The village, situated on the crest of a hill, six hundred feet above the banks of the River Tweed, consisted of one street with two rows of red-roofed laborers' cottages, a joiner's shop, a smithy, a school, and a police station. At the top of the street were the parish church and glebe, while the United Presbyterian Church was in the middle, with its manse at the bottom. Farmhouses nestled in the low hills round about, and near the parish church was the imposing gateway of the mansion house of the laird, George Alexander Baird, whose family had made its fortune by investing in the mining industry and the railways. While the young laird squandered his inheritance in a dissolute life, the agricultural community around him worked hard and thrived. Farming was mostly arable, although cattle and sheep were kept for the southern markets, and the Eden Water (a tributary of the Tweed) with its pools and waterfalls provided a plentiful supply of trout.[3]

Cairns's formal education began only two miles from home, in the village school in Ednam, where his father was a member of the school board. Even in old age, D. S. Cairns was able to recall both the layout of the interior of the building and the character of the dominie, David Pringle, who was much respected by children and parents, and had received some of his education at the university in Edinburgh. Pringle's reputation as being outstanding among the region's schoolmasters drew pupils from as far away as Kelso, and included a contingent from Stitchel. With two pupil teachers to assist him, Pringle might have between 120 and 150 pupils.[4] In the year after the 1872 Education Act made education compulsory for children between five and thirteen, Pringle records Cairns's first day at school as 2 October 1873, when he was eleven years old, and that he had not attended any other school before Ednam. It may be that he had been tutored at home until this point. There was a school in Stitchel, but its reputation fluctuated over the years, and in May 1875 a school inspector criticized it, recording, "Discipline bad. No geography, no history and no arithmetic books."[5] Less than a year after entry at Ednam, Cairns passed the new Standard V examinations (equivalent to the old Qualifying examination), and was ready to leave the school in September 1876, when he was fourteen years old.[6] As was the custom of the day, Pringle trained his students to memorize the Shorter Catechism. The authors had designed it for those who found the Longer

3. Cairns, *Autobiography*, 39–56 and 65–66, and Lewis, *Topographical Dictionary*, s.v. "Stirling-Stonehaven" (489–500).

4. Cairns, *Autobiography*, 57–61.

5. Carlaw and Ogston, *Stitchill Parish*, 89–90.

6. Admission Register for Ednam Primary School, School Records Collection, Scottish Borders Archive and Local History Heritage Centre, Hawick.

Catechism too difficult: "for those of weaker capacity"; although as Cairns pointed out, it was still quite beyond young children. He admitted,

> The idea was that when they grew up and their minds awakened, they could in moments of doubt or difficulty draw upon their memories and know how they should look up to God and out upon the Universe and discern the path of duty. Though I learned the Catechism thoroughly, I cannot say that I have found this come true in my case, for by that time a new age had begun.[7]

On a more humorous note, Cairns described Pringle's method of getting the children to learn the 107 questions, by dividing them into teams who vied for a money prize that would later allow the victorious squad to buy peppermints. "So the great system of Geneva, or at least the words of it, passed into our memories without stripes or tears."[8]

Following Ednam, Cairns attended Kelso High School, a fee-paying establishment for boys. Here the pupils' fees depended on the subjects they took, the most expensive being Latin, math, and Greek, which Cairns took along with science, French, and German. There was obviously some parental aspiration for him, although his ambition at this time was to be an architect or to go into business, as he "hoped to be the money-maker of the family." He did fairly well at the high school, winning some prizes including a medal for arithmetic; however, when he looked back on his time there he did not think very highly of the standard of education that it offered. He enjoyed cricket, football, and rugby although he did not excel at any of these, and throughout his school years there was no indication of the ill-health that was to plague his university years.[9]

Ecclesiastical Roots

An appreciation of the ecclesiastical tradition to which the family belonged, and of the issues that preoccupied its ministers and theologians in the second half of the nineteenth century, may shed some light on the religious atmosphere of the home. This was a family that was proud of its membership of the United Presbyterian Church, which Aileen Black describes as having a "vigorous religious culture" that originated in the industrialized villages and small towns of the Scottish lowlands.[10]

7. Cairns, *Autobiography*, 59.
8. Cairns, *Autobiography*, 60.
9. Cairns, *Autobiography*, 62–64.
10. Black, *Gilfillan of Dundee*, 4–5

In 1861, the year before Cairns's birth, the population of Stitchel village was 425.[11] Despite its small size, there were two churches: the established parish church and a Secession church. Cairns's father had been ordained in 1855, the seventh minister appointed to the Secession congregation that had existed there since 1733.[12] By this time the congregation identified itself as part of the United Presbyterian Church. To understand the character of this body, it is necessary to go back as far as the first half of the eighteenth century. Presbyterianism, as a form of church government, had developed in the later sixteenth century, and was established by law in 1690. By this law it was also agreed that heritors (local landowners) and elders would nominate clergy, and the congregation would have the right to accept or reject any minister who was proposed. In the event that the congregation disapproved, an appeal would be made to the presbytery, who would make the final decision. Following the Union of Parliaments in 1707, when the Edinburgh parliament ceased to operate, the Church of Scotland wanted to know that its religion was secure. Its safety seemed to be guaranteed by an Act of Security which was embodied in the Treaty of Union, declaring that the church's constitution would be maintained "without any alteration therof, or derogation thereto, in any sort, for ever."[13] In 1712, however, the government of Queen Anne passed a law, which Presbyterians saw as inimical to their democratic spirit. This was the restoration of Lay Patronage, which curtailed the power of the people to object to any clergy whom they saw as unacceptable.[14] The ecclesiastical historian S. J. Brown points out that "nearly every parish in Scotland had its patron, with about two-thirds of the church patronage belonging to the gentry and aristocracy and about one-third to the crown."[15]

With this transference of the authority for decision-making into the hands of those who were more often than not absentee landlords, a keen sense of injustice was felt. Drummond and Bulloch, historians of the Church of Scotland write: "Those to whom the right to nominate a minister had been given, and those who were to receive his ministrations, belonged to different worlds of thought, and out of this were to come the divisions of the eighteenth century."[16]

11. Dunstan, "Stichill and Hume."

12. Mackelvie, *Annals and Statistics of the United Presbyterian Church.*

13. Watt, "Ebenezer Erskine," 107.

14. Muir, *Church of Scotland*, 127.

15. Brown, *Providence and Empire*, 21–22.

16. Drummond and Bulloch, *Scottish Church*, 24.

That century saw the beginning of schism in the Presbyterian ranks. On some occasions, troops were used to keep order at the inductions of ministers whom congregations had voted to reject. Appeals to the general assembly grew so numerous that its sympathies turned away from the people, and according to A. Morris Stewart, it too became an oppressor, sending out committees to induct unwanted ministers.[17] In 1732, an overture limiting the rights of congregations to choose their own minister was passed by the general assembly, even though most presbyteries had voted against it. Petitions of grievance were ignored and complaints disregarded, fueling the sense of outrage and injustice.[18] Amid this maelstrom of popular feeling, on 10 October 1732, Ebenezer Erskine (1680–1754) preached a sermon at the Perth Synod, in which he declared that the restoration of patronage had rejected Christ "in his poorer members," in favor of the rich of this world.[19] In an effort to assert its authority, the ruling party in the church courts decided to use Erskine's case to deter others from questioning their decisions. They accused him of calling the ministers of the church corrupt, of charging their forefathers with a sinful silence or negligence, and of speaking disrespectfully of an act of the assembly. Erskine was not allowed to see the committee's report but defended himself assuring his hearers that he was innocent and that he was aware that "there is a great body of faithful ministers in the Church of Scotland, with whom I do not reckon myself worthy to be compared." Nonetheless, he and three supporters, William Wilson, Alexander Moncrieff, and James Fisher, were deposed from the ministry. They had not wanted to cause schism, or leave the church; rather they had opposed what they saw as the prevailing party's policy, and had hoped for reform.[20]

As disagreements over the nomination process increased, many people moved out of or seceded from the established church and formed new congregations. The seceding congregations operated the Voluntary principle, which meant that they had to raise the money they needed, thus freeing them from obligation to the state. However, James Rankin points out that they were not "Voluntaryists" in principle from the start, having at first no view of the connection between church and state as being intrinsically dangerous.[21] These congregations formed the Secession Church, begun in 1733 under the leadership of Ebenezeer Erskine and his brother Ralph (1685–1752). In the following year, 1734, dissenting members of Stitchel

17. Stewart, *Origins of the United Free Church*, 37–40.

18. M'Kerrow, *History of the Secession Church*, 37–45.

19. Barr, *Scottish Church Question*, 60.

20. M'Kerrow, *History of the Secession Church*, 43–66.

21. Rankin, *Handbook of the Church of Scotland*, 240–41.

parish church, including its chief heritor, Sir Robert Pringle, broke away and became a Secession congregation. While they waited for premises to become available for worship, services were held in the open air. The first church building was erected in 1739, just two hundred meters from the site of the open-air services.[22] By the end of the eighteenth century there were between three and four hundred Seceders in the parish.[23] Many of these Seceders had experienced "new light" on the teachings of the Westminster Confession of Faith on the relation of church and state; they had become Voluntaries in principle, believing that there should be a separation of Church and State, and that religious affiliation should be entirely voluntary, a matter of the individual conscience.

The controversy continued throughout Scotland, and came to a head with the Disruption in 1843, when a large part of the Church of Scotland (about one third of the ministers and perhaps half the lay members) left to form the Free Church. Unlike the previous seceders, these protesters were not Voluntaries, but believed in national recognition and support for religion, but they were willing to forego such support in what they viewed as the higher cause of spiritual freedom. They saw themselves as splitting from the state rather than from the church.[24] As the courage involved in leaving behind manses, church buildings, and salaries was recognized, money flowed in for Free Church support from all over the world, from those who identified with its principle of freedom from state interference in church matters. It became a vigorous and effective body of equal importance in the national life of Scotland, as one of the two main churches, with a collection of Secessionists outside. S. J. Brown describes how in spite of victimization by many landlords, who denied it land for building churches and manses and dismissed tenants and agricultural laborers who joined it, the Free Church flourished, and emerged as one of the most dynamic of Scotland's denominations. "Within five years, the Free Church had built 730 new churches, 400 manses, and 500 primary schools, while they were also in the process of building the New College in Edinburgh for the training of clergy."[25]

22. Carlaw and Ogston, *Stitchill Parish*, 83–85. D. S. Cairns's father ministered there from 1855 to 1910, following which a plaque was erected in memory of the service of this "beloved minister." Around 1930, in his honor, the church was renamed the Cairns Memorial Church. Today it is a private residence, but retains the name as Cairns House.

23. Statistical Account of Scotland, Stichell and Hume, County of Roxburgh (1791–99) vol. 3, 290, http://stat-acc-scot.edina.ac.uk/link/1791–99/Roxburgh.

24. Vidler, *Church in an Age of Revolution*, 60–61.

25. Brown, *Providence and Empire*, 116.

In 1847, the main body of the Secessionists, the United Associate Synod, and the Relief Church, founded in 1752 by Thomas Gillespie (1708–1774), rejoined to found what was to become the third significant body, the United Presbyterian Church.[26] In 1752, Thomas Gillespie, minister of Carnock, was deposed for his defence of six men in the Presbytery of Dunfermline, who had refused to ordain a patron's nominee who was considered unacceptable by the congregation. Described by James Barr as "the most splendid, the most striking of all the Secessions," Gillespie went on to found a church that was "by far the most Catholic ever seen in Scotland."[27] Barr quotes Gillespie's first words of invitation to Communion following his deposition: "I hold communion with all who visibly hold the Head [Christ], and with such only." The title "Relief" refers to the relief offered to those who had been denied the sacraments because of their perceived unorthodoxy. At the birth of the Relief Church, Gillespie saw the Secession as too narrow and the establishment as dead and oppressive, but as time went on he held communion with Seceders and Episcopalians, and for fifty years Relief students studied divinity under the professors of the established church, showing a truly ecumenical spirit. In this spirit, the Relief church was the first to make the move toward union with the United Associate Synod.[28]

More than three thousand people witnessed the birth of the union in Tanfield Hall on 13 May 1847 after a struggle to reconcile the various elements of the two traditions. The Secession Church had a longer history and consisted of four hundred congregations, while the newer Relief Church had only one hundred and eighteen congregations, but a basis for union was worked out, with what the church historian, J. R. Fleming, describes as "three notes of special testimony." The first was the disavowal of any "intolerant or persecuting doctrines that might be found in the Westminster Confession of Faith," respecting the struggle of both churches for civil and religious liberty. The second was an article on free communion, although it was couched in much more cautious terms than the invitation issued by

---

26. Historical note: the United Presbyterian Church and the Free Church later united to form the United Free Church in 1900, and then the UFC and the Church of Scotland entered a reunited Church of Scotland in 1929. It was not until the 1960s that the last three or four congregations of the Original Secession Church joined the Church of Scotland, indicating the perceived intractability of the issues for some people. What is called the Free Church today was begun by a small group of people, mainly in the Highlands, who refused to enter the 1900 union with the United Presbyterian Church, believing its theological views to be more liberal than they could accept. See Stewart, *Origins of the United Free Church* for a chronological account and explanation of the divisions and reunions within the Presbyterian Church in Scotland from 1690 to 1900.

27. Barr, *Scottish Church Question*, 63.

28. Stewart, *Origins of the United Free Church*, 57–70.

Gillespie, and required "satisfactory evidence" that communicants belonged to other denominations. The third was a declaration about the duty and privilege of Christian giving, asserting the Voluntary principle. Fleming notes a significant inclusion in the founding document: Presbyterianism was declared to be "founded on and agreeable to Scripture" rather than "the only form of Church government founded on and agreeable to the Word of God," as had been previously stated.[29]

The United Presbyterian Church had a synod with powers like that of the general assembly of the Church of Scotland and of the Free Church, but it differed in that it had ministers and representative elders from *every* congregation.[30] Fleming describes the United Presbyterians as over-emphasizing the popular element, for instance in leaving the choice of moderator to the rank and file of those in attendance on the first day of synod, resulting in an unwieldy annual meeting. However, he suggests that the large numbers of attendants and the moderatorial election process were consistent with the aims of the United Presbyterian Church to "liberalise Church politics, to give a democratic turn to the ecclesiastical machine that had run too long in the grooves of a stiff conservatism."[31]

The struggle for democracy, as perceived by the United Presbyterians, continued in different arenas. One example was the opposition to the Annuity Tax in Edinburgh, a tax that supported the clergy of the established church as well as the city's police. The campaign against the Annuity Tax began in the early 1830s and was still being waged three decades later. The proceedings of the presbytery that met in Berwick on January 19, 1864, moderated by Rev. Dr. John Cairns, recorded the legal prosecution of three men, Rev. Dr. George Johnston, and David and Thomas McEwan, for nonpayment of the tax. The men had stated their willingness to pay the portion that supported the police, but refused to pay the other portion for the established clergy. The presbytery recorded its approval of their willingness to play their part in opposing this "unjust, unscriptural, and oppressive system of civil establishments of religion."[32]

T. W. B. Niven describes the positive effects of the union of 1847, with its practical illustration of how strength is fostered by unity:

> Instead of barely existing as a number of weak and unimportant sects, the united church has grown to be a power in the country,

29. Fleming, *History of the Church in Scotland*, 1:81–89.

30. *Rules and Forms of Procedure of the United Presbyterian Church*, 11.

31. Fleming, *History of the Church in Scotland*, 1:84–85.

32. United Presbyterian Church, record of the Presbyterial proceedings at Berwick, January 19, 1864, 82–84.

wielding much influence by its numbers and by its wealth, including men of the highest character in its ministry, and setting a noble example to other churches, in the energy and liberality which it displays in the sphere of foreign missions.[33]

The general trend toward unity that pertained during the major part of Cairns's life is important to note, as it formed much of the backdrop to his thinking, and the United Presbyterian Church played a leading role in achieving reunification. Progress toward unity involved patience and perseverance, as the differences that separated the different factions had roused feelings that ran high on all sides. The Ten Years' Conflict that culminated in the Disruption, for example, had caused extraordinary bitterness.[34] As recorded in the *Annals of the Disruption*: "Families were divided, children at school took sides, bitter pamphlets were poured forth from the press, the whole frame-work of society was dislocated, and high above the turmoil were heard the voices of Scotland's most venerated ministers, engaged in keen debate."[35]

Two reminiscences in Cairns's autobiography allude to this time of bitter contention, and point to the difficulty of overcoming the strain in relationships caused by it. The first is an oblique reference in discussion of the name of his home village of Stitchel. Throughout its long history it had many variants of the name, which in his time were reduced to two—Stitchel and Stitchill, with the latter being the older of the two. He spoke of the different usage: "For some unknown reason the Auld Kirk name for the village and congregation was Stitchill. We in the Seceder, United Presbyterian and United Free Churches always spelt it Stitchel and to this I stick as a matter of loyalty. I have never spelt it in any other way and never shall."[36]

Elsewhere he said,

> Today many people take a surprised tone about this ecclesiastical exclusiveness and talk of it as due to mere narrowness and bigotry. But there was something a great deal more in it than that. There was something entirely anomalous in the position in which the historical development of the Church and State question in Scotland had put the members of these Churches [the United Presbyterian and Free Churches]. The *position* was unfair [for example, the Annuity Tax], and this

33. Niven, *Church from the Revolution to the Present Time*, 843.

34. Burleigh, *Church History of Scotland*, 394.

35. Brown, *Annals of the Disruption*, 190.

36. Cairns, *Autobiography*, 65.

caused a certain constraint, which it took unusual humanity
and spirituality to transcend.[37]

Cairns experienced at first hand such a positive approach. In 1877, the
Stitchel United Presbyterian congregation was well off enough to build a new
church with seating for 320, at a cost of £2,000.[38] The following year, 1878,
marked a significant event that was to create a relationship which affected
Cairns in a number of ways. That event was the arrival of a new minister to
the established parish church: George Gunn (1851–1900). A recent history
of the village relates how the two ministers consulted together on matters
affecting the spiritual and moral welfare of the area, and shared each other's
pulpits, with evening services alternating between the two buildings.[39] Up
until then there had been little or no contact between the two churches:
merely a relationship of "polite but guarded neutrality." From the time of
Gunn's arrival, a friendly cooperation began between the ministers and
their respective families. A joint Sunday School was started, with Elizabeth
Cairns taking the main responsibility, while Gunn was invited to meet any
distinguished visitors who came to the United Presbyterian Church manse.
A lifelong family friendship developed.[40]

Cairns later drew attention to the remarkable nature of such a relationship between Gunn and his father at a time when ecclesiastical
animosities throughout the country ran high. In the mid-1870s, disestablishment became the major political issue in Scotland, reviving the bitter
divisions between the Seceders and the Church of Scotland.[41] By respecting
each other's right to differ, Gunn and Cairns senior managed to maintain
good relationships throughout the late 1870s and early 1880s when the
disestablishment campaign was kept in the forefront of the public mind
by Cairns's uncle, Dr. John Cairns, and the Free Church theologian Robert
Rainy, principal of New College.[42] D. S. Cairns was sixteen when Gunn
came to Stitchel, and admits that the young minister's "fine, sincere and
generous character" had a great influence on the family. Cairns appreciated the "unusual humanity and spirituality" shown by his father and by
Gunn.[43] They provided him with an early practical example of cooperation as a way to respect the other and live with difference. D. S. Cairns's

37. Cairns, *Autobiography*, 78.
38. Groome, *Ordnance Gazetteer of Scotland*, 1882–84.
39. Carlaw and Ogston, *Stitchill Parish*, 85.
40. Cairns, *Autobiography*, 77.
41. Brown, *Providence and Empire*, 262–63.
42. Burleigh, *Church History of Scotland*, 364–66.
43. Cairns, *Autobiography*, 78.

ecclesiastical inheritance included both the independent thinking of the Non-Conformist, and the willingness to seek common ground with others. His theology would embrace both dispositions.

Theological Inheritance

According to J. H. Leckie, the early eighteenth-century controversy about patronage brought matters to a head and resulted in schism, but the real cause of strife lay much deeper. He describes the essence of Ebenezer Erskine's creed as a high Calvinism that led him to perceive the majority in the established church as having a lax attitude to doctrinal error.[44] A. M. Stewart also records a theological split between Erskine and the establishment, demonstrated in Erskine's reaction to the "Marrow Controversy" which divided the church into two theological camps, the Evangelicals and the moderates. The source of dispute was a book, *The Marrow of Modern Divinity*, published in England in 1644 by Edward Fisher, and in Scotland in 1718 with a preface by James Hog of Carnock, a preacher well-known for his espousal of the doctrine of free grace.[45] The book spoke of experimental [experiential] religion and was evangelical in tone. "It commended the Gospel in all its freeness and discountenanced the obtruding of Calvinistic tenets in the preaching of Salvation." The majority of the general assembly, which met in 1720, took the moderate position and ministers were forbidden to preach on the book or to recommend it. Erskine saw this as further proof that the establishment was drifting away from the love of truth and freedom.[46] The English historian D. C. Somervell points out, however, that among the things that Erskine wanted to retain were the penal statutes against witchcraft, indicating a darker side to the Secession movement of that time.[47] Drummond and Bulloch draw attention to further evidence of the Secession's own intolerance in its attitude to the visit to Scotland by the English evangelist George Whitefield (1714–1770). They were keen to invite this evangelical Calvinist preacher to the country, but wanted him to preach only to Seceders. By preaching to the congregations of the established church, the Seceders felt he would validate the opinions of those who were "corrupt clergy." When Whitefield found himself unable to support the

44. Leckie, *Secession Memories*, 54–65.

45. Drummond and Bulloch, *Scottish Church*, 36.

46. Stewart, *Origins of the United Free Church*, 40–56.

47. Somervell, *Short History of our Religion*, 302.

Seceders in this way, they rejected his ministry, denouncing him as "a wild enthusiast, who was engaged in doing the work of Satan."[48]

The social historian T. C. Smout records that the first decades of the nineteenth century were dominated by ideological and party struggles between the moderate and Evangelical wings of the established church. The moderates had been in the ascendancy since the 1790s, but by 1834, the Evangelicals had achieved the majority in the general assembly and thereafter set the dominant key in nineteenth-century Scottish spiritual life. He describes the two factions as follows:

> The Moderates were the party of the ecclesiastical and political establishment. . . . They stood, broadly, for a rational, impersonal and unenthusiastic religion, outwardly orthodox in Calvinist theology yet tolerant of intellectual deviation, and overwhelmingly polite and conformist in social tone. The Evangelicals were men of a less accommodating nature. . . . The core of their faith was a burning conviction of their personal salvation through the merits of Jesus, a conviction often reached only after a period of profound psychological agony: to "bring to Jesus," to bring men and women to the same spiritual climax they had experienced themselves, became the ultimate aim of Evangelicals, to which all secular and intellectual values had to take second place.[49]

As the century proceeded, the focus of conflict in the churches was the Westminster Confession of Faith, particularly as it defined the doctrines of atonement and predestination. Between 1820 and 1837, a further perceived assault was made on strict Calvinist theology through the publications of another Erskine, Thomas Erskine of Linlathen (1788–1870). Thomas Erskine was a lay theologian who numbered among his eclectic mix of friends and correspondents the philosopher Thomas Carlyle, Thomas Chalmers the leader of the Disruption, and the broad church dean of Westminster, A. P. Stanley, as well as the broad church theologians John McLeod Campbell (1800–1872) of Scotland and Frederick Denison Maurice (1805–1872) of England.[50] Erskine's theology had a profound influence on the latter two theologians, whom Cairns respected and who influenced his own theology. When F. D. Maurice published *The Prophets and Kings of the Old Testament* in 1852, he dedicated it to Erskine out of a sense of gratitude to him as the "spiritual progenitor" of the ideas it contained. Erskine and McLeod

---

48. Drummond and Bulloch, *Scottish Church*, 51–53.

49. Smout, *Century of the Scottish People*, 184–87.

50. Evidence of such friendships is found scattered throughout his correspondence as recorded in Hanna, *Letters of Thomas Erskine*.

Campbell reached the same theological position on the atonement, although they had worked independently. After they met in 1828, Erskine supported McLeod Campbell in the lead-up to his trial for heresy and after his deposition.[51] Although he was an Episcopalian, Erskine worshipped with people of a variety of Christian traditions. While admiring the deep reverence which Calvinism invoked, he rejected what he described as "the humanly devised doctrine of substitution," believing that Christ died for all.[52] The theological perspective of his first publication, *Remarks on the Internal Evidence for the Truth of Revealed Religion* (1820), is encapsulated in the following summary of the work.

> His theme in the *Internal Evidence* was the inwardness of the response necessary to salvation—the assent of conscience—and by conscience he means the whole consciousness, not just a moral detector. The Incarnation shows God's infinite love and within every man was the faculty to accept or to reject. Faith was not the acceptance of doctrines and events; it consisted of a total spiritual condition showing that a man had responded in his whole being to the love of God.[53]

Calvinist theology was enshrined in the Westminster Confession of Faith, which all ministers, except those of the Relief Church, were required to subscribe to on ordination Up to around the middle of the nineteenth century tension continued over strict adherence to the Westminster Confession, especially as it touched on the doctrine of the atonement. In the Scottish churches there were heresy trials, some of which lasted for years, during which time the various assemblies and synods debated the nature and extent of the atonement. However, the contemporary Irish theologian Alister E. McGrath suggests a subtle difference between Calvin and Calvinism as developed in later Reformed Orthodoxy with its preoccupation with the doctrine of predestination. McGrath explains that books 2 and 3 of Calvin's *Institutes* (1559) deal with the foundations of the doctrine of redemption and its application to the individual, but says that neither justification nor predestination was central to his thought, and that Calvin adopted a "distinctly low-key approach" to the latter doctrine.[54] Drummond and Bulloch suggest that the Westminster Confession had "created the conviction that uniformity of theological teaching was essential to unity," and that the moderates in the church worked hard to maintain this unity by keeping silent

51. Hanna, *Letters of Thomas Erskine*, 100–106.
52. Erskine rejected the substitutionary theory of atonement in *Brazen Serpent*.
53. Finlayson, "Aspects of the Life and Influence," 34.
54. McGrath, *Life of John Calvin*, 150–67.

on controversial doctrinal matters.[55] Those who could not subscribe to the absolute predestination of Calvinism, who found that they could no longer accept that God singled out some people for salvation and some for damnation, were accused of *Arminianism*.[56] Theirs was a God who wanted all to be saved and who forgives all who repent. For them, God is omniscient and therefore knows what response an individual will make to the offer of salvation, but has not determined or predestined such a response. An example of such a charge against James Morison will be discussed later in the chapter, in relation to his defence by one of Cairns's forebears.

When the Relief Church united with the United Secession Church in 1847, creating the United Presbyterian Church, it brought with it a more inclusive spirit, which checked the severe tendencies of the Secession. It embraced the principle of open communion for people of any sect who professed faith in Christ as Savior and Lord, affirming the essential unity of all Christians. At the institution of its presbyteries, there was no explicit declaration of belief.[57] The theological perspectives embodied in these two strands, the one ultra-Calvinist, and the other liberal, were not confined to the United Presbyterian Church, but scattered throughout the various Scottish Presbyterian denominations. On the whole, the churches in Scotland remained evangelical and broadly Calvinistic in belief, even if in some quarters this belief was seen as "lukewarm in temperature and not very vigorous in tone."[58] The next section will show how some in the Cairns lineage contributed to a move away from rigid Calvinism and toward a more flexible application of the Westminster subscription.

Family Heritage

David Sr. and Elizabeth brought to their young family a wealth of tradition from their own respective families. Already in his childhood there were at work influences which would help liberalize the church and shape the significant attitudes and dispositions that became characteristic of D. S. Cairns the theologian.

When Professor William Barclay wrote about the fame of the Cairns family name, he was most likely attributing its renown to D. S. Cairns and to

55. Drummond and Bulloch, *Scottish Church*, 37.

56. A view developed in the theology of the Dutch theologian Jakob Hermandszon (Jacobus Arminius, 1560–1609), denying absolute predestination, and declared a heresy by the Synod of Dort in 1618.

57. Leckie, *Secession Memories*, 82–94.

58. Leckie, *Secession Memories*, 63.

his uncle John Cairns, both of whom were highly distinguished academics and churchmen in their respective generations. Barclay was in effect saying that they had made the name famous, but D. S. Cairns already possessed a weighty inheritance going back several generations on his mother's side of the family. On the distaff side, the line stretched back from his maternal grandmother, Janet Brown (1800–1900), who was descended from a long line of well-known Browns that led directly back to John Brown of Haddington (1722–1787), who was the great-great grandfather of David Smith Cairns. In a sense the family easily fits into that category of "rambling clerical kinship dynasties" described by Aileen Black: "The Secession clergy tended to marry the daughters of fellow ministers and it was expected that at least one of their sons would follow his father into the ministry. Such practices enhanced the self-image of the 'clan' as the exclusive guardians of denominational traditions, linking back to the Four Brethren [Ebenezer Erskine and the three other founders of the Secession Church]."[59]

John Brown of Haddington lived at a time when moderatism was in the ascendancy, and when, to some, religion had lost its vitality. He was a minister of the Secession Church and a theologian, with an exhaustive knowledge of the Bible, and proficient in several languages including Greek and Hebrew. According to his biographer, Robert Mackenzie, "No better representative of its [the Secession's] spirit and genius in the second generation could be found than John Brown of Haddington." Mackenzie also credits him as follows: "It is to men of the stamp of John Brown we owe it that Scotland was saved from the dull effect of the strong current that was bearing religion to an arid desert. His work . . . did much to keep in full flow the stream of his evangelical truth that was in time to fertilize the land."[60]

Born into a humble but religious home, Brown was self-taught, achieving such an exceptional level of learning that he was accepted for training for the ministry without a university degree, and later served the associate synod of the Secession Church as its theological professor. Andrew Thomson described Brown's "wide and sustained reputation," based on the combination of intellect and deep piety which he embodied, and referred to him as "one of the most valuable contributors to the theological literature of his age."[61] He was a prolific author, and J. M'Kerrow describes Brown's publications as not original, but of "excellent practical tendency," and with a "high-toned piety."[62] His most substantial work was

59. Black, *Gilfillan of Dundee*, 17.
60. Mackenzie, *John Brown of Haddington*, 7.
61. Thomson, *United Presbyterian Fathers*, pt. 1, 169.
62. M'Kerrow, *History of the Secession Church*, 854–59.

The Self-Interpreting Bible (1778), by which he tried to make the Bible accessible to the lay majority. Mackenzie describes it as a monument to his wide and extensive reading, declaring that it was as familiar to Presbyterians, and as treasured by them, as John Bunyan's *Pilgrim's Progress*. It brought him a worldwide reputation, and passing through twenty-six editions, became known as "Brown's Bible."[63]

John Brown of Haddington was also an impressive preacher, the force of whose sermons was admired even by the philosopher David Hume, who said of him that when he preached, he spoke "as if he were conscious that the Son of God stood at his elbow."[64] Brown's first work was an effort to explain the Westminster Confession, especially so that young people could understand it.[65] Although a Calvinist, he was not of the sternest kind, but of the evangelical type, as illustrated in his reaction to one of his dying parishioners. In conversation with the woman on her deathbed, he asked her what she would do if, after all God had done for her, he let her drop into hell. He was pleased with her immediate reply, "E'en's [even as] He likes, if He does, He'll lose mair than I'll do." The woman was suggesting that if God behaved in such a way, then the divine reputation as a righteous and faithful God would be destroyed.[66] Brown obviously found the hyper-Calvinist stance on predestination intolerable, and on his own deathbed in 1887, reiterated that story in relation to his own situation: "I would not wish that foolish question ever put to me, 'Would you go to hell, if that were the Lord's will?' for it is God's promise, securing my salvation, that has much influence in making me resigned. God said to me, 'I am the Lord thy God'; and if He were not to be mine for ever, He would forfeit His word—which is impossible."[67]

Significantly too, John Brown of Haddington was one of the first of the antecedents of Cairns to speak for the right of women to vote, supporting his claim by quoting from the New Testament: "For as many of you as were baptized into Christ have put on Christ. There is neither Jew nor Greek, there is neither slave nor free, there is neither male nor female; for you are all one in Christ Jesus. And if you are Christ's, then you are Abraham's offspring, heirs according to promise."[68]

---

63. Drummond and Bulloch, *Scottish Church*, 111.

64. Mackenzie, *John Brown of Haddington*, 106, 185, 190.

65. Published in 1758, *A Help for the Ignorant; Being an Essay towards an Easy, Plain, Practical, and Extensive Explication of the Westminster Confession of Faith and Catechisms*, it went into four further editions in 1761, 1781, 1800, and 1811.

66. Mackenzie, *John Brown of Haddington*, 107.

67. Mackenzie, *John Brown of Haddington*, 306.

68. Gal 3:27–29.

John Brown of Haddington had a son and namesake who also became a prolific author, and who continued his father's highly evangelical style of preaching. This John Brown of Whitburn (1754–1832) was the great-grandfather of David Smith Cairns. In the early part of his ministry, such great numbers gathered to hear him preach that his services had sometimes to be taken out of doors, where there was enough room for everyone.[69] He had a son, another John Brown (1784–1858), who was a United Presbyterian Church minister and theologian, like his grandfather, but differed from him in that he was keen to engage with the controversial issues of the day. He put forward his views in religious journals, one of which he edited: the *Christian Repository and Religious Register*, the theological organ of the Burgher Church.[70] This was one of the more liberal groups within the Secession churches, and the one in which the family had its roots. There had been a split, popularly known as "The Breach" in the Secession in 1747, concerning a disagreement over whether it was lawful or sinful to take the oath required of the burgesses in Edinburgh, Glasgow, and Perth, acknowledging the true religion "presently professed within this realm." The Erskines were among those who agreed that it was lawful to take the oath, but the Secession split in two, with Burghers in favor and Antiburghers opposed. The Antiburghers excluded from communion all those who took the oath, seeing it as sanctioning the established church and its perceived abuses.[71]

In 1834 Brown was appointed to the chair of Exegetical Theology in the United Presbyterian Church Hall, making him, according to MacEwen, the first biblical professor in Scotland.[72] In an address to the synod at the celebration of the Jubilee of the United Presbyterian Church in 1897, Dr. Thomas Whitelaw described Brown as "the foremost New Testament exegete of his day in Scotland, a mastermind of advanced scholarship and true spiritual insight, in whose hands Bible exposition became a new art, and the sacred volume, instead of being compelled, as frequently before had been the case, to talk like the Westminster Confession or Shorter Catechism, began, through strict grammatical investigation and careful exposition, to speak with its own simple and liquid accents."[73]

One of Brown's most able students, James Morison, was expelled from the United Secession Church in 1841 for holding "erroneous" views in relation to the atonement, disputing the idea that Christ had died for

---

69. M'Kerrow, *History of the Secession Church*, 907–10.

70. This later became the *Christian Monitor* and was edited by Brown from 1816–26.

71. Burleigh, *Church History of Scotland*, 323, and MacEwen, *Life and Letters*, 28–29.

72. MacEwen, *Life and Letters*, 110.

73. Whitelaw, "Church's Home Work," 123.

the elect only.[74] In the following year, Morison published a work entitled *The Extent of the Propitiation or the Question for Whom Did Christ Die Answered,* in which he asked:

> If it were not true that Christ died for the heathen, pray, what gospel is the missionary to preach when he lands on a foreign shore? Is he to tell them that God loved a few men scattered somewhere or other throughout the world, and that therefore, for aught that he could know, there may happen to be some of these favoured ones among them, and for these Christ died?[75]

Brown, along with another colleague, Professor Robert Balmer, took up Morison's defence and they found themselves the target of charges of heresy by those who traced the "heresy" back to the teachers. Brown was cleared of the charges, but only after four years duration of a gruelling exchange. Analyzing the confession's teaching, he concluded that while the doctrine of particular elections and of particular salvation are very strongly asserted by it, the doctrine of a more general application is not explicitly condemned.[76] This controversy fixed attention on the Westminster Confession, to which, before licensing, students were required to declare to presbyteries their allegiance. This became something of an ordeal for some students, dreading accusations of heresy. "Presbyteries were on the alert, and students were in anxiety and distress."[77] According to A. R. MacEwen: "One of the leading figures in the Edinburgh of his day, Brown is accredited with the liberalisation of his Church. He was willing to state publicly that while there must be 'something above the dangerous laxness of a pledge to the scope of the Confession, something below the impracticable rigidity of adherence to every iota contained in it was sufficient."[78]

Brown was to have a great influence on another one of his students, John Cairns, and both were later to be connected by family ties. Both would play a vital role in the liberalization of their church in terms of adherence to the confession.[79]

D. S. Cairns also had a rich though more attenuated heritage on his father's side of the family, as far as theology was concerned. The history of the Cairns family mirrors the changing character of the United Presbyterian Church in the eighteenth century, from working class to middle class.

74. Cheyne, *Transforming of the Kirk,* 63–64.

75. Morison, *Extent of the Propitiation,* 64–65.

76. Hamilton, *Erosion of Calvinist Orthodoxy,* 38–57.

77. MacEwen, *Life and Letters,* 211–12.

78. MacEwen, *Life and Letters,* 212.

79. MacEwen, *Life and Letters,* 110–15.

On his father's side, the family was not far from its roots in the laboring classes. Cairns's grandfather, John Cairns (1799–1841) had been a Borders shepherd, but the following generation benefited through education, producing a schoolmaster (William), a parish minister (David), and an academic theologian and leading figure in the United Presbyterian Church (John). Cairns's uncle, the Rev. John Cairns (1818–1892), became a highly distinguished minister and preacher, a full-time professor of the United Presbyterian Church College in Edinburgh in 1876, and then its principal in 1879. In his biography of Principal Cairns, Alexander R. MacEwen describes him as one of the striking personalities of the United Presbyterian Church: brilliantly gifted, with literary and artistic sensibilities, and a large measure of speculative power.[80] John had had to leave school at thirteen to assist his father at herding. The local schoolmaster of the parish school at Cockburnspath, John McGregor, had qualified in theology at the University of St. Andrews, and tutored him part-time in preparation for entering the University of Edinburgh, where from the start he was conspicuous for his intellectual ability.[81]

Whereas John Brown as professor of exegetical theology had helped liberalize attitudes to the Westminster Confession, John Cairns was instrumental in securing a qualifying statement in the Declaratory Act of 1879. Some of the basic doctrines of Westminster Calvinism had remained under serious and sustained attack since the 1830s. Throughout the 1860s and 1870s, when D. S. Cairns was growing up, the three main branches of Presbyterianism remained conservative in their approach to the Westminster Confession, but many theologians and elders found subscription to it hard to bear, and the 1870s saw a spate of heresy trials.[82] In 1877, the United Presbyterian Church appointed a committee to consider subscription to the confession, and his uncle, John Cairns, was one of its four members. It was set up in response to changes in theology that affected all the Scottish churches, and which had seen many of the younger ministers wanting to move away from the rigid form of Calvinism, particularly in its pronouncements on the scope of salvation. On the opposing side were those for whom every sentence in the Westminster Confession is "taken from and approved by the Word of God."[83]

80. MacEwen, *Life and Letters*, 559.

81. MacEwen, *Life and Letters*, 13–41.

82. Cheyne outlines the perceived heresies, and the changes that developed in relation to subscription to the Westminster Confession throughout the nineteenth century in *Transforming of the Kirk*, ch. 3, "Confessional Revolution," 60–85.

83. Small, *History of the Congregations*, 2:724.

The task may have brought back memories of John Cairns's own student days, and the time leading up to his licensing. MacEwen describes how two months before licensing John Cairns studied the Westminster Confession and made notes on every article. When he came before the presbytery, he criticized some inconsistencies which he had found, but made a statement assenting to many of the articles. Where he found a questionable point with which he was not entirely in accord, he would not make a bald statement of disagreement, but rather say that he could not "dissent from this, but assent to the doctrine as elsewhere in the Confession." MacEwen also points out the intriguing fact that the presbytery records are silent on the discussion of the confession before John Cairns's licensing. He also notes that John Cairns "received explanations from the metropolitan [Edinburgh] presbytery which removed his difficulties."[84]

When John Cairns later presided over the United Presbyterian committee that was charged with examining subscription to the confession, he used the same points that he had used thirty years before when a student, and when his committee produced its final report, it inserted a final clause allowing for liberty of conscience on matters that did not enter into the substance of the faith, with the caveat that the church would guard against abuse of such liberty. This was enshrined in the Declaratory Act of 1879. Fourteen years later, in 1893, the Free Church passed its own similar Declaratory Act.[85] Following 1879, the formula for United Presbyterian ministers at ordination or induction, included at point 2, the following:

> Do you acknowledge the Westminster Confession of Faith, and the Larger and Shorter Catechisms, as an exhibition of the sense in which you understand the Holy Scriptures;—this acknowledgement being made in view of the explanations contained in the Declaratory Act of Synod thereanent?[86]

Such explanations included a recognition that the confession, being a human composition, is necessarily imperfect; salvation is a gift freely offered to all, and individuals are responsible for accepting or rejecting it; and although the ordinary way of salvation is through the gospel, those who die without accepting it are not necessarily condemned to be lost as the divine grace may be extended in any way that God sees fit. (This last point tried to deal with the anxieties of those who had found it impossible to reconcile the idea of a loving God with the idea of unbaptized babies or unevangelized

84. MacEwen, *Life and Letters*, 211–13.

85. The texts of both can be read at appendix B (United Presbyterian Church) and C (Free Church) in Hamilton, *Erosion of Calvinist Orthodoxy*, 192–95.

86. *Rules and Forms of Procedure of the United Presbyterian Church*, 124–25.

peoples being consigned to eternal damnation.) In discussing the significance of the act, Ian Hamilton reflects on the lack of dissent at any point
in its progress through the synod and presbyteries. He concludes that this
was because of the unanimity of the United Presbyterians on the subject:
"The available evidence points to a Church completely at one with its desire
to alter its relations to the Westminster Standards."[87] MacEwen agrees with
this, but also credits the diplomacy and sensitivity of John Cairns in presid-
ing over the transition.[88]

Parental Influence

When, in 1922, D. S. Cairns was called on to deliver an address on the unveil-
ing of a memorial to A. R. MacEwen, he described the dominant influence
on MacEwen's character as that of his family. There can be little doubt that his
words resonated with his own experience of family life: "From their earliest
youth they eat the bread and drink the wine of the great sacrament of family
love and duty, and through these they discern the glory of God."[89]

Memories of those early years at home, and of his parents, David
(1825-1910) and Elisabeth Williamson Smith (1829-1914), are depicted
lovingly and reverently in his autobiography. While his father had a good
sense of humor, he was usually grave, and not prone to physical expressions of affection. Although Cairns owned that all the children were aware
of his "deep and abiding love" for them, there was "a certain awe in their
affection for him."[90]

> On the one hand, Cairns senior expressed the deep convictions
> and unworldliness of the Seceder tradition, and its dignity and
> warmth of humanity in the daily business of living; content to
> spend his life in a small country church, with no ambition but to
> serve God. On the other hand he held to its austere view of life,
> with its sombre views of God and humankind.[91]

While they retained the traditional roles of minister and minister's
wife, his mother possessed a vitality that his father lacked, and was engaged
in activities which widened the interests of the family. She had inherited
from her father a deep interest in foreign missions, and missionaries were

87. Hamilton, *Erosion of Calvinist Orthodoxy*, 169.
88. MacEwen, *Life and Letters*. 664.
89. Cairns, address given in Claremont Church, Glasgow, 2.
90. Cairns, *Autobiography*, 44-53.
91. Cairns, *Autobiography*, 45-46, 73-74.

invited to come to the manse to share their experiences. One of her brothers had been a trader along the Calabar River in West Africa, and Cairns's mother encouraged in the Stitchel congregation a special interest in the Calabar mission of the United Presbyterian Church. The women of the congregation sent out trunk loads of clothes which they had made for the mothers and children there. In return, exotic gifts were sent to Stitchel, including birds' nests, colorful woven mats and parrots which became family pets. Their arrival was always a cause of great excitement, and on one occasion there was even what Cairns described as a "wooden heathen idol."[92] Cairns later recalled his mother's activities as humanizing and popularizing the missionary idea for him, long before he was able to understand it, and throughout his life he was to maintain his interest in and admiration for the missionary work of the church. In his mother he had also an early practical example of standing up for justice, when legal action was taken against her for warning a young widow against marriage with a certain man. The legal proceedings lasted a year and were very costly, but Elizabeth had promised the young woman's mother that she would look after her, and so felt that she could not retreat from her position. In a happy conclusion, the sheriff expressed his approval of her action.[93]

It was his mother who introduced Cairns to the theology of F. D. Maurice, Thomas Erskine and John MacLeod Campbell, who with their wider theological perspectives, particularly in relation to the doctrine of atonement, led him to feel "greatly emancipated" from the sterner Calvinism of his father.[94] At a time when academic theology was very much the domain of men, the influence of the women in the family was paramount for Cairns. The culture within his tradition supported such influence. Within the strand of United Presbyterian Church to which the Cairns family belonged, there was an attitude to women which was more liberal than in the other Secession groups. David Cairns senior was in a Burgher Church in Stitchel, and, according to Robert Small, the Burgher congregations granted equal voting rights to women almost from the start.[95] Such a vote would be used, for example, on whether or not to accept a new minister. Voting was open to "all in full communion," but this was usually interpreted as referring to the males in the congregation.

Cairns points out that in the forty-five years of his ministry in Stitchel, his father spoke only once in the United Presbyterian Synod, when he was

---

92. Cairns, *Autobiography*, 49–50.
93. Cairns, *Autobiography*, 51.
94. Cairns, *Autobiography*, 50–52.
95. Small, *History of the Congregations*, 2:711–16.

an old man, and that was in support of those who wanted to give extended influence in church affairs to women.[96] With such a background, the Cairns family produced some women who made significant intellectual contributions to its life. Cairns describes his maternal grandmother as "really the head of my mother's family" and she seems to have made a deep impression on him with her love of poetry, especially Byron, Cowper, and Milton, her interest in the world outside the church, and her questioning attitude.[97] "She read the *Scotsman* every day after her devotions. And strict Seceder as she was, she read the Bible with an open mind. I remember her look of serious questioning when she spoke to me about the imprecatory Psalms. Was it not strange to find such prayers in the Divine Word?"[98]

In spite of the happiness of his home life, and the loving nature of relationships there, Cairns saw in the theological and religious background of his childhood, the roots of "a profound religious upheaval" that was to cause him much agonizing and even a temporary loss of religious belief when he went to university. Although very deeply influenced by his father's character, he found his theology out of date and of little help to him. Of David Sr. he said,

> No one who knew him could fail to be impressed by his own humility before God, his deep sense of reverence for holy things and of the profound difference between right and wrong and the seriousness of life. I wanted to believe as he believed, and wrestled with the old Calvinism and its solutions of the problems of the world and of human life. But it was in vain. It seemed to me to make God unjust and something in me rose up in inextinguishable protest against it.[99]

In old age, Cairns recalled his childhood in the Borders as providing him with a solid foundation in the Christian faith, and he especially valued the influence of his parents. Of them he wrote, "I am not at all blind to their limitations, and even mistakes, but they both in different ways made it easier for me to believe in goodness and in God, and I can think of no better name for God than our Lord's name 'Father,' or for heaven than 'our Father's House.'"[100]

According to his son, throughout his long life D. S. Cairns maintained a simple ritual, which revealed the depth of this respect. Every time he

96. Cairns, *Autobiography*, 45–46.
97. Cairns, *Autobiography*, 72–74.
98. Cairns, *Autobiography*, 73.
99. Cairns, *Autobiography*, 85.
100. Cairns, *Autobiography*, 44–45.

traveled by train between Edinburgh and Berwick, when he got to a certain point near Cockburnspath, he stood in the corridor, and removed his hat and gave thanks, while passing the small cottage that was the childhood home of his father.[101] In his own words, Cairns explained: "I never pass his birthplace in the little forester's cottage among the trees in Penmanshiel wood without a glow of thankfulness in my heart and a reassurance about this Power behind the Universe and its meaning and its end. I look out for it always as I draw near it in the train and salute it as I pass!"[102]

Thus nurtured by their parents, the family developed strong and lasting bonds of affection and respect for one another, but they were not insular or exclusive in their relations. To their home came a constant stream of visitors that included some notable preachers and distinguished figures of the day, including writers and missionaries. J. H. Leckie, also a United Presbyterian theologian, and close friend of the Cairns family, is likely to have been thinking of them when he described the United Presbyterian Church homes of his day. "Some of these were homes of singularly wide intellectual interest, where a devout and tolerant type of religion dwelt in amity with knowledge and with letters. There are many of us who can witness to this; in whom the memory of their early home is one of constant gratitude and praise."[103]

Among the many frequent visitors to the Stitchel manse in Cairns's teenage years, was a young Free Church minister, William Robertson Nicoll (1851–1923).[104] Cairns described him as follows: "He had little respect for dignities, and was an odd blend of evangelical fervour and clear, practical realism, with a full dash of cynicism. He was a devout, well-informed and amusing young minister."[105]

In 1877, Nicoll was inducted as minister of the Free Church in Kelso. During his previous charge in Dufftown in Banffshire, he had written a number of reviews and addresses for a variety of journals, and in Kelso, he continued to develop his journalistic skills. According to his biographer, T. H. Darlow, his sermons and lectures made a particularly strong impact on the young people of the district. In his sermons he sometimes quoted lines of poetry, for which he was criticized by Edinburgh Presbyterians, who found this offensive. This particular group he described as "censorious," after they advised him that if must use poetry in the pulpit, he

101. David Cairns, "John Cairns," 204–13.

102. Cairns, *Autobiography*, 48.

103. Leckie, *Secession Memories*, 78.

104. Cairns, *Autobiography*, 79–81.

105. Cairns, *Autobiography*, 80.

should not mention the name of the author. He became the editor of some of the new journals of the day, including the *Contemporary Pulpit* and the *Expositor*. For this latter publication, which he edited from 1885 till his death in 1923, he secured contributions from nearly all the leading biblical scholars in the country, as well as from distinguished experts in America and on the European continent, presenting "the best thoughts of the best men on the best of books."

Following his contraction of typhoid on a visit to Norway in 1885, Nicoll gave up the parish ministry and moved to London, where he became editor of the *British Weekly*, founded by Hodder and Stoughton in 1886 as a Nonconformist "high-class weekly journal for the advocacy of social and religious progress." Through this, he became the de facto intellectual leader of Nonconformity exercising a wide influence.[106] According to Darlow, "Christian teachers as contrasted as F. D. Maurice and C. H. Spurgeon have agreed in their judgment that in these days no ministerial position is equal in importance to that of a man who can collect and hold a constituency which will read his religious instruction. In the *British Weekly* Nicoll never ceased preaching to a great and listening audience till he died."[107]

Spiritual Crisis

In his early teens Cairns first experienced doubts about his faith, and these brought him much unhappiness and anxiety. The anxiety manifested itself around the time of the Dwight L. Moody and Ira Sankey visit to Edinburgh (1873–74). Cairns's uncle John was an enthusiastic supporter of the campaign and in 1874, the Americans moved their base from Edinburgh to Berwick, where John Cairns ministered in Wallace Green Church, and he took on a leading role, taking part in some of the crowded evangelistic meetings and prayer meetings.[108] Many orthodox Calvinists questioned the integrity of such activity, which offered the gospel to everyone, in contradiction of the hyper-Calvinist doctrine of election and limited atonement.[109]

The evangelists' campaign which involved direct conversionist preaching, "inquiry meetings," and gospel music, produced gatherings that were theatrical and highly emotional.[110] Cairns did not appear to see the revival movement of the two American evangelists as the cause of his

106. Darlow, *William Robertson Nicoll*, 29–82.
107. Darlow, *William Robertson Nicoll*, 82.
108. John Cairns, *Principal Cairns*, 40. John Cairns was the brother of D. S. Cairns.
109. Cheyne, *Transforming of the Kirk*, 82–83.
110. Carwardine, "Revivals (British Isles)," 326.

distress at this impressionable age—he was eleven. On the contrary, he described their campaign as a much more genial movement than the one which had preceded it in 1859, which, according to Cairns, had played on people's fear of hell rather than on the love of God.[111] During his period of anxiety, Cairns felt aware of the presence of God, but feared that God was displeased with him. His problem was spiritual rather than intellectual. His anxiety may be described as a natural fear for someone living in a society in which the dominant theological view is the supralapsarianism of high Calvinism, even if such a view was being challenged by evangelical Calvinists.[112] Smout describes something of the mental anguish involved in subscribing rigidly to this doctrine.

> Such a doctrine was compelling and terrible. It was hard to accept it and remain sane without deciding that one was oneself already numbered among the Elect, and so destined to escape the everlasting fires. If so, it was clear that one would try to live a good life, to be obedient to the demands of the church, and to be a devoted church-goer. It was unthinkable that a member of the Elect would not be zealous in these matters: if he was not, then he could not be so sure that he really was counted among them.[113]

It is, perhaps, not difficult therefore to picture a boy, on the brink of adolescence, respectful of his family's tradition, and exposed to competing theological claims, succumbing to confusion and doubt. Unwilling or unable to speak to friends or family members about his distress, Cairns searched through the evangelical texts in the manse, but found them of no help. Eventually he came across what Donald Baillie, the writer of the *Memoir* that introduces Cairns's autobiography, described as an "obscure little book," and there found solace in the writing of Dr. William Landels (1823–1899), a Baptist minister and lifelong friend of his Uncle John. Born in Berwickshire, Landels later ministered for a short time in Cupar in Fife, before moving to Birmingham and then to London, where he spent most of his working life, becoming at one point president of the Baptist Union. He was frequently asked to preach in Wallace Green Church, when in the area on holiday.[114] Converted in his youth during a Methodist mission in

111. Cairns, *Autobiography*, 86.

112. According to the high Calvinistic view, God had first decided to elect some for salvation and others for damnation, and had then created humankind in these two categories. Christ's work of salvation was for the elect only.

113. Smout, *Century of the Scottish People*, 192.

114. This friendship is recorded in a biography of Landels written by his son,

Eyemouth, Landels had chosen to study theology under James Morison, who was later deposed for his views on the atonement. One of his fellow students was Fergus Ferguson, who was in 1870 tried for heresy by the United Presbyterian Synod for holding views of the atonement that included the possibility of salvation after death. Landels admired both Morison and Ferguson in their stand against what his son described as "the hard and unlovely Calvinism then in vogue."[115]

Although the book which Cairns found seemed obscure to Baillie, Landels was one of the popular preachers of the day, and because of John Cairns's friendship with him and high opinion of his tradition, it is not surprising that such a book should have found its way into the library of the Stitchel manse. The book was *The Gospel in Various Aspects: A Book for the Anxious*, and at the heart of its theology was the belief in God's unconditional love for all, quite different from the Calvinistic theology of predestination which, for Cairns made God seem unjust. The subtitle of the book must have made an immediate appeal to Cairns and its opening chapter, "What Is the Gospel?" got straight to the heart of the matter. Focusing on the definition of "the gospel" as "good tidings," Landels declares that anything that does not fulfill that expectation of something to our advantage, of something that dispels our fears and fills us with gladness, does not deserve the name of "gospel." He suggests that lack of peace may be the result of ignorance of what the gospel really is, and points out that while the Bible contains the good tidings, not everything in the Bible is the gospel. The gospel is not the history of Christ's life and death, nor is it the evangelical teaching which focuses on the doctrines of grace or of justification by faith. For Landels, the central truth of the gospel, and therefore of the world, is summed up in the three words *God is love*. This is the source of blessing and its outcome was God's sending Jesus into the world: *God so loved the world, that he gave his only-begotten Son*. All the other statements in the Bible are dependent on these two. "They are but repetitions, or applications, or explanations of these, showing how the Saviour accomplished the work which he came to perform, and what blessings he has brought nigh to us as a result."[116]

Landels's style was emotional, and his frequent use of the second person in articulating problems of faith gave it a very personal tone, and the author's association with John Cairns may have lent it enough authority to reassure an anxious teenager. "To try to believe that you have received him, is to prevent the reception taking place. It is to make your faith rest

Thomas Durley Landels, *William Landels*, 78.

115. Landels, *William Landels*, 13–15, 21, 78.

116. Landels, *Gospel in Various Aspects*, 19.

upon yourself, instead of Christ. It is to believe in your own belief, instead of believing in God's word."[117]

Cairns dated his conversion from this time, and in his last years affirmed that "all my later life has been deeply conditioned by it and today that faith is still my only enduring ground of hope either for myself or for mankind."[118]

Another ameliorating influence in his teenage period was one of Cairns's father's elders, George Melrose, a Kelso tailor. It was in the Melrose home that Cairns got his lunch when he attended the High School. George had been brought up in the Reformed Presbyterian Church, also known as the Cameronians, which rejected any state interference in church matters and were strict Sabbatarians. Cairns related that George Melrose's influence on him came through the theological talks they had, possibly made easier to imbibe because of the humor Melrose sometimes used to get his point across. For example, when refuting the idea of the Tay Bridge disaster (28 December 1879) being a punishment from God, he declared, "They talk as if He watched that train until He saw it on the brig and then gied it a shove—like that!, pushing out his hand. Man, to hear some folk speak, ye would think that God the Faither had been after ye wi' a knife."[119]

Melrose had managed to break free from the strictness of his religious upbringing, without dismissing religion entirely, and had embraced "Arminian evangelicalism," reinforcing in Cairns the hope of finding a similar faith that accommodated a broader view of God's justice. In the struggle against Calvinism, Cairns cited his mother's theology books and George Melrose as his main aids to freedom.[120] But there had been for some time, within his own United Presbyterian tradition, other voices that had been raised in the cause of a more inclusive theology. One such was George Gilfillan of Dundee (1813–1878), minister, public speaker, literary critic, essayist, and editor of several volumes of poetry. He argued that in an age of theological doubt and inquiry, people should be allowed to question and find reasons for their beliefs. He preached an inclusive Christianity, encouraging people to use their God-given reason in their search for religious meaning.[121] He was one of the first ministers in Scotland to preach on the theory of biological evolution and he encouraged people to consider the new theory even if

---

117. Landels, *Gospel in Various Aspects*, 20–21.

118. Cairns, *Autobiography*, 87.

119. Cairns, *Autobiography*, 86.

120. Cairns, *Autobiography*, 85–86.

121. Black, *Gilfillan of Dundee*, 106.

it shook their cherished beliefs.[122] Emphasizing the brotherhood of man, he preached a gospel of mercy and forgiveness and rejected the idea of a vengeful God who would send people to hell. He frankly admitted the difficulty of sustaining belief in such a divinity, opposing the doctrine of eternal damnation and emphasizing the liberty of the individual conscience.[123]

D. S. Cairns was sixteen when Gilfillan died, and so too late to benefit from his role as honorary director of the Society for the Sons of United Presbyterian Ministers, or from his role as honorary president of the Students' Theological Society. His wider influence would not have escaped Cairns, for as the demand for liberalization continued to grow within the United Presbyterian Church, the Dundee Presbytery described him as "undoubtedly the most representative Scotchman of his time."[124]

David Smith Cairns was born at a time when many people, lay and ordained, religious and secular, were developing an awareness of the inadequacies of the churches in their response to the intellectual and scientific developments of the day, such as evolution and biblical criticism. In this new world, scholastic Calvinism with its rigid doctrine of predestination began to be questioned, and many came to see the idea of a God who would bestow favor in an arbitrary manner on a select group as repugnant. From the 1830s the basic doctrines of the Westminster Confession of Faith came under attack. Attention focused on the doctrine of atonement, its nature and scope, and on questions related to the authority of the Bible. From the time of John Brown of Haddington, Cairns's antecedents had played their role in the liberalization of the church in terms of its subscription to the Westminster Confession of Faith, culminating in John Cairns's work in securing within the United Presbyterian Church, the Declaratory Act of 1879. However, as Cheyne points out, in the 1860s, the decade of Cairns's birth, "the weight of numbers in every Presbyterian communion was still very much on the side of theological conservatism," and heresy trials continued into the 1870s.[125] By 1880, when he was ready to go to the University of Edinburgh, Cairns had experienced his first crisis of faith, finding practical help outside his own tradition, in the evangelical message of the Baptist theologian William Landels. Within two years, in common with many thinking people of the day, he was to undergo a much deeper crisis of faith.

122. Black, *Gilfillan of Dundee*, 100.

123. Black, *Gilfillan of Dundee*, 217

124. Black, *Gilfillan of Dundee*, 223

125. Cheyne, *Transforming of the Kirk*, 68–70.

Conclusion

Of all the childhood influences to which Cairns later referred, perhaps the highest was the piety of his parents, and particularly that of his father. Although Cairns later distanced himself from aspects of his father's theology, he continued to revere his father's devotion to his parish and the profundity and integrity of his faith. Cairns's family life was characterized by the evangelical piety, ethos of hard work, liberal politics and serious scholarship of the United Presbyterian tradition. Further intellectual stimulation was provided by the many visitors who came to the Stitchel manse, and Cairns could see, in the examples of his grandmother and mother, and in such people as William Robertson Nicoll, that religious faith could coexist with questioning, and that it was related to events in the wider world.

The parish of Stitchel had produced one of the earliest dissenting congregations, and Cairns grew up in a family steeped in the old Secession tradition, out of which had grown the United Presbyterian Church. Characterized by its struggle for spiritual independence, its emphasis on individual autonomy, and its strong sense of mission, the United Presbyterian Church provided the backdrop and inspiration for his thinking. His church's theology was evangelical, with an emphasis on personal religious experience, and, strongly influenced by the Relief church, it was liberal and in some senses inclusive, and allowed for some accommodation of divergences from the dogmatic Calvinism of the Westminster Confession of Faith. As the nineteenth century progressed, the churches in Scotland encountered growing questioning of some of the doctrines of the Westminster Confession, and both sides of the debate were represented within Cairns's own family. While his father and his uncle John found it difficult to move away from traditional dogmatic Calvinism with its belief in double predestination, his mother embraced the more inclusive theology of the Broad Church theologians such as F. D. Maurice in the Church of England and John MacLeod Campbell in Scottish Presbyterianism. Repelled by ultra Calvinist views, Cairns too was attracted to more liberal, inclusive views on the atonement. During his period of youthful spiritual crisis, he also found solace in the theology of William Landels, whose belief in the unconditional love of God for all freed him from the Calvinist doctrine of predestination for good, and provided him with the foundation for all his later thinking.

Chapter 2

Breakdown and Restoration, 1880–1892

Following in the Family Tradition

CAIRNS MATRICULATED IN THE University of Edinburgh in 1880, just before his eighteenth birthday. The family had discussed his entry into the Indian Civil Service, but rejected this ambition, as it required too long and costly a training.[1] Their initial ambition would account for their payment for tutoring in the most expensive subjects on offer at Kelso High School because entry into the Indian Civil Service involved a very competitive open entrance examination, followed by a two-year probationary period and a final examination. The nature of the open examination meant the employment of a "crammer" to supplement a candidate's knowledge to a level that would ensure success. According to J. M. Compton, in the 1870s, when the family might have begun to consider this path for Cairns, almost every successful candidate had attended a crammer.[2] Following success in the open examination, the probationary period consisted of residence at one of the universities prepared to provide the specialist tuition that would ensure similar success in the final examination: in practice these were Oxford, Cambridge, and London. In the 1870s the maximum age limit for departure to India was nineteen, which meant that training began at a very young age.

A handbook of the time for parents who were trying to make up their minds about a suitable career for their son or daughter, included information about the Indian Civil Service and set out details of the examination and selection process, with the costs involved at each stage.[3] Although financial assistance was available for the probationary period, money was paid retrospectively at the end of each six-month period, and the funds had to be repaid if a candidate did not in the end go to India. On passing the final examination candidates had to attend at the India Office "with the view

1. Cairns, *Autobiography*, 82.
2. Compton, "Education of a Ruling Caste," 269.
3. Philp, *Index Scholasticus*, 158–60.

31

of entering into covenants and giving a bond for £1,000, jointly with two sureties": this latter amount on its own would surely have been beyond the means of the Cairns family. The training itself was only for two years in Britain, but would of course continue in India, as the young entrants made their way up the career ladder. Its attractions may have been strong for some, especially as described by Compton:

> The emoluments of a writership [referring to the allowance for probationers]; the steady advancement in the service of those who devote themselves to it with zeal and perseverance; the infinite opportunities of public usefulness which it presents; the dignity, honour and influence of the positions to which it may not improbably lead; and the liberal and judicious provision for retirement at a moderate age; all render the Indian civil service a career full of interest and of pecuniary advantage.[4]

One would imagine that while the young Cairns dreamed of making money for the family, such financial remuneration would not have been the motivation for his parents. Whatever the thinking behind their consideration of such a career for him, the prospect proved too much, and although the training for ministry was long, the costs were less and there were opportunities for scholarships, as well as the long months during which there were no classes, which provided opportunities for tutoring. In recruiting for the Indian civil service, great emphasis was laid on the need for candidates to be robust in health, with no "constitutional affection, or bodily infirmity unfitting him, or likely to unfit him."[5] Considering the poor health that was to dog Cairns for the next few years, it seems unlikely that he would have had the stamina to sustain a career in India.

It was not until he had matriculated that he decided to train for the ministry. In old age, he found it difficult to recall the chronology of the decision, but the actual moment of decision remained clear in his memory, and was one that he never regretted.

> I have in my memory one of those snapshots which accompany mental or emotional crises. The decision was taken one afternoon in the Greek classroom in the class of the assistant Greek professor, Mr. Gardner. It is an isolated snapshot. I see myself in one of the front benches (we were arranged alphabetically, not by merit), Gardner and a mist of faces round me. I cannot remember what led up to it; there was no very strong feeling, but

---

4. Compton, "Education of a Ruling Caste," 269.

5. Philp, *Index Scholasticus*, 158.

just a quiet resolve, which has determined the whole course of my life ever since.[6]

Those who wished to train for the ministry, had first to undergo a four-year arts course, consisting of humanity [Latin], Greek, mathematics, physics, English literature, and moral philosophy. The course might be shortened to three years for those who passed a preliminary examination in humanity and Greek, but Cairns's education in Ednam and Kelso had not provided him with that capability. His time in Edinburgh began inauspiciously in the failure to win a bursary, due to a lack of mathematical prowess, which dogged his university career. He describes himself as undistinguished in Latin in spite of the efforts of his scholarly teacher, Professor William Young Sellar; and poor in Greek, although he attributed this to the poor teaching of Professor John Stuart Blackie, whose classes were often out of control. In spite of that, Cairns had a favorable opinion of Blackie's character and of his pastoral role in the university.[7]

John Cairns had become principal of the United Presbyterian Divinity Hall in 1879, just before his nephew went to university. According to MacEwen, the four Cairns siblings were as dear to John Cairns as if they had been his own children.[8] Throughout childhood, they maintained a close relationship with their Uncle John, staying with him in his manse in Berwick during summer holidays, as well as enjoying his frequent visits to the Stitchel manse. When the three sons went to university in Edinburgh and then to the divinity hall, their uncle's house was always open to them, and they spent at least one afternoon a week in his company there. D. S. Cairns remembered his uncle as a venerable figure whom the family loved and of whom the children were very proud.[9]

Theological Education in the United Presbyterian Church

According to A. R. MacEwen, the Seceders from the beginning had seen as of paramount importance the education of its ministers. A theological hall fund was set up, as was a scholarship fund to provide bursaries for students at the university or hall.[10] They wanted their students to attend university with those training for other learned professions, before training for the

6. Cairns, *Autobiography*, 82.
7. Cairns, *Autobiography*, 84.
8. MacEwen, *Life and Letters of John Cairns*, 598.
9. Cairns, *Autobiography*, 67–68.
10. *Rules and Forms of Procedure of the United Presbyterian Church*, 112.

ministry in their own theological hall.[11] The first theological seminary had been opened in Perth in 1737, and for the next century moved to wherever its single professor had his parish, with the students attending for two months of the year. For the rest of the year, the students sought opportunities to earn money to support their studies, usually through private tutoring. Aileen Black describes how the United Presbyterian Church struggled to maintain this part-time peripatetic professoriate, drawn from the parish ministry, with teaching conducted in the ministers' homes. In a speech to the Jubilee Synod of the United Presbyterian Church in 1897, Dr. Thomas Whitelaw of Kilmarnock looked back at the development of the education of the clergy, remarking that it would have been easy, given the difficult circumstances of the early days of the Secession, to have succumbed to the temptation to employ an untrained ministry. With foresight, and in the tradition of John Knox, they had rejected that path. He declared that by the time a permanent base had been established in Edinburgh in 1876, the church had produced "a splendid succession of theological doctors."[12]

Referring to the nineteenth century, MacEwen declares, "It would be difficult to exaggerate the isolation and insularity of British theology during the first half of this century."[13] Engaged in its own ecclesiastical disputes, Scotland looked inwards, and up until the 1840s it engaged little with theological developments in France and Germany, cutting itself off from the currents of thought prevalent on the wider European continent. From the 1840s things began to change through a developing interest in German theology. During the ten months of the year when there were no classes, students were encouraged to visit the great theological faculties in Halle, Berlin or Bonn. In 1843, John Cairns took the opportunity to spend almost a year in Berlin, taking classes in theology and philosophy, and mastered German to such an extent that he was invited to remain as an instructor for the next year.[14] Succeeding members of the family, including D. S. Cairns, would make many visits to Germany, learning from the great German theological schools of the day. The family dedication to learning was also evident in the fact that Cairns's sister, Jessie, spent an educational year in Germany, although her life later followed the domestic model that provided the orthodox role for middle-class women of the time.

11. MacEwen, *Life and Letters of John Cairns*, 109.

12. Whitelaw, "Church's Home Work," 117–20, and Black, *Gilfillan of Dundee*, 24–25.

13. MacEwen, *Life and Letters*, 148.

14. MacEwen, *Life and Letters*, 148–52.

When she was sixteen years old, Jessie went to boarding school in Kreuznach, a picturesque spa town located on the Nahe River, a tributary of the Rhine, in an area noted for its wine-making. Setting sail from Newcastle on 28 September 1875, she was accompanied on the journey by her father and by her Uncle John, who was able to interpret for them. Lessons in the school included music and French, added to which were many outings for walks and concerts. In a letter to her mother shortly after her arrival at the school, Jessie related that she found the other girls and staff members friendly, adding that she thought she would like it there; but her diary reveals a longing for home and family, and the high point of her week was always Saturday when letters arrived from Scotland.[15]

Jessie's going to Germany must have been unusual for a family living on a minister's salary. However, David Cairns Sr. had been left the sum of five hundred pounds to be distributed over ten years, for the education of his family. He inherited the money from Thomas Wilson of Haymount, whom he had supported through prayer and visitation during a long illness.[16] Perhaps Jessie's parents considered it democratic practice to make sure that their only daughter had as good an education as was possible at a time before women were allowed to matriculate in the universities.[17] Her year in Germany may have been seen as preparation for one or other of the few career openings for middle-class women—tutoring or working as a governess. This idea is supported by an anonymous family record. A diary "probably of a Cairns daughter" kept between 1880 and 1893, is almost certainly Jessie's and in it she speaks of her own continuing education, taking lessons in painting and Latin. She also speaks of getting her first pupil in October 1879, and of two more pupils in the following December.[18]

Historically the village of Stitchel had a more positive record regarding the education of girls than many places in Scotland. According to local history records, a system of compulsory education was established there as early as 1688, and parents who did not send their children to school were fined. Also, when the common view in Scotland was that education was less important for girls than for boys, the parish of Stitchel stipulated that the tenants

15. Jessie Cairns, in a letter to her mother, 12 October 1875, and her diary, 1875–76, respectively at Acc. 66825/9 and Acc. 6787, Cairns Papers in National Library of Scotland. Her journey to the school is also described in MacEwen, *Life and Letters*, 598.

16. Cairns, *Autobiography*, 50.

17. See Macdonald, *Unique and Glorious Mission*, 262–90, for a description of the campaign, from 1870, to extend equal educational opportunities to middle-class women.

18. Acc. 10584/5 in Cairns Papers, National Library Scotland.

and cottars who had daughters must not send them to a sewing school until they had completed two full years reading at the public school.[19]

At the outset of his university studies, Cairns was required to take an oath that he would not take part in "tumults," although he does not elaborate on the nature of such theoretical possibilities.[20] Elsewhere he points out that the 1870s and 1880s had produced a number of heresy trials, during which the ecclesiastical leaders had tried to avoid "disastrous cleavages." For some of the able theology students their academic leaders were too cautious and the intellectual atmosphere too narrow, and they moved out into other spheres.[21] However, in spite of the restriction of the oath, the students of Cairns's day would have found more freedom due to some significant developments in the preceding decades. Of immediate consequence for prospective divinity students, was the passing of the United Presbyterian Church Declaratory Act of 1879, which allowed for a degree of flexibility regarding subscription to the Westminster Confession of Faith. Freedom of conscience was allowed on points which did not constitute the "substance of the faith."

There was also the liberalizing of Free Church theology during the 1860s by some of its professors who introduced to their students the works of the Continental theologians.[22] According to Black and Chrystal, the Free Church theological hall, New College, was the center of evangelical propaganda, and "the level of reputation and even of celebrity enjoyed by the staff, was at this time very high." Among the staff were two men who jointly occupied the chair of Hebrew Language and Old Testament Exegesis: Dr. John (Rabbi) Duncan and Dr. A. B. Davidson. Duncan represented evangelical orthodoxy on the one hand, while Davidson was part of the new generation of teachers, and "brought the first light into the dark age in Biblical Criticism and Biblical Theology in Scotland."[23] In the academic career of one of their most erudite students, William Robertson Smith (1846–1894), a major battle was fought with repercussions for freedom of inquiry. Its outcome was decided around the time that Cairns went to the University of Edinburgh,

19. Carlaw and Ogston, *Stitchill Parish*, 86.

20. Cairns, *Autobiography*, 82.

21. Cairns, *Autobiography*, 125.

22. Brown, *Providence and Empire*, 246–47.

23. Black and Chrystal, *Life of William Robertson Smith*, 72–77. John Sutherland Black (1846–1923) was an author and editor. Among his works was a translation of Wellhausen's *Prologomena* which discussed the origins of the Pentateuch. George Chrystal (1851–1911) was a distinguished mathematician who lectured in Cambridge and St. Andrews, before holding the chair of Mathematics at the University of Edinburgh from 1879. Both also wrote for the Encyclopaedia Britannica.

and was crucial to the establishment of the climate in which teaching and learning were conducted in all the divinity halls.

The William Robertson Smith Case and Its Outcome

William Robertson Smith was influenced by the German biblical scholar Julius Wellhausen (1844–1918) and his work on the structure of the Pentateuch. He was also heavily influenced by the German theologian Albrecht Ritschl (1822–1889), whom he met when he was a student, and with whom he maintained a lifelong friendship and correspondence. Both men were influenced by another German theologian, Richard Rothe (1799–1867), who affirmed a supernatural divine revelation, but who refused to assign a special supernatural character to the records that convey the revelation: they were willing to admit that as a human work, the Bible may not be free of error. In 1870, at the age of twenty-four, Smith was ordained and appointed to the Hebrew chair at Aberdeen's Free Church College. Ritschl was among those who recommended him for the post, although according to Black and Crystal the decisive recommendation came from Davidson, who described Robertson Smith as the "most distinguished student I have ever had in my department."[24] Smith spelled out his vision for the task in his inaugural address, appealing to the authority of Calvin's example of "believing courage" when dealing with the Scriptures. Applying historical method to the study of the Bible, he concluded,

It is impossible to pass from this topic without in one word pointing out that a necessary consequence of this way of treating the Bible is the honest practice of a higher criticism. The higher criticism does not mean negative criticism. It means the fair and honest practice of looking at the Bible as a historical record, and the effort everywhere to reach the real meaning and historical setting, not of individual passages of the Scripture, but of the Scripture records as a whole; and to do this we must apply the same principle that the Reformation applied to detailed exegesis. We must let the Bible speak for itself. Our notions of the origin, the purpose, the character of the Scripture books must be drawn, not from vain traditions, but from a historical study of the books themselves. This process can be dangerous to faith only when it is begun without faith—when we forget that the

24. Black and Chrystal, *Life of William Robertson Smith*, 119.

Bible history is no profane history, but the story of God's saving self-manifestation.[25]

For the next few years, Robertson Smith continued his work at Aberdeen, earning the respect of international scholars in science and theology. It is interesting to note that William Robertson Nicoll entered the theological course here in the year of Robertson Smith's arrival. In 1874, Professor Thomas Spencer Baynes of St. Andrews, editor of the *Encyclopaedia Britannica*, asked Smith to contribute some articles, including one on the Bible, for the third volume. Following its publication in 1876, an article entitled "The New Encyclopaedia Britannica on Theology" appeared in the *Edinburgh Courant* on April 16, anonymous but widely believed to have been written by A. H. Charteris, professor of biblical criticism at the University of Edinburgh. Although he belonged to the established church, Charteris was respected as a "sincere and fervent Evangelical" by the Free Church, and his sensationalist criticism, with accusations of "Moses in danger" and "Predictive prophecy denied," began a four-year campaign against Robertson Smith. Four years of accusation and counter-accusation, false allegations of plagiarism against Robertson Smith, political maneuvering and bitterness, it resulted in him being charged with "dangerous and unsettling" statements and losing his chair at Aberdeen in 1881. Strangely, although he was considered unreliable as a teacher of students, there was never any effort to depose him as a minister.[26]

Throughout this time of trouble for him, Robertson Smith was offered chairs at Harvard and Cambridge, and letters of support arrived from many eminent people, including Ritschl, President Eliot of Harvard, and Sir Richard Burton, the explorer and ethnographer. From the beginning of the campaign against him, Robertson Smith was supported by his former teacher, Davidson, whose commentary on Job, published in 1862, had been considered by the more conservative Free Church minds "almost the first example in English of Hebrew erudition of the 'dangerous' variety."[27] Davidson had escaped controversy at that earlier time; something his favored student did not. In later years, when asked to list the books which had influenced him, first on his list of authors was A. B. Davidson: a fitting tribute by Robertson Smith to the teacher who had endured public criticism for defending him.[28]

25. Black and Chrystal, *Life of William Robertson Smith*, 128–29.

26. A full account of this time, the issues and the characters involved and their role in the dispute, is found in Black and Chrystal, *Life of William Robertson Smith*, 179–451.

27. Black and Chrystal, *Life of William Robertson Smith*, 130.

28. Black and Chrystal, *Life of William Robertson Smith*, 534.

William Robertson Smith went on to have an illustrious career as professor of Arabic at Cambridge, traveling to lecture in America, and receiving a doctorate in theology from the University of Strasbourg, an honor rarely conferred by German universities on foreign scholars. Tragically he died when he was only forty-eight, but not before the University of Edinburgh had conferred on him the degree of doctor of laws. In one sense, he was vindicated by the response of his intellectual peers, but even more so by the fact that from then on intellectual freedom was guaranteed for students of divinity. Following Smith's deposition from the chair, a protest meeting was held in the Masonic Hall in George Street, Edinburgh, on Saturday, 28 May 1881. Although it was hastily convened, over three hundred people met; professors and teachers, ministers, elders and others, including most of his prominent lay supporters. Of the speeches made, the most notable was that of the organizer Professor Thomas Martin Lindsay, who held the chair of Church History in the Free Church College in Glasgow. Lindsay had supported Robertson Smith during the four years of controversy, and now, while admitting that he did not agree with Smith on every point, declared that his new critical method was the way forward. A document was drawn up, condemning the general assembly's violation of the church's constitution in the manner in which it had gone about the trial, and dissenting from its findings. It concluded thus: "We also declare that the decision of the Assembly leaves all Free Church ministers and office-bearers free to pursue the critical questions raised by Professor W. R. Smith, and we pledge ourselves to do our best to protect any man who pursues these studies legitimately."[29]

The English academic Bernard Reardon points out that liberty of critical biblical scholarship was not secured immediately as at the end of the 1880s, Professor Marcus Dods of New College and Dr. A. B. Bruce of Glasgow were examined regarding their opinions on biblical inerrancy and inspiration.[30] In 1900, George Adam Smith, professor of Hebrew and Old Testament at Glasgow, was involved in a similar procedure, but was acquitted in 1902.[31] The general assembly of the Free Church emphasized the infallible truth and divine authority of Scripture, although it stopped short of asserting its verbal inerrancy, and of condemning the professors. In spite of the continuing controversy following the Robertson Smith case, it was into a more liberal atmosphere that D. S. Cairns came to Edinburgh as a student in 1880, just before his eighteenth birthday. The Robertson Smith case seemed to have been settled and the professor had been admonished,

29. Black and Chrystal, *Life of William Robertson Smith*, 449–50.

30. Reardon, *Coleridge to Gore* 415.

31. Bebbington, *Evangelicalism in Modern Britain*, 185.

but was allowed to return to his post. It was to be another year before he would be deposed by the general assembly. Reflecting on his own past crisis and describing his state of mind as he entered this new phase, Cairns wrote: "I had got my head above water before I went to the University. I had some real faith in Duty and in God's grace in Christ and a rather cumbrous armour of theology painfully laboured out on an inherited basis . . . but I was definitely away from Calvinism and fatalistic doctrine."[32]

Collapse of Faith

According to the English theologian and philosopher Clement C. J. Webb (1865–1954), there were four "outstanding assumptions" in currency in the first half of the nineteenth century: (1) that God was a transcendent being; (2) that the origin of the material world was an act of creation in time; (3) that Scripture was an authoritative revelation of truth which was otherwise unattainable by human rational powers; and that happiness and salvation of individual souls were the supreme concern of religion.[33]

As the century progressed, science challenged the idea of a teleological interpretation of the universe, the idea of a providential God and a purposive world. New developments in archaeology, psychology, anthropology, comparative religion, science (particularly the popularization of the theory of evolution), and history (especially as the historical method was applied to biblical criticism), led to skepticism and to questioning of these religious assumptions by some within the religious establishment. Two publications in the 1860s had contributed to the controversy and helped create what Stephen Bevans describes as one of the greatest religious debates in nineteenth-century Britain. The first, *Essays and Reviews*, published in 1860 by a group of six eminent Anglican clergymen and one lay contributor, the Egyptologist and lawyer Charles Wycliffe Goodwin. All were well-known scholars. The other was the first volume of a seventeen-volume work *The Pentateuch and the Book of Joshua, Critically Examined*, published in 1862 by John William Colenso, bishop of Natal in South Africa. These publications called into question belief in the inerrancy and literal truth of Scripture, and the assumption that Scripture was an authoritative divine revelation.

The Convocations of York and Canterbury condemned Colenso's work and requested his resignation. When he refused to comply, he was deposed by a synod of bishops convened by the bishop of Cape Town.[34]

32. Cairns, *Autobiography*, 87–88.

33. Bevans, *John Oman*, 26, cites Webb, *Study of Religious Thought*, 9.

34. Withrow, *Religious Progress of the Century*, 208.

Essays and Reviews was condemned by the Anglican Convocation in 1864.[35] Nonetheless, the latter book in particular "proved in the event to be a turning-point in the history of theological opinion in England."[36] The same issues had surfaced again in Scotland during the Robertson Smith case which was in its third year when Cairns went to university. The English historian George Malcolm Young describes this period in a way that allows us to empathize with the confusion that a young theology student of the time may have felt: "A sense of vagueness, of incoherence and indirection, grows on us as we watch the eighties struggling for a foothold in the swirl and wreckage of new ideas and old beliefs."[37]

Whatever emotional comfort Cairns had found through his conversion experience, it did not bring complete resolution; rather he found that "thought could not stop with this intuition of faith." The challenges raised by *Essays and Reviews* and biblical scholarship did not go away. At university, the study of philosophy raised further questions for him, and in his third year he had a sudden and complete collapse of faith. A century before, the German philosopher Immanuel Kant (1724–1804) had set out to show the limits of human reason by analyzing the conditions of knowledge. For Kant, the business of philosophy was to answer three questions: (1) What can I know? (2) What ought I to do? and (3) What may I hope for?[38] In Cairns's description of his feeling of desolation at his loss of faith, we can hear echoes of Kant's questions:

> I have a vivid snapshot of myself standing beneath a flaring gas-jet in my bedroom at Lonsdale Terrace, absolutely dismayed. How did I really *know* that anything in that inherited theology or such a construction of it as I had made was *true*— what *reason* had I for believing in God or Christ or immortality? I had, I thought, none. I had been laboriously building on a foundation which had now collapsed and brought with it the entire superstructure as well. But if there were no God, there was only a horror of great darkness, "a wide, grey, lampless, deep, unpeopled world."[39]

35. Bevans, *John Oman*, 27–29. *Essays and Reviews* was a theological symposium edited by H. B. Wilson, and contributed to by six well-known scholars: Frederick Temple, Rowland Williams, Baden Powell, Mark Pattison, Benjamin Jowett, and C. W. Goodwin. For a fuller account of this controversy, see also Brown, *Providence and Empire*, 234–41, and Reardon, *From Coleridge to Gore*, 321–59.

36. Reardon, *From Coleridge to Gore*, 321.

37. Young, *Victorian England, Portrait of an Age*, 165.

38. Wallace, *Kant*, 33, 61.

39. Cairns, *Autobiography*, 88–89.

There followed a deeply unhappy time, when Cairns kept his doubts and worries from friends and family, unable to understand his own reasons for this, but believing at some subconscious level that he had to work things out for himself. He suspected that his father knew and prayed for him, but there is no suggestion that he knew that his father too had suffered a similar experience in his student days in the late 1840s, and early 1850s, or that his uncle had in a letter to David Sr. greeted his anxieties with the reassurance, "I am pleased to hear that you are beginning to doubt all things." John Cairns saw such doubts as a necessary test of those who would go on to teach others. In a second letter, to his brother, he urged him to keep up his usual religious habits while examining rigorously the Christian arguments and doctrines, and declaring that "the ethics of doubt consisted in hope, prayer, and humility." Refusing to provide his brother with any answers, he assured him, "Nothing so chimerical is required as bringing your mind into a state of equilibrium before you proceed to examine the evidence."[40] Whether or not Cairns knew of this advice, he instinctively followed a very similar path through his own perplexity.

Donald Baillie's memoir, which introduces Cairns's autobiography, records that such comprehensive doubt was common among devout intellectuals of most Christian traditions in the nineteenth century.[41] Cairns wanted to believe, and his search for answers included reading the Scottish classic of the day, *Theism*, in which Professor Robert Flint (1838–1910) of the University of Edinburgh discusses the roles of science and religion in explaining the world, and defends theism as a reasonable theory that fits with scientific developments. In defining the theory he writes: "Theism is the doctrine that the universe owes its existence, and continuance in existence, to the reason and will of a self-existent Being, who is infinitely powerful, wise, and good. It is the doctrine that nature has a Creator and Preserver, the nations a Governor, men a heavenly Father and Judge."[42]

Reardon describes Flint as having an unshakable confidence in reason as the pillar of faith.[43] For Flint, there were aspects of faith discoverable by reason, and this natural theology was the foundation of all other theology, and the basis of all religion. He saw as foolish any attempt to teach a faith that denigrates reason, or relies blindly on authority, and declared that such methods would not convince people to believe in God. Reason could access countless evidences or proofs of God's existence: "They are to be found in

40. MacEwen, *Life and Letters of John Cairns*, 295, 340–42.

41. Cairns, *Autobiography*, 10.

42. Flint, *Theism*, 18.

43. Reardon, *From Coleridge to Gore*, 421.

all the forces, laws, and arrangements of nature—in every material object, every organism, every intellect and heart. At the same time they concur and coalesce into a single all-comprehensive argument, which is just the sum of the indications of God given by the physical universe, the minds of men, and human history. Nothing short of that is the full proof."[44]

For those beset by doubt and confused by the different theories, Flint concludes with advice from Robertson of Brighton. They should hold fast to the "simple landmarks of morality," as faith in duty will help restore faith in God.[45] Cairns reported that he found *Theism* of little use, as its traditional and scholastic apologetics with its very logical approach failed to convey the conviction necessary to revitalise his faith. However, the advice to hold fast to duty was one that he seemed to take, perhaps encouraged by the fact that Robertson of Brighton was one of his mother's favorite Broad Church divines, and therefore, someone whose views might be trusted. Cairns kept up his attendance at Palmerston Place Church, where a family friend, Armstrong Black, was minister. Feeling himself to be no longer a part of the faith community, he absented himself from Communion, and felt an acute sense of accompanying loss. Although this time of abject darkness and isolation, in which he felt cut off from Christian fellowship, did not last long, the mental anguish that resulted from it, coupled with a bout of pleurisy, led to a breakdown in his physical health, for which his doctor recommended a voyage. Before this breakdown, however, there was a first glimmer of hope when he underwent what he describes as "a genuine religious experience" during a subsequent Communion service.

> As I took the cup I realized that whether Christ was alive or not now He certainly had been alive at the first Communion, that He had instituted it then and had through many hundreds of hands placed it now in mine and that He must have meant it to convey some vital meaning and message; and what could that message have been? Was it not very simple, "My brother, the way of the cross is the way of light" (*Via Crucis, Via Lucis*). Face it, take up the Cross and follow me. I believe He did speak to me then.[46]

44. Reardon, *From Coleridge to Gore*, cites Flint, *Theism*, 62f.

45. Flint, *Theism*, 261–63.

46. Cairns, *Autobiography*, 90.

Egypt—a Search for New Foundations

The dogmatic foundations of his religion may have crumbled, but there was some faint reemergence of faith. At the end of January 1883, aged just twenty-one, Cairns set off for Constantinople. His father accompanied him on the train journey to Swansea, from where he sailed on the *Oakdale*, a ship owned by a friend of his brother John. He had congenial company in the captain and his one fellow passenger, a Congregationalist minister, who was also recovering from a breakdown in health. Experiencing a long bout of seasickness, the continuing pains and discomfort of his illness, and sleeplessness, Cairns found comfort in poetry, through which he was still looking for spiritual reassurance. He believed this journey changed the entire course of his life, and included as significant in the healing process a quiet experience which he had during the voyage. Lying on the deck in the sunshine one day, looking out over the vast space of sea and watching the waves rise and fall, he felt a conviction that it was absurd to suppose these movements were aimless, and concluded that "each wave in its movement had not only a *cause* but an *end*." As well as this growing sense of purpose, Cairns was becoming surer of the reality of moral obligation, and felt that the natural universe must be in harmony with these two realities.[47] In his focus on moral consciousness we see again the influence of Kant, for whom humankind's sense of unconditional moral obligation (the categorical imperative), which says "thou shalt do this" or "thou shalt not do that," only makes sense in terms of God, freedom and immortality.

Such subjects continued to be the focus of Cairns's mind, as he journeyed further from home. About two weeks after setting out from Swansea, the *Oakdale* docked in a sun-drenched Alexandria to exchange its cargo. Cairns admitted in a letter to his sister, Jessie, that on that first morning he "didn't feel up to much—a nasty stitch in the side and a troublesome asthma."[48] In spite of this, and of feeling unwell, he found the city a heady mixture. Little traveled as he was, he felt sheer wonder and delight at the scene before him, with a multitude of brown-skinned Arabs in their long robes and their (to him) strange speech. The British had bombarded Alexandria in July 1882, and then invaded Egypt and imposed British rule in September of the same year. Much of the city lay in ruins as the result of the riots and massacre which followed. When Cairns arrived in February 1883, it was an exciting place for a young man, with the presence of Kitchener and other high-ranking British officials. When Henry Drummond passed

47. Cairns, *Autobiography*, 92.

48. Letter to Jessie Cairns, from Cairo, 1883. MS3384/5, Box 1, D. S. Cairns Papers, Special Collections Centre, University of Aberdeen.

through the city four months after Cairns, in the summer of 1883, on his way to Africa, his biographer reports that "they found traces of bombardment on every hand, and saw the battle-field of Tel-el-Kebir still thick with cartridges; the desert all round is streaked with the marks of gun-carriages as if our canon had rolled over them yesterday."[49]

S. J. Brown points out that with the occupation of Egypt, Britain had become ruler over more Muslims than any other state in the world.[50] However, there is no indication that Cairns was aware of the underlying complexity of the situation in Egypt, in terms of the identification of Christianity with Western imperialism and the perceived undermining of indigenous culture and religion.

Meaning to return to the ship and continue his journey, Cairns took the evening train to Cairo so that he could see the pyramids. The city itself, with its mosques, minarets, ancient windmills, and distant pyramids, and with its striking views of the Nile Valley flanked by the Mokkatam Hills, entranced him and he decided to stay there.[51] Just before he had left home, one of his father's friends had given him an introduction to Rev. Dr. Julian Lansing of the United Presbyterian Church of the United States, which had a mission in Cairo. Lansing and his wife agreed to take Cairns as a boarder, and he remained with them for the next three months, first in the large house in Cairo which was the headquarters of the mission, and then in a small mission house in Helouan, a new town which had been built beside sulphurous springs, sixteen miles south of Cairo, and surrounded by desert on three sides, and on the other by the Mokkatam Hills. At the end of the nineteenth century it appears to have been a resort for wealthy Egyptians and a few international visitors, among whom was an American, Dr. James Lee, who wrote:

> The bright and sunny sky of Egypt is in itself an incentive to cheerfulness and pleasure which, combined with the amount of healthy open air exercise necessary to attain the enjoyment of sight-seeing, cannot fail to produce favourable results whenever that is possible. Indeed, in all cases where a dry and bracing air, bright sunshine, freed from rain and atmospheric impurities, are to be desired, the Egyptian winter's climate claims an important, if not the most important, place.[52]

49. Smith, *Life of Henry Drummond*, 178.

50. Brown, *Providence and Empire*, 301–3.

51. For photographs and descriptions of Cairo around this period, see Lee and Bain, *Photographic Views of Bible Lands*. This book is not page numbered, but follows chronologically the geography of the life of Christ.

52. Lee and Bain, *Photographic Views*.

Between 1878 and 1879, during the period of his heresy trial, William Robertson Smith had made two extended visits to Egypt and the Middle East, and had written a series of ten letters that appeared in the *Scotsman* between February and June 1880. In one of these letters, Smith had mentioned the magnificence of the desert air and its health-giving qualities.[53] Cairns was to experience a similar effect during his stay in Cairo and Helouan, and there he began to see his way out of his mental confusion.[54] In a letter to Jessie he claimed to have fallen on his feet in finding the Lansings, and described the pure, clear air of Egypt as having an "enlivening effect" on him. He sent her vivid descriptions of the landscape, of humorous encounters with guides and beggars, and of travels to the pyramids, including one ten-mile "gallop and canter" on donkey-back to the pyramids of Ghiza, in the blazing sun—from which, surprisingly he had no ill-effects other than stiffness.[55]

Dr. Lansing belonged to a church which had grown out of the Scottish Secession, but which was by that time connected to it only by name. Cairns described its theology as Calvinist and its view of the Bible as orthodox. They sang only psalms, but according to him, were ingenious enough to give sections of the psalms modern headings, such as: "THE LIQUOR SELLER," who "shall sit in the villages to slay the innocent!"[56]

In spite of what he saw as the limits set by their doctrinal framework, he admired the practical work and witness of the missionary families, for whom God and Christ were living realities. In particular he came to admire a Scottish missionary who came to stay with the Lansings, Dr. John Hogg of Assuit (1833–1886), who was a lowland Scot like himself, and whom Cairns later described as one of the most notable personalities that he had ever met. Hogg combined learning, devotion, and practical service in a way that Cairns had witnessed in his parents, reinforcing his belief that "every good man and woman is a witness to the structure of the universe and the nature and purpose of its Creator." Cairns relished the good company, and the general experience in which everything was "novel and wonderful" to him. The days were for exploring, often walking into the desert hills in the mornings and afternoons with Lansing's shotgun, and hoping to shoot a vulture so that he could "have his enormous wings," or using binoculars to view the pyramids forty or fifty miles away.[57] The evenings were spent in reading and

53. Black and Chrystal, *Life of William Robertson Smith*, 302–13, 333–38.

54. Cairns, *Autobiography*, 94–101.

55. Letter to Jessie Cairns, from Cairo, 1883. MS3384/5, Box 1, D. S. Cairns Papers.

56. Cairns, *Autobiography*, 95.

57. Letter to his father, from Helouan, April 1883. MS3384/1, Box 1, D. S. Cairns

study, with an hourly interval for singing and conversation. There was little talk of religion, but a genial atmosphere, which had a steadying and healing influence.[58] Nurtured in this way, Cairns continued his theological quest, describing his feelings during this period:

> I was still groping about in the ruins of my dogmatic con-
> victions, which had been undermined, as I have said, by the
> shaking of the very foundations. I had by now to get firmer
> foundations in the new conviction that things must have a
> meaning, that even the waves of the Mediterranean were there
> for some purpose as well as some cause. And I felt more and
> more that moral obligation was at least as inescapable a real-
> ity as anything to which the waves could bear witness and that
> the natural universe must in its depth and reality be such as to
> contain and be in harmony with these things.[59]

Dr. Lansing was an Oriental scholar, and did not have much in the way of the philosophical or theological literature that Cairns felt he needed, but the young student had brought a few books with him. During the long journey southward from Waverley Station, there had been several stops, and at a bookstall in one of the railway stations Cairns bought two books by Dr. Newman Smyth (1843–1925), an American Congregationalist pastor and theologian with a national reputation as a preacher and scholar. Throughout his working life, Smyth refused many offers of prestigious professorships, in favor of the ministry, and remained one of his country's most widely read and respected liberal theologians.[60] His books, *The Religious Feeling* (New York, 1877) and *Old Faiths in New Light* (New York, 1879) provided read-ing material for Cairns's stay in Egypt, and seemed to fit with his develop-ing thoughts. They made a deep impression on him, and in retrospect he regarded them as of more help than many of the more famous texts of the day, setting out a theology that seemed to him reasonable. Smyth was sym-pathetic to the historical-critical approach to Scripture, and in *The Religious Feeling* he attempted to synthesize the theology of Friedrich Schleiermacher and Charles Darwin's evolutionary theory, calling for a Christianity that welcomed modern thought: for a faith that was "more in harmony with the present condition of our knowledge."[61] He was optimistic, interpreting the *zeitgeist* not as a force destructive of faith, but as "an earnest spirit, at heart

---

Papers.

58. Cairns, *Autobiography*, 94–101.
59. Cairns, *Autobiography*, 100.
60. Gowing, "Ecumenical Dreams and Deeds."
61. Smyth, *Religious Feeling*, 8.

reverent of truth and searching for its Lord."[62] For Cairns, searching for a new theological framework, Smyth's ideas were inspiring and reassuring.

New Light—the Influence of Newman Smyth

In *The Religious Feeling*, Smyth begins by pointing out the persistence in human history of faith in spiritual and divine realities and agrees that the problem of the times is to decide whether or not we can justify belief in a spiritual dimension to life. Smyth saw the *Zeitgeist* as an earnest spirit of inquiry that had reverence for the truth, and like Kant, he asked if humankind is capable of coming to a knowledge of God. Having been used to defensive reactions in theology, it is easy to see how the author's positive approach would have appealed to the young Cairns. Describing the opportunity that contemporary skepticism offers, Smyth declares:

> It is surely not a loss, but a great gain, that in the discussions of modern times the main religious question becomes more and more disentangled from the minor perplexities of theology. It is a sign of progress that the religious question upon which the printing presses in these days are most busy, is not a question of sect or school. . . . The question facing us to-day, which we can avoid only be retreating from the nineteenth century, is a question of the very life of religion itself, a question between any theology and no theology; between faith in the spirit and the Father of all spirits, and faith only in the visible order of things.[63]

Smyth embraced the theology of Schleiermacher, for whom truth was not just a matter of logic and reason, but something that could be apprehended through an innate spiritual faculty in humankind. The German theologian ascribed the basis of all religions to a feeling of absolute dependence on something other; he saw such feeling as integral to humankind's consciousness of existence, and always preceding any conscious thought of God. Humankind feel their dependency on the Other, then try to conceive what the Other is like, and find a way to describe this Other. For Schleiermacher, reason may give shape to a conception of Divinity, but it has not created in the human mind the idea of God. People intuit something that is there already, and reflecting on this feeling or intuition, use reason to help them shape doctrines and beliefs, usually belief in some kind of overruling

62. Smyth, *Religious Feeling*, 11.

63. Smyth, *Religious Feeling*, 10.

Providence. In the case of Christianity, the sense of dependence is conceived of and expressed as dependence on God who is a loving Father.[64]

Reminding his readers of the advice of science to make sparing use of the word "impossible," Smyth reflects on the possible modes of relationship between the Spirit of God and the spirit in humankind, and on the influence of the Divine over the human which cannot be subjected to scientific analysis. He describes such influence as "the felt *magnetism* of the Unseen Presence over the human heart," which may come through the created order . . .

> and, in this case, we should still have, not merely our own conclusions, or reasonings toward God from His works, but through these we should receive directly the inflowing influence of the Creator upon His creatures;—His works may be not merely dead memorials of His activity, proofs to the reason that once there has been a God, but also living means of God's present self-revelations, the channels, as it were, of the incoming of God's presence and power to human hearts.[65]

According to Smyth, the source of religious faith was the immediate feeling of God, but faith was only complete when it had "passed through, unscathed, the process of reasoning."[66] The logical powers had to examine the feeling and the beliefs that grew out of it, and either show the inadequacies of such faith or accept it as a genuine source of knowledge. Unless God can be proved to be an impossibility, the most that skepticism can say is "that the Divine is beyond our mental reach, and incomprehensible."[67] For Cairns, struggling to recover faith in a world that had come to see science as coextensive with rationality, Smyth's work declared confidently that it is not "unthinkable, or inconceivable" to accept a view of the world in which there is a spiritual power at work.[68]

Turning to Smyth's later publication, *Old Faiths in a New Light*, the dedication of the book to "an honored father and a revered mother," must have resonated deeply with Cairns's own feelings; likewise Smyth's description of the book as the "result of the endeavour to keep the birthright of a Christian childhood through the doubts and questionings of after years."

This dedication echoed so clearly his own situation, and the book was probably the inspiration for his quiet conviction of purpose, as will be seen in the next paragraph. Like Cairns, Smyth had grown up in an academic and

64. Smyth, *Religious Feeling*, 23–29.
65. Smyth, *Religious Feeling*, 108–9.
66. Smyth, *Religious Feeling*, 117.
67. Smyth, *Religious Feeling*, 119.
68. Smyth, *Religious Feeling*, 108.

evangelical family, and was greatly influenced by the thinking of his mother. He too was frustrated by "the sheer unreality of orthodox dogmatism." As a student, Smyth spent time in Germany, and came under the influence of Friedrich August Tholuck, who taught his pupils to embrace historical criticism, and that experience, not doctrine, is the central element in Christianity. According to Tholuck, "It was possible to pursue theology in a reflective, nondefensive, historical manner that was both modern and evangelical."[69] His teaching had a life-changing impression on Smyth, and its influence is seen in these books that appeared around a decade later.

In *Old Faiths in New Light*, Smyth focuses much of his attention on the issue of scientific and religious approaches to biblical criticism, pointing out that the discrepancy in views about the Bible between scholars and church members has had a corrosive effect on faith. "The mere suspicion that the advanced scholarship and the old faiths are to-day at variance, is itself a fruitful cause of popular indifference and unbelief." People have a little knowledge, but not enough on which to make sound judgments. He wants to meet what he sees as the "growing need of intelligent people" for reasoned argument and explains that the purpose of his book is to "bring together the material and the spiritual, the natural and the supernatural, in one continuous and rounded whole of knowledge." In order to pursue this ideal or "ultimate philosophy" he will draw on the work of specialists in the religious and scientific fields. Smyth sets the tone for his work by suggesting that while we cannot be blind to modern thought, any criticism of the old faiths should be done cautiously, and with a desire to get at the facts. "We are justified in pulling down as we cherish the purpose of building up."[70] His book reveals a wide knowledge of British and German theologians from Erskine of Linlathen to Schleiermacher, of the philosophies of Kant and Hegel, as well as familiarity with the work of specialists in other fields, including Charles Darwin, Hugh Miller, T. H. Huxley, Herbert Spencer, and the Scottish physicists Balfour Stewart and P. G. Tait. Smyth's criticism of the theories of the English philosopher and sociologist Herbert Spencer, appears likely to have contributed to Cairns's restored belief in the idea of a purposive universe. Smyth describes Spencer's social evolutionism as a mechanistic interpretation of history which "seizes the form, and misses the spirit of history," and goes on to say,

> It observes the uniformity of the waves, and the regularity in their rise and fall; but it does not measure the tides, and their higher law. It may be an accurate science of the relation and

69. Dorien, *Making of American Liberal Theology*, 284–85.

70. Smyth, *Old Faiths in New Light*, v–viii, 13–32.

succession of social phenomena; but it is not a philosophy of history, for it holds no plummet by which to fathom the deeper currents, and has no means of determining the destiny toward which the life of man is swept on.[71]

Calling for a new apologetics based on modern ideas of development, he encourages his readers to renounce the demagogic interpretations of both science and religion, to forego the temptation to use proof-texts to support favored dogmas, and to "rejoice in beholding the wonderful treasures of the kingdom of truth."[72]

> A faith that leans upon its own prejudices cannot stand long in the days when all things are shaken. There is only one state of mind which in such investigations is truly and profoundly reverent and religious, and that is, the desire to find the facts as they are. Whoever is afraid of science does not believe in God![73]

Smyth goes on to suggest that the discoveries of each discipline have their part to play in the search for truth. Each may offer fragments of knowledge which today appear unconnected, but will one day reveal a "grand, connected story." He sees the science-religion debate as an ongoing development that is reaching its "third epoch." In the first stage there had been a violent attack on the Bible from science, followed by a violent defence. The second epoch had been marked by attempts at reconciliation by both sides. The question for the third epoch is not can religion and science be reconciled, but:

> How are we to use the help of both—the light of science, and of the spirit—in a rational interpretation of the universe? It is, in short, the age of critical review and of judicial reconstruction.[74]

It seems likely that this challenge acted as a call to arms for Cairns, for he would spend the coming years reading widely in a variety of disciplines, constructing a new theological framework, and as it turned out, preparing for his first work of apologetics. However, while Smyth's work had an affirming effect on Cairns, it had the opposite effect on some American

71. Smyth, *Old Faiths in New Light*, 24.

72. Smyth, *Old Faiths in New Light*, 16–19. For Smyth the great contribution of evolutionary theory was its investment of the idea of development with a new power, making development the dominant idea of modern thought. Everything, including Christianity, the Bible, and the concept of immortality had to be subjected to the test of that idea.

73. Smyth, *Old Faiths in New Light*, 63–64.

74. Smyth, *Old Faiths in New Light*, 27.

theologians, who distrusted his liberal ideas, and particularly his doctrine of "future probation," in which he declared, "The possibility of a progressive sanctification after death deserves to be part of the faith of a progressive Christian orthodoxy."[75]

Return to University Life

In spite of his experiences in Egypt, Cairns was not well enough to return to university until 1886, and did not finish his arts degree until 1888, eight years after matriculating. As a child he had been healthy, apart from one bout of rheumatic fever, but in his teenage years he experienced what he describes as "a period of rather depressed health," which made him timid in regard to physical exercise, and in turn exacerbated his feelings of weakness. Egypt may have cured his pleurisy, but he was still not in full health. A letter to his father from Helouan indicated a preoccupation with a variety of symptoms which individually do not appear to be of a serious nature: for instance he spoke of "uneasiness about the right side" which a doctor diagnosed as indigestion. He also referred to an enlargement of his right lung, which he had been told will never be completely cured, but will cause no trouble if he is not reckless and looks after his digestion. He was advised that he must take special care of himself for three or four years until his physique is matured, and concluded, "This, I think, is as much as I can look for reasonably, practical health for work."[76]

On his return from Egypt he was advised to call off the strenuous work of the university, and for the next two years he became tutor to the family of William Hilson, a tweed manufacturer and provost in Jedburgh. Life in this Seceder household was happy but quiet and there was plenty of time for reading. Never quite free from chest pain and a feeling of weakness, and realizing that his university friends were moving on ahead of him, Cairns found little help from the church. According to the English cleric and author Charles W. Stubbs (1845–1912), many people in the nineteenth century looked to the poets rather than the theologians for insight, because there could be found "the true warm religious emotion of men's hearts rather than the cold conventional thoughts of their minds."[77] A. C. Cheyne endorsed this view that the clergy had been replaced as intellectual leaders, with Christianity on the defensive since the higher criticism had destroyed its foundation

75. Dorrien, *Making of American Liberal Theology*, 291–92.

76. Letter to his father, from Helouan, April 1883. MS3384/1, Box 1, D. S. Cairns Papers.

77. Stubbs, review of *The Poetry of Robert Browning*, 363–73.

doctrine of the inerrancy of Scripture.[78] In his continuing debilitated state of health, Cairns found solace in the poetry of Robert Browning (1812–1889), whom he described as his "main prophet."[79] Having picked up a Tauchnitz four-volume edition of Browning in Cairo,[80] he continued to read the poet while in Jedburgh, and through his subsequent years at university Browning remained "a companion to my solitude."[81] "Browning, with his immense vitality and knowledge, and above all with his blend of analytic scepticism and fundamental but unconventional faith, appealed irresistibly to me as the teacher who met my needs as had no one else. I cannot forget that debt and I do not think that there is any book-writing teacher of my youth to whom I owe so warm a feeling of gratitude as Robert Browning."[82]

To a young student, undergoing a crisis of faith, Browning offered optimism and hope, and according to Reardon, "he offered the cosmos as an adventure rather than a scheme."[83] His belief in striving as one of the highest human virtues, even if seemingly ineffective,[84] must have held an irresistible attraction for the young Cairns who was "temperamentally inclined to be apprehensive."[85]

On his return to the University of Edinburgh in 1886, Cairns went, with his brother Willie, to live at the home of his grandmother and aunt at 6 Lonsdale Terrace. Although she was in her late eighties, his grandmother was the dominant personality in the house, and he admired her character and strength. He and Willie went every Saturday to have dinner with his uncles John and Willie and with his aunt Janet, who acted as their housekeeper at 10 Spence Street. Although he lived with his grandmother, Cairns did not attend her church at Lauriston, choosing instead to attend Palmerston Place Church where the family friend, Armstrong Black, was minister. When Cairns began worshipping in Palmerston Place, he was invited to sit in the manse pew for the two services, morning and afternoon, and between times, he joined Black's family for lunch in the manse in Lennox Street. According to Cairns, Black was never entirely at home

78. Cheyne, *Transforming of the Kirk*, 184.

79. Cairns, *Autobiography*, 104.

80. The Leipzig-based publisher Christian Bernhard Freiherr von Tauchnitz (1816–1895) produced cheap paperback versions of English-language classics, which were to be sold only in countries outside the UK and USA.

81. Cairns, *Autobiography*, 120.

82. Cairns, *Autobiography*, 105.

83. Chesterton's comment on Browning's hopeful activism in Reardon, *From Coleridge to Gore*, 370.

84. Dunn, *Robert Browning*, 37.

85. Cairns, *Autobiography*, 111.

in the United Presbyterian Church, nor sure that he should have become a minister, but to him Black was a deeply religious man to whom he owed a big spiritual and mental debt.[86] Black's tentativeness in the face of so much Presbyterian dogmatism may have had a reassuring effect on Cairns as he struggled with his own doubts.

Other significant relationships developed too. From his earliest days at university, Cairns developed an enduring friendship with a childhood acquaintance, Ivor Roberton, whose naturally optimistic character was a foil to his own anxious temperament. Roberton was the son of a Free Church minister. After university, Roberton was ordained to the ministry of the Church of Scotland, and from 1907 to 1925 was minister of Regent Square Church in London. In later life, he served a term as moderator of the Presbyterian Church in England and was for some years president of its Foreign Mission Committee. Before moving to London, Roberton had ministered in Galashiels in the Borders, and there he was again to come to the rescue of Cairns in a time of great personal difficulty.[87] Another friend from this period was Thomas Kirkup (1844–1912), whom Cairns visited on a regular basis. Kirkup, a shepherd's son, was also from the Scottish borders, and had begun theological training but decided against going into the ministry when he gave up the traditional theology that he had inherited, becoming a well-known author of books on socialism. *An Enquiry into Socialism*, published in London in 1888, remains one of the definitive works on the subject. Among Kirkup's other works was a primer of socialism (1908), cowritten with Edward Reynolds Pearce, secretary of the Fabian Society. Following Kirkup's death in 1912, Pearce updated Kirkup's *History of Socialism*, first published in 1892. Cairns admitted to learning a lot from this friendship, particularly about the importance of the economic interpretation of history, and about the nature of British and Continental socialism.[88] When he published his first book, in 1906, *Christianity in the Modern World*, he included mention of this indebtedness to "Mr. Thomas Kirkup, from whom, of all modern authorities upon the Social Question, I have learned most."[89]

Such friendships sustained and challenged Cairns as he tried to get back into academic life. Neo-Hegelian philosophy dominated the universities, but did not attract him, apart from T. H. Green's *Prolegomena to Ethics*. Even there the attraction was limited, for while he agreed with Green's demonstration that "all thought implied a human self above the flux of

86. Cairns, *Autobiography*, 117.
87. Cairns, *Autobiography*, 110–11.
88. Cairns, *Autobiography*, 117–18.
89. Cairns, *Christianity in the Modern World*, vii.

sensations," he found Green's concept of the "universal self" inadequate as a substitute for the idea of God as Father. Neo-Hegelian philosophy seemed to Cairns to be "bleached and impoverished" but he lacked the physical stamina for rigorous study and as a consequence was unable to engage fully in the philosophical debate, and "so had an inferiority complex on the whole question."[90] Apart from moral philosophy and English literature, he struggled through his classes, especially mathematics, which he eventually succeeded in passing only at the very end of his theology course.

Henry Drummond and the Religious Awakening in the University

Cairns recorded that in his first period at university the religious life of the students had been at a low ebb. Most arts students had church connections and some were involved in missions, but there was little or no corporate religious life, not even a regular service in the university chapel. When he returned to his studies in 1886 he found the whole spiritual atmosphere changed, with many students meeting in prayer groups during the week, and around six hundred of them attending evangelistic meetings on Sunday nights in Oddfellows Hall on Forest Road.[91] The location was chosen because it was the nearest building to the university capable of holding such large numbers. The meetings often reached the hall's capacity of nine hundred.[92]

Two main factors led to this change at the university. First, since the late 1850s, student Christian associations had been growing in Scotland, and their members devoted themselves to prayer and personal spiritual growth.[93] Such associations would later form the basis for the Student Christian Movement in Britain. Second, the American evangelist Dwight L. Moody had visited Britain during 1873–75. During this time a group of Free Church ministers, led by James Hood Wilson, invited Moody and his partner in mission, Ira D. Sankey to Scotland.[94] S. J. Brown describes the campaign, which began in Edinburgh. The evangelists held three meetings a day, including a midday prayer meeting at which the average congregation numbered two thousand. Focusing on the need for conversion, Moody's Bible teaching had a style that incorporated illustrations from everyday life, many of them humorous. Sankey's music was sentimental and his tunes were

90. Cairns, *Autobiography*, 108.
91. Cairns, *Autobiography*, 112.
92. Smith, *Life of Henry Drummond*, 298–99.
93. Boyd, *Witness of the Student Christian Movement*, 2–3.
94. Drummond and Bulloch, *Church in Late Victorian Scotland, 1874–1900*, 9.

catchy. Together they provided an experience that was warm and emotional without the kind of sensationalism that accompanied some kinds of revivalist meetings. Their mission strategy involved holding inquiry meetings after the services, at which volunteers would speak to any anxious inquirers who chose to stay behind. Among those who helped in the inquiry rooms were many respected church leaders, including John Cairns. By the time of their final Glasgow meeting in the Botanical Gardens, April 1874, an estimated twenty thousand gathered to hear them, and about two thousand stayed behind for the inquirers' meeting.[95] In contrast to Sunday morning church congregations, many men were in attendance at the revivalist meetings, sometimes exceeding the number of women.[96]

Into this milieu arrived Henry Drummond (1851–1897). He had entered New College in 1870, just as William Robertson Smith was leaving the city to take up his chair in Aberdeen. Moody recruited students to stay behind to discuss with inquirers issues raised during the meetings, and Drummond was among the students who offered to help. Moody also sent out speakers on deputation to other parts of the country, to address meetings and describe the work that was going on. On seeing the impact that Drummond's addresses had on a meeting in Elgin, Moody asked him to continue the work among young men in places that he and Sankey had already visited.[97]

Finishing his theological studies in New College in 1876, Drummond felt a strong pull toward work as an evangelist, but had difficulty deciding on the precise nature of his vocation. He worked for a few months as assistant to the minister at the Barclay Church, but the congregational routine did not appeal to him, although he enjoyed the evangelistic meetings on Sunday nights, with the opportunities to speak to those who stayed behind to inquire. Drummond had seen the importance of individual conversations, even before he encountered Moody's techniques. In a paper to the Theological Society at New College, near the start of the 1873–74 session, he had "electrified" his audience with his essay on "Spiritual Diagnosis," in which he suggested that ministers would achieve a more powerful effect by "buttonholing" individuals rather than by preaching sermons.[98]

Following another of his main interests, science, when a vacancy occurred in the area of natural science in the Free Church College in Glasgow,

95. Brown, *Providence and Empire*, 278–82; Smith, *Life of Henry Drummond*, 54–100; and Drummond and Bulloch, *Church in Late Victorian Scotland, 1874–1900*, 9–18.

96. Smith, *Life of Henry Drummond*, 56.

97. Smith, *Life of Henry Drummond*, 62–68.

98. Smith, *Life of Henry Drummond*, 50.

Drummond applied and was appointed to the lectureship. Donald Carswell points out that with only four classes a week for five months of the year, he was able to teach there while conducting a ten-year evangelistic movement among university students in Edinburgh. Carswell also indicates Drummond's lack of academic qualification for the post, having never completed his BSc course.[99] However, Drummond appealed to his former teacher, Professor Archibald Geikie, who had the chair of Geology and Mineralogy at Edinburgh, and received a reference that he believed got him the job.[100]

According to William Robertson Nicoll, the Free Church was at this time in danger of surrendering its intellectual life. While it was "refusing to shape the dogmas of traditional Christianity in such a way as to meet the subtle intellectual and moral demands of an essentially scientific age," like Robertson Smith, Drummond showed that it was possible to embrace science and the new criticism and still be a "convinced and fervent evangelical."[101] Drummond had wrestled with the great theological issues of the day, especially those related to biblical scholarship and to evolutionary theory and the relation of science to Christian faith. His thinking on these two areas was very much influenced by Dr. Marcus Dods, at the time minister of Renfield Free Church in Glasgow. Dods had ordained Drummond as an elder and put him in charge of his church's mission station at Possilpark, where he worked for four years from September 1878. Drummond's biographer writes that Dr. Dods's knowledge provided the younger man with "numerous opportunities for repairing the defects of his own education."[102] Drummond developed an attitude of openness and he encouraged others to adopt a positive approach to science. For Boyd, it was this honesty and openness that made students flock to hear him, including many who had previously found their faith discredited by the churches' defensive posturing. When Drummond called on students to volunteer for overseas missionary service, hundreds responded positively.[103]

George Adam Smith sets out Drummond's views on the relationship between science and religion in a short chapter in his biography.[104] Summarized, they are as follows: (1) Science and religion do not have to be in conflict, in fact religion could put to good use the instruments of "scientific

99. Carswell, *Brother Scots*, 21-22.

100. Smith, *Life of Henry Drummond*, 117.

101. Nicoll, "Henry Drummond." Nicoll also points out that since the 1860s, the Hebrew scholar A. B. Davidson had been quietly teaching his New College students that the old views of revelation would have to be seriously altered.

102. Smith, *Life of Henry Drummond*, 132.

103. Boyd, *Witness of the Student Christian Movement*, 3-4.

104. Smith, *Life of Henry Drummond*, 227-44.

method" and "the concept of evolution." However, scientific method must be used in conjunction with the scientific spirit, the former being characterized by fearlessness and originality, and the latter tempered by caution, modesty, and reverence. Science has given Christianity a theory of the method of creation (evolution), which thoughtful minds can accept, but it cannot give proof of its hypothesis, nor provide any answers about the ultimate mystery of origins. Neither scientists nor theologians are unanimous in their views, but the evolutionary principle is widely held by theologians, and for Drummond, it increases the sense of worship. (2) As far as revelation is affected by the theory, he points out that creation is a form of revelation, the oldest and most universal form of revelation, and based on the law of the uniformity of nature a strong presumption may be made that any other revelation, in this case the Bible, might also be evolutionary. Applying evolutionary theory to the Bible has made it more meaningful to the modern person. For instance, seeing it in its historical and cultural context has helped resolve what some see as the moral difficulties raised by some sections of the Old Testament. Such difficulties have led to skepticism about religion in general, but the new methods of scholarship remove some significant barriers to faith. The problem of reconciling the findings of geology with the first book of Genesis, for example, is irrelevant when one adopts the new, nonliteral approach to the Bible. Science and religion present their truths in very different ways.

Carswell describes Drummond's thinking as vague and incoherent, but suggests that that was part of its appeal. According to Carswell, the average man of the 1880s wanted to hear somebody "who would save his soul without insulting his intelligence," and Drummond met this need.[105] Even Smith, his biographer, questioned some of the assumptions on which he tried to build his Christian apologetic, but nonetheless admitted the inspiration and practical help his writing provided for hundreds of thousands of readers.[106] By the time Cairns had returned to university, Drummond had been appointed to the new chair of Natural Science in Glasgow in 1884, and had already published his first book, *The Natural Law in the Spiritual World*, which brought him widespread fame. Later in 1894, he would publish *The Ascent of Man*. Cairns admitted that Drummond was no theologian or philosopher, but his Christian faith, combined with a charismatic personality contributed to his ability to captivate hundreds of young men, and to convince them that their decision whether to accept or reject Christ was a matter of life and death.[107] To the end of his life Drummond saw his evangelistic

105. Carswell, *Brother Scots*, 27–48, 50.

106. Smith, *Life of Henry Drummond*, 142–46.

107. Cairns, *Autobiography*, 114.

work among students as his main work.[108] "It haunts me like a nightmare. The responsibility I feel almost more than anything in my life. I do not think I would exchange that audience for anything else in the world."[109]

Moody and Sankey had returned to Britain from 1881–83 for another campaign, and in 1882 a group of seven young Cambridge men had volunteered for work with the China Inland Mission. In December and January 1884–85, two of the "Cambridge Seven," Stanley Smith and C. T. Studd, came to speak to the students in Edinburgh, encouraging and inspiring others to dedicate themselves to missionary service. Robin Boyd describes the Seven as "a group of popular if somewhat elitist young graduate sportsmen,"[110] two of whom were army officers.[111] The willingness of young men of brilliance who were willing to give up prestigious careers at home for the sake of the gospel had a powerful motivating effect on young students, showing that manliness and Christian witness were not incompatible.[112] Moody's evangelistic campaign had also had the effect of leading many of the students to seek conversion.

"Young Christianity had found a cause, a channel for bounding energies to: 'burn out for Christ' in the world which both within and beyond the growing British empire, was opening up to exploration and adventure."[113]

By this time, Drummond had published his first book, and had been appointed professor at Glasgow. Some felt that he was the one to lead this new movement of the spirit, and he was invited to address a meeting in Edinburgh, following the departure of Smith and Studd. This turned out to be the first of many, as he returned every Sunday except one to the end of the session.[114]

According to Smith, "It was simply announced that 'Professor Drummond would give an address,' and an audience gathered that nearly filled the hall."[115] His Sunday night addresses in Oddfellows Hall were evangelistic, but not sentimental in the way that Moody's had been, with his em-

108. Smith, *Life of Henry Drummond*, 295.

109. Smith, *Life of Henry Drummond*, 301. Smith has amalgamated quotes from two of Drummond's letters. The first two lines are from a letter to Lord Aberdeen, January 6, 1887, in which Drummond refers to his impending work among students in Edinburgh. The last line is from a letter dated March 3, 1887. These letters are respectively on pp. 272 and 319 in Smith.

110. Boyd, *Witness of the Student Christian Movement*, 3.

111. Clements, *Faith on the Frontier*, 27.

112. Smith, *Life of Henry Drummond*, 298.

113. Symonds, *Oxford and Empire*, 250; cited in Clements, *Faith on the Frontier*, 27.

114. Smith, *Life of Henry Drummond*, 298.

115. Smith, *Life of Henry Drummond*, 299.

phasis on the Judgment of God and on public declarations of repentance and conversion. Rather, Drummond encouraged thinking things over in the quiet of one's bedroom at home. He believed strongly in speaking on a one-to-one basis, believing this personal approach more effective than the sermon, and he spent much time being available for discussion after his meetings.[116] Cairns had felt uncomfortable with Moody's approach when once they met in a Kelso church and Moody had asked him outright if he was saved. He felt that this approach did not suit the Scottish students, and thought that Drummond intuited this, realizing that the students were struggling to find a way to maintain faith without sacrificing intellect or reason, and were already under a great deal of pressure.[117] The size of these meetings, their intensity of atmosphere, and their effects on the students are described in detail in Smith's biography.[118]

Drummond's addresses were not welcomed universally, for, according to Nicoll there were those who saw his reconciliation of science and religion as premature, and based on insufficient knowledge of the nature of either. Some judged that he did not give due consideration to the concepts of personality, freedom and conscience.[119] Cairns related that the older evangelicals accused him of giving a superficial view of the gospel.[120] There were those also who questioned his doctrine of the atonement, and the fact that he did not talk about it at the Oddfellows gatherings. Smith documents some letters that asked pointedly about Drummond's position on the matter. He includes one that recounts a private conversation in which Drummond was asked for a "yes" or "no" to the question, "Do you believe that the sacrifice of Christ is the essential and basal thing in the Christian religion?" His reply was "No," but he added, "If I may venture a supplementary remark I would say that in my opinion the sacrifice of Christ is a part of the very essence of Christianity, but the basis of Christianity is the eternal love of God."[121]

In his short life Drummond traveled to many countries, and in 1890 he was invited to a tour of Australian colleges, planning to come back to Scotland via China and Japan, where he could also visit students. In a letter to a friend, written as he was preparing for the journey, he spoke about the reading material he was planning to take, including George MacDonald's *Robert Falconer*, but he continues, "My *piece de resistance*, however,

---

116. Smith, *Life of Henry Drummond*, 50–51.

117. Cairns, *Autobiography*, 112–13.

118. Smith, *Life of Henry Drummond*, 295–339.

119. Nicoll, "Henry Drummond."

120. Cairns, *Autobiography*, 112.

121. Smith, *Life of Henry Drummond*, 335.

will be Browning. I am taking him complete, and mean to go through with him thoroughly. None can approach him for insight into life, or even into Christianity."[122]

A companion on board, an Italian count, was also an admirer of Browning, and the two spent time reading the poet aloud together.[123] Four years after this voyage Drummond published his best-known sermon, based on 1 Corinthians chapter 13. In "The Greatest Thing in the World," he describes the supreme good as love, with its source in God—God is love. For Drummond love is the answer to every moral and social predicament, and he describes in very practical terms how it might be put into practice through the nurturing of the qualities specified in his text: patience, kindness, generosity, humility, courtesy, unselfishness, good temper, guilelessness and sincerity. He agrees with Browning that "Love is energy of Life," to be accessed by humanity, and in quoting the following he seems to agree with him that life is more than anything an opportunity for developing this capacity.

> For life, with all it yields of joy and woe
>
> And hope and fear,
>
> Is just our chance o' the prize of learning love—
>
> How love might be, hath been indeed, and is.[124]

Drummond also declares that love is the test of all religion, not belief; it is how people relate to the needs of those around them, how they treat humanity, that is the decisive factor. As for God's love for people, it is expressed in a detailed Providence in every part of life. It was this aspect of his teaching that Cairns found most challenging. How might this be harmonized with the scientific conception of nature as an impersonal system of law? This problem haunted him in the years to come and in making a first attempt at a solution he produced the first printed article he ever wrote for the *Contemporary Review*.[125] The article, "Science and Providence," was one of a series Cairns wrote on the problems connected with belief in Christianity in the intellectual milieu of the day. This and the other subsequent articles were revised and published as his first book, *Christianity in the Modern*

---

122. Smith, *Life of Henry Drummond*, 293.

123. Smith, *Life of Henry Drummond*, 359–60.

124. Drummond, *Greatest Thing in the World*, 26.

125. *Contemporary Review*, founded in Oxford in 1866, was a quarterly journal devoted to discussion of important issues of the day. It was liberal in outlook and independent in character, attracting contributors of distinction, like Ruskin, Huxley, F. D. Maurice, and Matthew Arnold.

World, Studies in the Theology of the Kingdom of God, in 1906. Cairns also attributed the roots of this article to the conviction of purposiveness which he had experienced on board the *Oakdale* when traveling to Egypt.[126]

Like Browning, Drummond tried to reconcile the idea of a loving God with the existence of pain and suffering. His thoughts were later to be delivered as the Lowell Lectures in Boston, and published as *The Ascent of Man* in 1894. Nicoll describes this as Drummond's last and greatest book. In it, he discusses the commonly accepted version of evolution as an individualistic system in which nature is morally indifferent. By contrast, Drummond postulates an intrinsic altruism at the core of the evolutionary process. For him, there can be no dualism between the physical and moral order of the world; the natural law must be moral.[127]

Whatever the shortcomings of his science or philosophy, Cairns always felt gratitude for Drummond's teaching, which helped him make the transition from inherited theology to a new perspective of faith that fitted with his own generation. In old age, he still remembered the day of Drummond's death, with "its whirling snow."

"I am certainly thankful to have had him as one of my teachers in spiritual things, for he helped me greatly in a transition time at once to hold fast to what was permanent in the old tradition and at the same time go on into the new world of thought with a new freedom."[128]

There was a strong social dimension to Drummond's theology. The American theologian Walter Rauschenbusch declared him to be one of the early prophets of the kingdom idea,[129] and George Adam Smith described him as one of the principal exponents of the day of the social duties of religion.[130] Drummond's social theology and his love of work among students were to be echoed in Cairns's own life.

United Presbyterian Hall and Marburg

By the time he went to study at the United Presbyterian Hall in October 1888, while Cairns had not yet developed a comprehensive theology, he had recovered enough faith to allow him to continue his plan to study for the ministry. He was one of about eighty students brought up in the same church tradition, sharing a common outlook, and preparing for the

126. Cairns, *Autobiography*, 115–16, 168–69.
127. Nicoll, "Henry Drummond."
128. Cairns, *Autobiography*, 116–17.
129. Rauschenbusch, *Theology for a Social Gospel*, 56.
130. Smith, *Life of Henry Drummond*, 14.

same vocation. This and the small classes meant that students could get to know each other well, and made it possible to enjoy a strong sense of fellowship. Reflecting on his training in his autobiography, Cairns felt it had two elements essential to ministerial training: having to take an arts course broadened the perspective of the candidates, while the specialized theological training nurtured a sense of corporate loyalty and esprit de corps that would serve the men well as they served the church together in the future.[131] According to Cairns, the professors (including his uncle John, who was principal) belonged to "a less troubled age" and were therefore unable to identify with the intellectual struggles of the students. The narrow worldview of the staff had contributed to the loss of some able students who had made their way into other spheres of intellectual life. He felt that he and his peers learned more from their friendships and discussions than from their formal classes. Nonetheless, they saw their professors as "devout and earnest men and good scholars."[132]

Among the students was Joseph H. Leckie, who like Cairns, suffered from ill-health: Leckie's condition was described vaguely as related to a "nervous constitution." Cairns described him as the "unquestioned leader of our year in theology," and the two began a lifelong friendship. While Cairns admitted to Leckie's theological influence in relation to his ideas about atonement, the moral Fatherhood of God and about universalism, he described Leckie as conservative in political and social matters, in contrast to his own developing perspective, which embraced the teaching of Albrecht Ritschl on the theology of the kingdom of God and its expression in social reforms.[133] Leckie was to become a minister, serving only in the Boston Church in Cupar, Fife, where he was ordained in 1892, but his health eventually broke down and he had to retire to Edinburgh, where he engaged in theological writing.[134] The prefaces in both his publications, *Authority in Religion* (1909) and *The World to Come and Final Destiny* (1918), included thanks to D. S. Cairns for encouragement and helpful criticism. The Semitic scholar, Principal Skinner of Cambridge, declared the second book to be the "best of its kind in the language."[135]

In the summer after his first year at the Hall, Cairns tutored two boys who boarded with his grandmother. In the next summer, 1889, their parents came to Scotland from the Transvaal, and took the boys on holiday to

131. Cairns, *Autobiography*, 123–24.
132. Cairns, *Autobiography*, 124.
133. Cairns, *Autobiography*, 127.
134. Cairns, *Autobiography*, 128.
135. Cairns, *Autobiography*, 127–28.

Nethybridge, inviting him to accompany them. In his new surroundings, suffering from insomnia, and worried about the possibility of another break-down, Cairns consulted a local doctor who told him bluntly that he was imagining things. Reflecting on the doctor's lack of sympathy, he refers to his condition as one of the "nervous" diseases about which little was understood at the time. However, the doctor's response stung him into action, and he wrote to an old student friend, J. Lorrain Smith, who was by this time a pro-fessor of pathology in Belfast, asking if he was suffering from hypochondria, and wanting an honest answer. Lorrain reassured him that his illness was not imaginary, but could be treated by adopting a positive attitude: "Regi-men and fight for all you are worth! But fight with your brain. Don't overdo it."[136] Unable to continue in Nethybridge, Cairns went home and began a fitness regime, of which the main feature was a daily walk which increased in distance each day. This change in approach, from accepting his infirmities to fighting his way to fitness, was considered by him as a significant milestone, bringing him hope of an active and useful life. By the middle of October, he was fit to resume his studies, and he came through his second year without illness, but also without any academic distinction.[137] The spring semester in 1890 brought another new experience, when Cairns set off for Germany with two college friends, John Sinclair and James Wark.

Another college friend had returned from Marburg the previous year, and had given a glowing account of the beauty of the place and of the inspir-ing teaching and personality of the liberal theologian, Wilhelm Herrmann (1846–1922). In spite of restricted funds, poor diet, and little knowledge of German, this proved to be a significant time for Cairns. For the next three months he worked hard at learning German, and attended a variety of classes, but focused mainly on those of Herrmann, in whose classroom he "shared in the general hero-worship," finding his influence stimulating and provocative. Following his morning lectures, he went walking in the woods in the afternoon, enjoying the solitude and glorious weather, as well as the wildlife—deer, lizards and dragonflies, describing all with interest and keen observation when he wrote home to his father.[138] In the same letter Cairns described a visit to the Marburg Observatory, which crystallized some of his thoughts on the science-religion debate. The observatory was situated on a hill, just under the imposing *Schloss*. The gallery of its cupola allowed a panoramic view of the town and its beautiful landscape; but what went on

136. Cairns, *Autobiography*, 130.

137. Cairns, *Autobiography*, 130–31.

138. Letter to his father, from Marburg, 1888. MS3384/2, Box 1, D. S. Cairns Papers, Aberdeen.

inside the observatory was also impressive. One telescope allowed visitors to examine the surface of the moon, with its shadows and volcanoes, and to watch its movements. Even more "singular" to Cairns was a transit instrument, through which he was able to track the movement of a certain star at a time predicted precisely by the observatory assistant. He described this visit in great detail to his father, including the layout of the observatory and drawing a diagram of the special telescope. On the wall of the gallery was a table of heavenly bodies and the times when they would cross nearest the field of vision of the transit instrument. The assistant adjusted it and told them the "given minute a certain star would appear," and Cairns reported: "Then I went back to the cupola and sat down by the transit instrument, and there in the field of vision sure enough was a minute twinkling star flitting across the glass before our eyes . . . a marvel of the first magnitude surely it is, when one thinks of the vast spaces through which the planet [sic] was flying on its path, a path along a curve thought out by mathematicians in Alexandria long before Modern Astronomy mapped the heavens."[139]

The whole experience of that evening brought home to him "the pure wonder of the world in a most vivid way," but it left him wondering about the role of faith in a world in which the precision and certainty of its methods granted science a power and prestige that was very attractive. Over forty years later, he would recall this incident clearly, when writing his final work of apologetics.[140]

Among other significant events during this time, was a visit to the home of Herrmann, which he considered one of his pleasantest memories of Marburg. He and his friends spent a long time in conversation with the professor, finding that smoking together "relaxed the strings of speech," and discussing the state of German theology and the Ritschlian School in particular.[141] Herrmann was the leading figure in the school with its emphasis on ethics on the one hand, and personal experience of God on the other. For them, personal experience ought to be the ground of faith, rather than doctrine, which according to Herrmann may contain a lot of dead matter. Cairns saw in Herrmann not so much a theologian, but more of a prophet and preacher who was distressed by the conflict between science and religion, and who often had tears in his eyes as he spoke about the problems that science raised for faith. Cairns described the professor as exhibiting two characteristics that he felt do not often go together: intellectual honesty and

139. Letter to his father, from Marburg, 1888. MS3384/2, Box 1, D. S. Cairns Papers.
140. Cairns, *Riddle of the World*, 61–62.
141. Letter to his father, from Marburg, 1888. MS3384/2, Box 1, D. S. Cairns Papers.

a deeply religious nature.[142] Such a combination may or may not be rare, but it is evident in all the major influences mentioned in this chapter. Cairns admitted that the Ritschlian theology never really captured him, mainly because he disagreed with its Christology. In spite of theological differences, Cairns saw Herrmann as a spiritual genius, admitting: "And I learned a lot from Herrmann that has influenced me since then not a little. . . . And this knowledge, however imperfect . . . opened my eyes to much at home which I would otherwise never have noticed. It set me *comparing*, and comparison, as philosophers tell us, is of the very essence of *thought*."[143]

His time in Germany also sharpened Cairns's political consciousness, and his theological questions were taking on a political hue. Having read J. S. Mill's *Political Economy*, he had begun to question the dichotomy between the values of the kingdom of God, and those of the prevailing economic system which was motivated by enlightened self-interest.[144] Germany was an impressive and progressive state, leading the way in learning and science, successful in commerce and industry, with students from all over the world flocking to its universities. It had introduced national insurance and social service, but in spite if these positive measures Cairns questioned whether its practical ideals were Christian, concluding that they were at most influenced by Christianity, but not in themselves Christian. That in turn begged further questions: (1) Is Christianity essential to the life and progress of a national state? (2) Has God given us the principles for the creation of a healthy society? (3) The nations of the world, ignoring the Christian ethos, and operating on the principals of self-seeking nationalism, seemed to be very successful; is this not a problem for faith? These were among the many questions that were forming in Cairns's mind as he made his way back to Scotland to continue his college course.

Conclusion

In 1892, Cairns was ready to leave university and undertake the role of probationer minister. Throughout his student days, two problems had dominated his thinking. The first was his experience of poor health, on which comment must be made as it had the effect of drawing out his period of study to twelve years instead of eight, and was a major factor in leading

142. Cairns, *Autobiography*, 135.

143. Cairns, *Autobiography*, 136.

144. John Stuart Mill, British philosopher, economist and moral theorist (1806–73) published *Principles of Political Economy and Some of the Applications to Social Philosophy* in 1848, challenging the idea of an immutable economic law.

him to give the existence of pain and suffering a central place in his theology. He confesses in his autobiography that he knew nothing of illness till his student days, except for a bout of rheumatic fever. Between the ages of eleven and fourteen he walked the four-mile round trip from Stitchel to the school in Ednam. Having visited the parish myself, I can confirm that the homeward journey involves a long stretch where the gradient is very steep. In describing this walk, however, Cairns gives no indication that it was difficult for him, rather he says that the journey in almost all weathers was "good for healthy children," and goes on to recollect the road with its farms, flora and fauna, expressing the delight he felt in its environment. Presumably, he had not yet suffered rheumatic fever at that stage, and he gives no account of when it occurred except that it was earlier than his student days. Reading his autobiographical account one has a sense of someone who worried excessively over his health, and he did worry that he was a hypochondriac. Nowadays it is accepted as medical fact that rheumatic fever can lead to complications in the form of heart disease, the symptoms of which include chest pain, shortness of breath, and tiredness—all symptoms which Cairns suffered for many years. As it can take many years for the symptoms to develop after an episode of fever, it is easy to see why he did not connect his years of poor health to his contraction of this illness, and perhaps doctors at the time had not made the connection, but this seems the most likely explanation for his debilitation.

The other problem was the spiritual crisis which descended in the third year of his arts degree, and which engulfed him in mental confusion that only began to dissipate on the voyage to Egypt, and from which he took a long time to recover completely; but by 1888 he had gone from a collapse of faith to the discovery of a foundation on which to reconstruct it, and was ready to return to university. Supported by family and friends, Cairns progressed through his university days, trying to establish his own *weltanschauung*. His three major influences—Smyth, Browning and Drummond, had much in common. They did not recoil from the questioning attitude of the age, but saw it as a genuine seeking after truth. They embraced scientific endeavor, while acknowledging the limits of scientific analysis, and being prepared to question some of its findings. In defending the existence of a spiritual dimension to life, they did not go on the defensive, but questioned exclusive reliance on reason in the search for truth, thus making a place for intuition. The three were anti-sectarian and anti-dogmatic, seeing the divisions in the church as destructive. Central for them was the Providence of a loving God in a purposive universe, where a spiritual power was at work. They emphasized experience over doctrine, and central to each was a personal relationship with Christ.

In the teaching of each man, it seems that there was a particular emphasis which may have further focused and shaped Cairns's own thinking. In his belief that each discipline has its part to play in the search for truth, Smyth called for science and religion to come together to interpret the universe, a project in which Cairns contributed through his teaching and writing. As for Drummond, it was perhaps his love of the young students and his passionate desire to equip them with a reasonable personal faith that was one of the most lasting legacies for Cairns, who was to spend so much of his own life involved in work with young people. Browning's emphasis on the development of the soul and the moral life found its counterpoint in the idea of the immanence of the divine in the human, and the characterization of the divine as love allowed for confidence and optimism. These two qualities were to remain distinctive characteristics of Cairns's own theology.

Chapter 3

Building on the New Foundations, 1892–1906

Probationer

HAVING SPENT TWELVE YEARS and not the usual eight as a student, due to his bouts of illness, Cairns got off to a late and an inauspicious start as a probationer. At the age of twenty-nine, he was licensed by the Kelso Presbytery in the summer of 1892 and went onto the "preachers' list" as he was now eligible for a call by a congregation. Cairns recalled that the standard United Presbyterian practice was that when a vacancy arose, unless a congregation wanted to call a minister already in a charge, an appeal was made to the committee in charge of probationers. Although the congregation might indicate a preference, they usually had to take whomever the committee sent. Every quarter the committee produced a four-page leaflet with the names of all the probationers and congregations, and a calendar showing all the preaching allocations. The probationer went to preach on two consecutive Sundays, and the congregation then decided whether to call him or not. Cairns pointed out that the intervening week was a difficult period during which sensitive candidates, if they remained among the congregation, felt under intense scrutiny. He seemed to suggest that he usually disappeared during that time, returning on Saturdays. He described the process as a "mechanical" system, which nonetheless was highly democratic with all probationers receiving the same treatment. On the one hand, the congregation had to judge whether they would benefit from a man's preaching, and on the other, the probationer was free to refuse a call on the grounds that he felt he could not do his best work there.[1]

For Cairns, the years of his probationary period proved "an anxious and depressing experience."[2] According to his autobiography, he "preached

1. Cairns, *Autobiography*, 139
2. Cairns, *Autobiography*, 153

in fifteen or sixteen vacancies, without persuading any one of them that I was the minister they wanted."[3] However, a letter from his father indicates that in the autumn of 1894, Cairns declined a call to Springburn in Glasgow.[4] Robert Small also documents the call, in his account of United Presbyterian congregations.[5] Cairns senior divulges no reason for his son's refusal to go there, but it may be that he considered a city charge of about seven people would prove too demanding on his still fragile health. It is also likely that by this time he was working as an assistant minister in Selkirk, in his home territory of the Borders, and he may have entertained hopes of that position becoming permanent. Other letters from the family reveal something of the emotional drain of the period, with hopes raised and dashed on a regular basis. At one point Cairns received an invitation to preach for a vacancy in Biggar, where his maternal grandfather, David Smith, had been minister, encouraging his father to speculate on the possibility of the Brown-Smith "dynasty" moving into the manse again.[6] Cairns recalls that this was a difficult period for probationers in general as there were so many men looking for parishes; Moody's second visit to Scotland and the work of Henry Drummond had inspired increasing numbers to apply for training for the ministry. In spite of the difficulties, he felt that there were compensations. His sense of humor allowed him to admit that the disappointments prevented any overconfidence on his part, and that it made him familiar with the landscape of Scotland, as he traveled its length and breadth, going as far north as Orkney. On a more serious note, he felt that the unpredictability of the probationer's life was forcing him to develop his faith in the "Providence of God."[7] Up until then, this concept had been central to his theological speculations, but now he found that he had to put his belief into practice, as he waited for a way ahead to open up. During his three-year probationary period, Cairns held assistantships in three quite different congregations: Morningside in the south side of Edinburgh, Burnmouth in Berwickshire, and Selkirk in Roxburghshire.

Morningside

In the winter of 1892, his uncle John Cairns, experiencing declining health, retired from his professorial chair but remained principal of the United

3. Cairns, *Autobiography*, 151.

4. Letter from David Cairns, 17 October 1894, Cairns Papers, MS3384/3/1.

5. Small, *History of the Congregations*, 96.

6. Letter from David Cairns, 17 October 1893, Cairns Papers, MS3384/3/1.

7. Cairns, *Autobiography*, 155.

Presbyterian College. Dr. Archibald Duff, professor of church history, had died during the previous summer, so two interim lecturers were needed at the college. Dr. Alexander Mair, minister of Morningside, was appointed to one of the posts. Mair had taken advantage of the expansion of the city southward and westward, and had built up a sizeable Morningside congregation, which held him in great affection. Cairns spent a happy six months as Mair's assistant minister, having only a light workload which involved pastoral visits to those who were ill, running a Bible class, and preaching a monthly sermon. He enjoyed a close relationship with the minister, referring to Mair as his "bishop," lunching with him every Sunday, and describing him as a "good scholar" whose line was church history.[8] Cairns makes no mention of the fact that Mair had in 1889 published a work of apologetics, aimed at helping lay church members and teachers who struggled with intellectual doubts about their Christian faith.[9] Mair's stated aim in the book was to show the reasonableness of progressing from Theism to faith in the central truths of Christianity. Among the issues discussed were evolution, higher criticism, revelation, miracles, and the unique personality of Christ: and the extensive notes in his appendix show evidence of reading widely in such authors as philosophers J. S. Mill and Hermann Lotze, theologians David Strauss and Heinrich Ewald, and the Old Testament scholar Ernest Renan. From the start, Mair took a positive approach to science, pointing out its limitations, but advising Christians to be grateful for its discovery of truth.[10] It is unlikely that Cairns did not know about the book, but in any case, the author is likely to have provided a rich seam of topics for discussion at their Sunday lunches, and Mair's approach to science reinforced the attitude that Cairns had already encountered in Newman Smyth's writing. Mair also included a long section on the subject of miracles,[11] which he described as one of the "burning topics" of the age: a topic which came to preoccupy Cairns and led to the publication in 1928 of what Donald Baillie describes as "his most distinctive contribution to theology."[12]

It was during the Morningside period that his uncle John died. Cairns had been visiting him regularly while at Morningside, enjoying the closeness of family relations and affections, and the cheerfulness and happiness of the household in Spence Street, where John Cairns lived with his sister Janet and brother William. John Cairns had been a highly respected figure in the

8. Cairns, *Autobiography*, 139–40.
9. Mair, *Studies in the Christian Evidences*.
10. Mair, *Studies in the Christian Evidences*, 1–33.
11. Mair, *Studies in the Christian Evidences*, 157–222.
12. Cairns, *Autobiography*, 23.

church and in civic life, but the family was unprepared for the widespread emotional reaction to his death. The town council took over arrangements for the funeral, which was attended by many public dignitaries, and by representatives of the numerous societies and organizations to which John Cairns had belonged; but also by individuals from every station in life.

> Every street was lined with thousands, who respectfully saluted the funeral car. Traffic was suspended. Shops were generally closed. On public buildings flags were half-mast high, and the blinds of private houses were drawn.[13]

Burnmouth

During the following winter, 1893, in complete contrast to his first assistantship, Cairns took on a mission station in Burnmouth, a fishing village on the rocky Berwickshire coastline, close to the border with England, and marking the eastern boundary of the parish of Ayton. Surrounded by three hundred–foot cliffs, the settlement was located in three sites. At the top of a deep gorge, in Upper Burnmouth, a scattering of buildings included cottages, a school, a railway station, and an inn; three separate hamlets (Partan Ha', Coodrait and Ross) stretched along the foreshore below in Lower Burnmouth; and in between, halfway down the very steep brae, were the church, coastguard station, and a row of old cottages. From here one looks out over a vast expanse of the North Sea to an empty horizon. The entrance to the church, still in use today, is at the back of the building, probably designed to protect the worshippers and the building from the salty gales. In the first half of the nineteenth century, there was a thriving fishing community in Burnmouth. A harbor had been constructed in the 1830s and extended in 1879. One writer of the period described the place as "the romantic fishing village of Burnmouth."[14] Cairns's autobiography indicated that the community was no longer thriving by the time he went to work there.[15] Upper Burnmouth had a small population linked to the farm at the top of the hill, and to the railway. The main part of the village, Lower Burnmouth, had a population of between four and five hundred fisher-folk, but fishing now brought only uncertain returns. While other communities embraced the mechanization and industrialization of fishing, the men of Burnmouth

13. MacEwen, *Life and Letters*, 787.
14. Tough, "Parish of Ayton," 133.
15. Cairns, *Autobiography*, 141–48.

stuck to their traditional line-fishing methods, which could not compete with the capacity of the new trawlers.

As he approached the start of his ministry in Burnmouth, Cairns admitted that it was "almost like going among a foreign people again."[16] Up until then he had led a rather sheltered and comfortable life in the manse in Stitchel and at the university. Now he met people who had to eke out a living from fishing, in which sudden death was a constant threat. The dependence on one another among the crews, intermarriage and geographical isolation had bred a close-knit community, which may have made it hard for some probationers to enter into village life, but family associations brought Cairns acceptance among the people of Burnmouth.[17] His grandfather had worked as a boy on the nearby farm of Greystone Lees, and had then spent most of his married life on Ayton Hill, where his uncle John had been born. However, in spite of this acceptance it proved a hard winter for Cairns. He lived alone in Flemington Cottage, beside the inn at the top of the brae, without much company apart from the members of the little church, which had its own distinctive history.[18] Up until 1888, the people of Burnmouth had walked to Ayton where they were part of the Summerhill Burgher congregation—one of two secession congregations in the village—the other anti-Burgher. However, problems arose over a proposal to unite the two secession churches in Ayton, and the quarrelling led the fishing community to stop attending services there. It was agreed to treat Burnmouth as a mission station with a missioner in charge, and that the missioner and minister would exchange pulpits once a month to keep the link. When Cairns went to Burnmouth, the minister at Ayton was Rev. John Duncan. Cairns felt sorry for Duncan as his congregation had split and he was in what Cairns described as "an almost impossible position."[19] Four years after Cairns went to Burnmouth, the congregation purchased the hall and persuaded the general assembly that they needed a full-time minister, and the hall, which had originally been a Good Templars' Lodge,[20] was refitted as a church. Looking back on his time there, Cairns wrote, "I had never before come so close to human need and privation and the bare-handed struggle with Nature, and this had its reaction upon my own heart and mind."[21]

16. Cairns, *Autobiography*, 142.
17. Cairns, *Autobiography*, 143.
18. Cairns, *Autobiography*, 141–42.
19. Cairns, *Autobiography*, 142.
20. The Good Templars was a nineteenth-century temperance organization.
21. Cairns, *Autobiography*, 146.

He began to see the importance of the physical and economic environment for a community. He was not blind to the fact that in some poverty and constant danger bred recklessness and brutality, but he saw that in others it bred an intense religiosity in which the church meant much to them. During his short spell in the mission station, Cairns reported, "I became genuinely attached to many of these brave, simple, kindly folk. At its best, character rises very high among fisher-people and some of these rank among the finest types I have ever known."[22]

On a personal level, he was able to engage emotionally with the people, talking to them about their families and lives, and listening as they recounted the losses that were common to all fishing communities. One particular east coast storm on 14 October 1881, had resulted in the loss of twenty-four men from Burnmouth. Cairns's warm human touch and his capacity for systematic thinking and organization revealed themselves at this early stage in his ministry. He began his work by visiting all the church members in the village, and made a register containing their names and the names and ages of their children, with notes of information that he thought relevant: a practice that he later recommended to all young ministers. An indication of the warmth of relationships which Cairns enjoyed with his congregation is evidenced in a letter sent to him by one of the fishermen, Alexander Aitchison. Written in poor grammatical style but in beautiful script, it is very affectionate and signs off, "my best love to you Dear David."[23]

However, for a young man living alone, at a distance from family, former friends, and peers, there was an emotional toll, and he became depressed. He also continued to suffer from a stomach complaint—dyspepsia—which he had developed when in Germany. One wonders if this latter condition was not related to the fact that he lived alone and would therefore have had to cook his own meals. A thirty-year-old man of the day is unlikely to have had much in the way of culinary skills, and his trouble in Germany had begun at a time when he and his friends were cooking for themselves in the evenings! Added to that, much younger college friends were receiving calls and settling into their own churches. He struggled with a feeling that "fortune" was against him,[24] confessing to his mother at one point that he wished he could say, "I have finished my course."[25] Presumably he meant that he wished he had finished his time in Burnmouth, rather than something more sinister. He had thrown himself into meeting the needs of the

22. Cairns, *Autobiography*, 145.

23. Letter to Cairns from Alexander Aitchison, 15 June 1893 or 1894. MS3384, Box 3/2, D. S. Cairns Papers.

24. Cairns, *Autobiography*, 146.

25. Cairns, *Autobiography*, 147.

people, but found it physically and mentally exhausting, and feared another breakdown; however when the time came to leave, he went with some regret at leaving a community he had grown fond of. As for his remarks about "fortune" being against him, such thinking was part of his struggle to work out what Providence might mean in practical terms. "Fortune" carries with it the idea of arbitrariness, and since his visit to Egypt, he had become aware of what he described as purposiveness at the heart of life. He longed to live trusting in such a purpose in spite of outward circumstance. In his own words, "I felt more than ever the need of having a life independent of fortune and whether 'successful' or 'unsuccessful' yet contributing something essential to the fulfilment of God's purpose in the world."[26]

At the same time, his was not a fatalistic approach, as can be seen in his reaction to advice from a friend. Margaret Hardie had given him spiritual counsel before, and when he wrote to tell her of his ailments, she advised him "to submit," that is, to accept it as God's will. Cairns found this unhelpful.[27] He had been following the advice of his Belfast friend Lorrain Smith to assume a positive mental attitude, and he had begun developing a fitness regime that went a long way to restoring his stamina. He became convinced that illness was not something sent by God. Rather, he saw good health as God's will for people. The question of illness and suffering would become more central for him in the next few years, but for now he had established a basis on which he would build his own theological position. While Burnmouth had brought more awareness of the sociological and economic causes of suffering, his university friend, Thomas Kirkup, provided him with an intellectual foothold for his thinking in this area. In 1887, Kirkup had published *An Enquiry into Socialism*, in which he drew attention to the need to examine the principles underlying the contemporary social and economic systems. Comparing the fundamentals of socialism with those of the prevailing system of economic individualism, he promulgated socialism as the new economic basis for society.[28] Kirkup was from the United Presbyterian tradition and had begun training for the ministry, but had lost his faith. Cairns regarded him as "one of those men who, while nominally outside the Church, really belong to it in the deep foundations of their character," and admitted, "What I got intellectually from him was the importance of the economic interpretation of history and a great deal of information about Continental as well as British Socialism."[29]

26. Cairns, *Autobiography*, 146.
27. Cairns, *Autobiography*, 146.
28. Kirkup, *Enquiry into Socialism*.
29. Cairns, *Autobiography*, 118.

Selkirk

After six months at Burnmouth, Cairns was offered the post of assistant to the elderly Rev. John Lawson in Selkirk. Lawson was about seventy years old at the time, and was the fourth consecutive member of his family to have ministered there, beginning with his grandfather, Dr. George Lawson. George Lawson had been a biblical scholar, who studied at the Associate Synod Divinity Hall under John Brown, and published several Bible commentaries. He became minister in Selkirk in 1771, retaining his position there when he succeeded Brown as professor of theology. Following his death in 1820, his son Andrew became minister, and on Andrew's demise, his elder brother George took charge of the congregation in 1837. The family name was enough to convince many of the suitability of the candidate, but over a hundred members petitioned against George's induction. (He had refused two calls by them at the time of his father's death.) When the younger George Lawson died in 1849, a difficult situation arose when it was proposed that his nephew be appointed. This time there was more opposition: nearly half the members voted against, and John Lawson's appointment was the occasion of the building of another Burgher church, Selkirk West. Those who had not agreed to the call went to worship in the new church.[30] It was into this historically fraught situation that the new assistant arrived in 1894, and the "Lawson dissidence" mentioned by his father in a letter to Cairns probably refers to that.[31]

Notwithstanding congregational politics, the new situation presented a significant contrast to Burnmouth. Instead of working in isolation, he now had a colleague with whom he enjoyed good relations; and he had satisfactory lodgings also. His workload was not heavy, and consisted in a certain number of pastoral visits, occasional preaching, and a special focus on the young people of the congregation. Selkirk was a thriving market town on the banks of Ettrick Water, forty miles from Edinburgh. Its triangular marketplace was dominated by Handyside Ritchie's almost thirty-feet-high monument to Sir Walter Scott, and was surrounded by handsome civic buildings, elegant private residences and busy mills. Along with several churches of different denominations, there were a number of schools, banks, and a railway station, and organizations and institutions of various kinds, from the sporting to the religious and philanthropic.[32] Cairns described it as one of the most attractive towns in the Borders, with its population consisting

30. Small, *History of the Congregations*, 286, 440–45.

31. Letter from D. Cairns to D. S. 29 November 1894. MS3384, Box 3/1, Cairns Papers.

32. Groome, *Ordnance Gazetteer of Scotland* (1882), 2328–30.

mainly of comfortably off shopkeepers, artisans and young mill-workers. He took pleasure in the countryside around, presumably keeping up his walking regime.[33] His autobiography does not intimate much about his time in Selkirk, but in a letter to his sister, Jessie, he admitted that he was not overworked by Lawson, that his physical condition was improving or at least stable, and that "consequently I have a certain pleasure in living which I have not had for many years."[34] Cairns remained in Selkirk for nearly two years. A letter from his father implied that Lawson wanted Cairns to continue as his colleague and then as his successor, but that the congregation felt itself pushed too hard and called someone else.[35] Perhaps, in light of the history of the Selkirk church, the members felt that it was time that they had a wider and freer choice of minister, and Cairns was by then too closely associated with the Lawson dynasty. However, his time as a probationer was about to come to an end with a call to Ayton.

The Search for an Ideal

In his work on Christology, the Scottish theologian John Macquarrie comments that although the concept of the kingdom had been central in Jesus' teaching, it had never been the focus of the church's teaching until the nineteenth century. The social problems associated with industrialization forced the churches in Britain and America to develop a new theology focused on the transformation of human society into the kingdom of God.[36] In 1865, Robert Flint, then professor of moral theology and political economy at the University of St. Andrews, had published a sermon on "The Nature of the Kingdom of God on Earth" in which he declared the kingdom of God as a realm in which brotherhood was the defining relationship, and where there was no oppression of others.[37] Those outside the ecclesiastical establishment could be bearers of the kingdom, and the church itself could be in opposition to the kingdom, if it adopted worldly aims. Flint saw the energy spent on controversies about the constitution and government of the churches as an example of worldliness which prevented them going about the true work of establishing the kingdom of God out of the struggle between good and

33. Cairns, *Autobiography*, 148.

34. Letter from Jessie Cairns to D. S. 12 June 1893. MS3384, Box 3/1, Cairns Papers.

35. Letter from D. Cairns to D. S. 17 October 1894. MS3384, Box 3/1, Cairns Papers.

36. Macquarrie, *Jesus Christ in Modern Thought*, 267.

37. Flint, *Christ's Kingdom upon Earth*, sermon 3, 53–82.

evil. Flint's refusal to dichotomize the sacred and the secular, and his empha-sis on brotherhood, would become dominant themes in Cairns's theology. According to Johnston MacKay, kingdom theology was central for Flint, and during his time as professor of divinity at Edinburgh, from 1876–1903, he always included it in his teaching.[38] It was wider than the church, which he, like Ritschl, saw as a means to an end, and not an end in itself.

From 1890, there was a similar theological focus in American Prot-estantism. H. Richard Niebuhr has pointed out that the idea of the king-dom of God had always been central to American Christianity, but that in the late nineteenth century it became identified with a kingdom on earth, a social order.[39] The Kingdom Movement, led by George D. Herron and George A. Gates, tried to develop the social consciousness of the church.[40] As in Britain, rapid industrialization and urbanization had created social and economic difficulties. Members of the Kingdom Movement called for the application of Christian principles to the social and economic problems of the day. Their aim was to reorganize society on the basis of Jesus' teach-ings, replacing self-interest and competition with self-sacrifice. For them, the kingdom of God was the ideal of human society, and it could be realized on earth by applying this teaching, which provided the ultimate authority for social practice. Due to the perceived extremism of some of its leaders, the movement did not last after 1896, but it paved the way for the Social Gospel movement and its exponents, for example Washington Gladden (1836–1918) and Walter Rauschenbusch (1861–1918), who continued to advocate the application of Christian principles to the social context. While Cairns was working on the text of his first book, Rauschenbusch was pre-paring the text of his most well-known book, *Christianity and the Social Crisis* (1907), in which he pointed to the problem of human suffering in the light of divine Providence: a theme which was to become central in Cairns's own thinking. For Rauschenbusch, transforming the social context was an essential part of the good news for the poor, because Jesus had been moti-vated by the doctrine of the kingdom of God at war with the powers of evil in persons and social systems.[41]

In the 1870s and 1880s, Cairns had welcomed the swing away from the individualism of evangelical Christianity, with its emphasis on personal and otherworldly salvation, to a more social piety, which focused on the concept of the kingdom of God, and viewed the church as the instrument

38. MacKay, *Kirk and Kingdom*, Chalmers Lectures 2011, ch. 2.

39. Macquarrie, *Twentieth Century Religious Thought*, 162–65.

40. Handy, "George D. Herron and Kingdom Movement," 97–115.

41. Shriver in the introduction to Rauschenbusch, *Theology for the Social Gospel*, xiv–xxii.

for the restoration of a nobler form of human society. The influence of F. D. Maurice and Charles Kingsley, two of his favorite theologians, had already prepared the way for him. In 1848, along with John Ludlow and Thomas Hughes, they inaugurated the Christian Socialist movement, which promulgated the view that Christianity was not simply about the individual's relationship with God, but also was concerned with relations between individuals in society. In his probationary period, Cairns embarked on an impressive program of reading, from which began to emerge the intellectual framework for his own theology. Realizing that his knowledge of languages was scanty, he relied on the advice of the English author Frederic Harrison (1873–1928), whose *The Choice of Books* suggested good translations of significant texts. The significance of reading for Cairns, and the vital part it played in his development, is indicated by his own judgment: "It was not simple aesthetic delight in these great writings that lured me on to their study. I felt that they were initiating me into the meaning of human life and destiny and God's purpose with mankind—and with me."[42]

In Morningside, in the winter of 1892, Cairns enjoyed George Adam Smith's articles on the historical geography of the Holy Land, which appeared as a series in the *Expositor*, a monthly theological magazine edited by Cairns's former neighbor, William Robertson Nicoll. Evoking memories of his own time in Egypt, Smith's articles provided him with a vivid background to his reading of the Bible. In Burnmouth, he had had less time for reading, but found "some escape" in it when the occasion arose, reading the French Egyptologist Gaston Maspero's *L'Histoire Ancienne des Peuples de l'Orient*. Cairns was impressed by the great sweep of history portrayed by Maspero, as one empire after another rose and fell. "It gave a picture of mankind on the march, with nation after nation in turn as leader of the world."[43] In Selkirk Cairns had plenty of time for reading, and it was there that he "fell in with" the ten-volume report of the missionary conference held in London in June 1888, and through which he saw the potential of the missionary enterprise in delivering the kingdom throughout the world.[44] Its 1,600 members and delegates from at least 138 societies told of achievements in countries in every continent, including places as diverse as Ethiopia Alaska, Afghanistan, Hawaii, Syria, Burma, and Venezuela, and according to the editor of volume 1, represented an area "little short of the whole habitable globe."[45]

42. Cairns, *Autobiography*, 154.

43. Cairns, *Autobiography*, 145.

44. Cairns, *Autobiography*, 152.

45. Johnston, editor, *Report of the Centenary Conference on the Protestant Missions of the World*, xiii.

Drawing upon Harrison's *Choice of Books*, Cairns planned a program of systematic reading that would teach him about the different phases of civilization from classical antiquity, through the medieval period, and on to the secular individualism of the modern era: he read from Aristotle, through to Dante and on to Goethe. He expressed his evolutionary approach to history in the arrangement of his books in chronological order on his desk, symbolizing for him "the education of mankind in the way it should think and go. . . . The ideals of different phases of civilisation were the guiding stars of each people."[46] Naturally for Cairns, the ten volumes of the missionary conference stood at the end of the row, symbolizing the establishment of the kingdom of God as the zenith of human development, with the message of Jesus, the gospel, as its guiding star. According to Brian Stanley, nineteenth-century evangelicals saw the primary purpose of history as the fulfillment of God's plan of salvation, with themselves having a special role to play in bringing it about. For them there could be no other explanation for the huge spread and wealth of the British Empire, than that God had bestowed "Britain's imperial role as a sacred trust to be used in the interests of the Gospel."[47]

At the same time, Cairns had a growing awareness that the kingdom of God might not be synonymous with Christendom, and that prosperity and righteousness were not symbiotic. The missionary conference report had asserted the importance of "using commerce as a means for the spread of truth and righteousness," but had acknowledged that this was a mixed blessing as commerce came to be associated with religion, but not all those involved in commerce were of good or moral character.[48] Through the socialist critique expressed by his friend Thomas Kirkup, Cairns was beginning to see for himself the "non-Christian element in our so-called Christian civilisation," and to realize that it could not be God's will for society that so many people lived in hardship and poverty.[49] In his student days in Germany, Cairns had already begun reflecting on the relationship of Christianity to the secular institutions. There he had seen in operation a very successful state, but one that was becoming increasingly militaristic. Like Britain, it professed itself to be a "Christian country," but, like most Western nations, it operated on principles of self-seeking and national interest, in complete contrast to Jesus' teaching about the kingdom of God.[50]

46. Cairns, *Autobiography*, 151.

47. Stanley, *Bible and the Flag*, 68. This idea of Britain as an elect nation is also described in Brown, *Providence and Empire*, 196.

48. 1888 Report, xxix–xxx.

49. Cairns, *Autobiography*, 149.

50. Cairns, *Autobiography*, 137.

A more positive influence from his time in Germany was the theology of Albrecht Ritschl (1822–89). Ritschl had studied at Bonn and Halle, and finally in Tübingen under F. C. Baur, head of the famous school of New Testament Criticism. The Scottish theologian and historian James Orr (1844–1913) described Ritschl's theology as an attempt to find a ground of certainty in religion: one that was unassailable by metaphysical speculation and critical theories. To achieve this Ritschl excluded everything outside the range of human experience. Orr described his theology as a religious positivism which began with the data of experience—the facts of the life and work of Christ as recorded in the gospels.[51] For Ritschl, only in the faith of the first Christian community and its religious consciousness can we discern the significance of Jesus.[52] The German theologian Leonard Stahlin portrayed Ritschl's idea of Christ's mission as "the founding of that universal moral community of men which is designated the kingdom of God."[53] Cairns was attracted to Ritschl's concept of the kingdom as an ethical ideal, with twin foci of task and gift. The gift is Christ's redemption of the world in his work of establishing the church through his patient obedience to God's will, even at the cost of his own life. For Ritschl, reconciliation is to be understood as the right of the Christian community to relate to God as toward a loving Father.[54] The task belongs to the church, as a community, to continue the work of extending the kingdom of God. For Cairns, reacting against the evangelical stress on personal sanctity and "sound conversion," the focus on an essentially social task was compelling. "We were all feeling out for a comprehensive theocratic ideal which should embrace the whole of human life, a Divine Order instead of the social, economic and political disorder of which we were all becoming growingly conscious, some more than others, in those days."[55]

H. R. Mackintosh, professor of dogmatics at New College, Edinburgh, from 1904–36, also attested to the appeal of Ritschl's christocentric theology. Ritschl's insistence that religion must feed on concrete facts and events resonated with the scientific spirit of the times, and according to Mackintosh: "He was felt to be building theology afresh on the bedrock of actual events which could be ascertained, and men were encouraged to investigate all such events with perfect freedom. Life owes to the past all that makes it

51. Orr, Ritschlianism Expository and Critical Essays, 6–25.

52. Ritschl, Christian Doctrine of Justification and Reconciliation, 2–3.

53. Stahlin, Kant, Lotze, and Ritschl, 213, in which Stahlin cites Ritschl, Christian Doctrine of Justification and Reconciliation, 416.

54. Ritschl, Christian Doctrine of Justification and Reconciliation, 211.

55. Cairns, Autobiography, 172.

rich. . . . An age hungry for fact was taught by Ritschl that true Christian religion, not less than literature, science, art or political knowledge, has its roots in bygone events and is nourished by their sap."[56]

Cairns saw the Ritschlian "recovery" of the Jesus of history as one of positive gains of the movement, and though there were aspects of Ritschlian theology with which he disagreed, he admitted to learning much from the school, and continued to admire it throughout his life.[57] Orr observed that for Ritschl the idea of the kingdom of God was the key to understanding the whole gospel revelation.[58] Cairns continued his explorations of the concept, deepening and extending his reading, but his circumstances were about to change in a radical way, following a call to minister to the Springbank congregation in Ayton.

First Charge

Only two miles from Burnmouth, this was, for Cairns, familiar territory. *The New Statistical Account* described Ayton toward the middle of the nineteenth century as a picturesque village, deriving its name from the River Eye, on whose banks it stands. Its rocky southeast boundary where Burnmouth stands, contrasts starkly with the undulating tree-covered contours of its northern side. The fertile banks of the Eye made it at that time an attractive location for country mansions, including Atyon House with its fine plantations; and flour mills and a paper mill benefited from the river's flow. The area's past strategic importance can be seen in place names that indicate encampments from Roman times, and in the ruins of medieval castles. In the nineteenth century its land was well cultivated, growing several kinds of grain, turnips and potatoes, which among other uses, provided the basic ingredient for the local distillery. There was also a successful tannery. As well as the Parish church there were two Secession churches, which had begun as Burgher and Anti-Burgher congregations, but were now United Presbyterian churches: Summerhill and Springbank.[59] It was to the union of these two churches that Cairns was called.

Dr. D. K. Miller of Eyemouth, was moderator of the Presbytery of Duns and Chirnside during the vacancy, and Cairns's ecclesiastical referee. He had served previously as minister in the congregation next to Stitchel, in

56. Mackintosh, *Types of Modern Theology*, 156.

57. Cairns, *Autobiography*, 133–35. One major area of disagreement concerned the interpretation of the divinity of Christ.

58. Orr, *Ritschlianism Essays*, 23–24.

59. Tough, "Ayton, County of Berwick," 130–49.

Leitholm, so had known Cairns since childhood, being a frequent visitor to his father's manse. Cairns's shepherd grandfather had once lived in Ayton, and his uncle John had been born in Ayton Hill, and for a few years had lived in the village and taught in the school. Best of all, his father and Miller were nearby to give support and advice. Such were the advantages Cairns enjoyed, but potential problems within the congregation counterbalanced them. Due to falling numbers it was becoming difficult to finance both United Presbyterian congregations, and a union had been suggested. During protracted deliberations, bad relations developed with the presbytery, to the point where the Summerhill congregation, in 1888, sought admission to the Free Church. Only after this request was turned down did the representatives of the congregation agree to meet with the presbytery officials, although by this time the office-bearers were described as indifferent or "spirit broken." Good relations with the presbytery were restored, but the financial situation remained precarious, and the two congregations merged and became Ayton United. Springbank exhibited a significant degree of dissension over the proposed union, but both sessions decided to proceed. The united congregation had 212 members, and worship alternated monthly between the two buildings, but Summerhill was the larger, and was eventually settled on.[60] This was the situation inherited by Cairns when he became the first minister of the united congregation in March 1895. Discussing the prospect of Ayton in a letter to his father, he admitted that Atyon had attractions that he "could not easily explain to an outsider."

The work, the associations, the district, all these go to make it a singularly good place in which to move one's soul, and, I trust, to do useful work, and at the same time gain an increased measure of physical vigor.[61]

Cairns had been invited to preach along with another candidate, James B. Fleming of Glasgow, so an election was called. Some days after his letter to his father, an item appeared in one of the local newspapers, describing the election process, and detailing the way the votes had been cast. He had secured 50 votes to Fleming's 25 Although the vote had not been unanimous, the congregations then decided to make it a unanimous call. However, out of around 200 members, just over half (111) signed it.[62] From the start, then, Cairns entered a divided church. No wonder he accepted with "a good deal of trepidation."[63] His ordination, on March 12, 1895, was covered extensively in the *Berwickshire News*, headed by a portrait of Cairns by the paper's

60. Small, *History of the Congregations*, 1:406–12.

61. Letter, 25 January 1895. Cairns Papers, Box 1, MS3384/1/5.

62. *Berwickshire News*, 29 January 1895.

63. Cairns, *Autobiography*, 156.

"representative."[64] A large crowd attended the service of ordination in the church at two o'clock in the afternoon. There was much mention of his local associations: his paternal grandparents had worshipped in the church fifty years before, and his grandfather was buried in the churchyard. Frequent references were made to his uncle John of "saintly memory" and "fragrant associations." The annual visits of his uncle William were recalled fondly, and his departures that had made it seem "as if some of their own sunshine had gone along with him." There were not so many memories of Cairns's father, but the hope was expressed that he would make many visits now that his son was living in Ayton.

Later in the afternoon, the ordination was celebrated with a dinner in the Red Lion Hotel, where Rev. W. Wilson presided over gathered members, friends, and family, pointing out that the new minister came "with a character and reputation of his own." He came with high intellectual qualifications and moral purposes, committed to minister to the congregation. He had a wide experience of life and "ample stores of knowledge gathered from the wide field of human literature, and a devout knowledge of the word of God." He had come to a congregation "perfectly unanimous," and where union was progressing "most cordially." The congregation's recorded applause presumably implied their wish to maintain such cordiality. In responding, Cairns admitted his awareness that his generous reception owed much to the family reputation, and he promised to try to keep up the good name. He pointed out that while his family association was a privilege and an honor, it was also a disadvantage in that he had to live up to certain expectations while having his own ideals, and having to make up his own mind about situations as they arose. He was consoled by the fact that he was not altogether unknown to those present, remembering the kindness of the people in Burnmouth. Cairns might be moving to a quiet Borders village, where the way of life was familiar to him, but he was not opting for the quiet life in every sense. From the very beginning of his ministry, he kept the wider perspective in sight. In closing his speech he drew attention to Ayton's situation as it related to the national context of the search for unity. He said that he was glad to come to a united church, and he saw the cordiality of the people as auguring well for Ayton's future. He reminded people that their struggles represented "that larger hope and ambition which was animating the Church of Christ everywhere"—the movement in Scotland for Church union, especially the immediate union

---

64. All the information about the ordination, dinner, soiree and Sunday services, including content of speeches and sermons, from the *Berwickshire News*, 19 March 1895. The writer is unnamed, and referred to as "our Representative."

of the United Presbyterian Church with its sister churches, and, he hoped, in years to come with the Church of Scotland.

The day of ordination closed with a *"soiree"* in the Volunteer Hall, where there was a musical program, with more words of welcome and commendation for the new minister. Also important were the well-attended services on the following Sunday, when David Cairns senior preached at the morning service, and Cairns preached in the evening. At the end of his sermon, Cairns senior addressed the congregation with some personal remarks about their new minister, saying that he was a dutiful son and a loving brother, and although he was young in years, he had "gone through various experiences." His words reveal a deep sense of empathy with his son's intellectual struggles, and admiration for his perseverance in working out his personal faith perspective:

> Like most open-minded young men in the present critical and questioning age he has not escaped times of mental and spiritual struggle. These I believe are unavoidable and to be expected in the case of many. I believe he has got through these difficulties and has reached a foundation on which he has securely built up the structure of his faith and hope, even that foundation on which no other can be laid, which is Christ, and having found a gospel for himself, he has come at your invitation to preach that gospel also.[65]

His father's final words echoed Cairns's own earlier in the day, when he had indicated that he might not always choose the same paths as his illustrious antecedents had done. His blessing seems designed to free his son from the burden of such expectations: "May he be enabled to combine these old memories with others still more fragrant and tender . . . proving that the gospel has lost none of its ancient power, and that instead of the fathers there shall be the children whom the Lord shall make rulers in the earth."[66]

When he looked back on this event in his autobiography, Cairns remembered the solemnity of the service with its ritual of the laying on of hands. Afterwards he recollected shaking hands with all the people at the church door, followed by a dinner at the manse, with friendly speeches and letters. There is no indication of the formality and length of proceedings recorded in the newspaper, but he did recall the text he used for his first sermon that following Sunday evening—the one which his father had used to open his own ministry in Stitchel more than forty years before, with its

65. *Berwickshire News*, 19 March 1895.
66. *Berwickshire News*, 19 March 1895.

central theme of the cross and its meaning.[67] Decades later he recalled coming into the vestry after his first sermon, and wondering, "How can I ever keep this up?" and "Will they come back and keep coming back?"[68]

On a more mundane level, Cairns had inherited between two and three hundred pounds, which his mother and his sister, Jessie, spent on furniture for the manse. Thanks to this gift, he began his ministry free of debt, which he acknowledged was not the case for all ministers.[69] As far as his work was concerned, he adopted a practical plan of action for his new situation.[70] His first priority was "to minister to the souls of the men and women and children." He was not confident about his preaching ability, so had to focus hard on this, devoting mornings solely to study and writing his sermons. With a sense of humor, he recalled his shortcoming in this area: "I cannot say that judging by the evidence of my own eyes I could in common decency ever persuade myself that I have any considerable gift as an arresting preacher!"[71]

Cairns had two weekly sermons to prepare, and in winter additional work for a weekly prayer meeting and a Bible class for the young people. Life in Ayton "humanized and deepened" his outlook as, through his pastoral work, he shared the joys and sorrows of his people; and he often wrote sermons that he hoped would speak to the needs of particular individuals. He found that it took much hard work to put his ideas into the language and form that would speak to his congregation of "plain country people."[72] He also had to ensure that the union of the congregation was affected in a way that was more than superficial. Things appeared united externally, but internal divisions remained, and a sense of community was lacking. Getting to know his congregation was a necessary part of this, and he found pastoral visiting interesting as well as essential. The elders accompanied his first visits, but he then set himself the task of visiting every member once a year, with more frequent visits to those who were ill or elderly. This was his method of getting to know the family histories, personalities, and the daily life and work of the people. Evaluating his own ministry he later felt that lack of prayer was his main weakness. The aspect he enjoyed most was his work with the young people, who were mainly farm servants, and not very articulate, but whose cheerful approach to life often restored his own confidence when things were not going as well as he would have liked.

67. Cairns, *Autobiography*, 157.
68. Cairns, *Autobiography*, 160.
69. Cairns, *Autobiography*, 157.
70. Cairns, *Autobiography*, 157–66.
71. Cairns, *Autobiography*, 160.
72. Cairns, *Autobiography*, 160.

A brief selection from the session minutes during the early years in Ayton gives some flavor of the life there, and of the positive response to the new minister.[73] On 13 October 1898, Cairns presented a plan for "Our Young Men," which the session approved with gratitude. (His autobiography recorded the difficulty of getting young men to church.)[74] The session also gave their general approval to the plans for union with the Free Church, following Cairns's explanation of the general principles involved, particularly as they related to the Formula. The following month, on 26 November, the session met on behalf of the congregation to "give expression to the pleasure, and spiritual profit, which had been derived from the varied services of the Communion Season." Other minutes record the existence of a variety of societies and classes, including a reading society, a singing class, and a Christian union.

As well as his Bible study and reading for sermon preparation, Cairns continued what he described as his "solid reading," with the kingdom as his continuing focus. He read all six volumes of British historian Edward Gibbon's *The History of the Decline and Fall of the Roman Empire*, which spanned the vast period between the second century AD and the fall of Constantinople in 1453. Several summer months were spent reading the *Literary and Philosophical Essays* of the Italian activist and writer Giuseppe Mazzini, whom Cairns thought of as the great European liberal, and whose ideas about a free and yet associated world seemed vital for the survival of the world.[75] Previously he had read *about* Darwin, now he began to read his works for himself, finding the scientist's arguments convincing, highlighting for him the "red thread of pain and evil that runs through nature as well as human life."[76] In contrast to focusing on the great sweep of history, he tried to enhance his understanding of the main Christian denominations in Britain, by reading biographies of some of their great representatives. Of the English theologians he included Edward Bouverie Pusey, Henry Manning, and F. D. Maurice, the latter attracting him most. He also admired John Wesley. As far as Scottish theologians were concerned, there was none greater than John MacLeod Campbell, especially in his work *The Nature of the Atonement*. For recreation, D. S. turned to poetry, and besides Browning, he read Tennyson, Wordsworth, Keats, and Shelley.

73. *Principal Minute Book* of Ayton United Presbyterian Church 1898–1902, National Records of Scotland, CH3/932/1.

74. Cairns, *Autobiography*, 160.

75. Cairns, *Autobiography*, 167.

76. Cairns, *Autobiography*, 167.

A Nascent Apologetics

When Cairns had contemplated, in his student days, the idea that there may be no God, life had presented itself to him as "a wide, grey lampless, deep, unpeopled world" which filled him with horror.[77] During his time in Selkirk he had intimated in a letter to his sister, Jessie, his hopes of developing the "power to speak in the light what has been learned in the darkness."[78] Having known the pain of loss of faith, and faced up to the intellectual difficulties presented to religion by science, he wanted to be able to help others who found themselves in similar situations. In Ayton, while producing his weekly sermons, he continued to work independently to develop his theology of the kingdom of God, but he came to feel the need to articulate his thinking to the wider constituency of his academic peers. Two opportunities presented themselves. One came as the result of a visit by a friend from student days in the United Presbyterian Hall, David Connor.[79] He had impressed his friends by having an article accepted for the *Contemporary Review*, a prestigious monthly journal devoted to intellectual discussion of religious, philosophical, and social issues, and including articles by notable figures such as John Ruskin, William E. Gladstone, Matthew Arnold, and F. D. Maurice. According to Connor, he had just sent his article in and the editor, Dr. Percy Bunting, had accepted it right away. Cairns decided to follow his friend's example, and sent in a short article entitled "Science and Providence," in which he tried to show how the two worldviews could be brought together in the idea of the kingdom of God.

His thesis had been worked out over the long period since his experience during his voyage to Egypt, when he had intuited a sense of purpose behind the mechanistic movements of the waves. His reading program had given him an evolutionary perspective of history, in which development was synonymous with progress. The American historian Arthur Herman describes the idea of progress as fundamental to the Scottish notion of history in the post-enlightenment period.[80] Cairns claimed a teleological aspect to evolution: like religion, it admitted of a Supreme End, and assumed that some form of human society is its goal.[81] Both the religious and scientific views converge on a great "world-end of a social order."[82]

77. Cairns, *Autobiography*, 89. Here he quotes Beatrice in Shelley's "Cenci," act V, Sscene iv, line 66, in which she, having been condemned to death by her demonic father, contemplates the horror of a future world without God.

78. Letter to Jessie from Selkirk, 12 June 1893, Cairns Papers, Box 1, MS3384/1/5.

79. Cairns, *Autobiography*, 168.

80. Herman, *Scottish Enlightenment*, 11.

81. Cairns, *Christianity in the Modern World*, 233–45.

82. Cairns, *Christianity in the Modern World*, 244.

In support of his argument for the teleological nature of evolution, Cairns quoted the American botanist and Harvard professor Asa Gray (1810–1888), with whom Darwin had had a long correspondence. Cairns selected from this correspondence a response of Darwin, which suggested that he was pleased with Gray's teleological interpretation of his work.[83] However, Darwin's position was ambiguous. He vacillated in his response as he wrestled with the whole concept of design, finding it difficult to reconcile the idea of a loving Creator with the pain, suffering, and death involved in the apparent randomness of natural selection.[84] Following Darwin's death, his family had suppressed details of his agnosticism. His granddaughter, Nora Barlow, restored the account of his loss of faith in a revised edition of his autobiography in 1958.[85]

In his article, Cairns claimed optimistically that the introduction of the principle of the kingdom of God removed many difficulties and went a long way toward the solution of the central problem. "If the ends, then, of the two *Weltanschauungen* tend to identify, can there be any real contradiction between the means?"[86] He submitted his article, describing it as part of a proposed series in which he would apply the idea of the kingdom in other ways. He was on holiday in Zermatt, Switzerland, in April 1899, when he received the news that it had been accepted; his first publication appeared in March 1900. Several related articles followed.

Cairns's other opportunity to disseminate his ideas within the academic sphere, came from the Theological Society in New College. He had introduced his *Contemporary Review* article by declaring that Christianity had to come to terms with the new thinking of the day if its aim of world conquest was to be realized. Cairns was referring to the meeting in Kyoto in 1889 of the Student Volunteer Movement for Foreign Missions, at which the theme was "Christian Students United for World Conquest."[87] The idea of world conquest echoed the "watchword" of the student movement—"The Evangelization of the World in this Generation."[88] There had been a vibrant mission-centered movement among British university students since the middle of the nineteenth century, enlarged and energized by Henry Drummond in the 1880s and 1890s. Several manifestations of the movement later merged in 1905 to become the Student Christian Movement. In his history

83. Cairns, *Christianity in the Modern World*, 237–38.
84. Miles, "Charles Darwin and Asa Gray," 196–201.
85. Barlow, *Autobiography of Charles Darwin*.
86. Barlow, *Autobiography of Charles Darwin*, 365.
87. Boyd, *Witness of the Student Christian Movement*, 5.
88. Boyd, *Witness of the Student Christian Movement*, 6.

of the SCM, Robin Boyd describes its four themes: the Bible; the missionary call; academic integrity; and commitment to the church. Academic integrity had included, since the time of Drummond, openness to science and to biblical criticism.[89] One of those who had become involved in the movement as a student in Oxford was Joseph Houldsworth Oldham (1874–1969). After graduating with a second-class degree in Greats, he had worked for a year as the first full-time general secretary of the Student Volunteer Missionary Union (SVMU) and in 1897 had received an invitation from the Scottish National Council of Young Men's Christian Associations to work as YMCA secretary in Lahore in India. During his three and half years in India, he had married Mary Fraser, who was also involved in the student movement in Oxford, but the two succumbed to typhoid and had to return to Britain.[90] In 1901, Oldham was accepted as a theological student at New College, where from 1903–4 he was president of the Theological Society.

At some point during this period, an invitation came to Cairns to speak to the society, and he agreed, taking the kingdom of God in the Bible as his theme, set in the context of the historical ideals of humanity, and of the various interpretations of it throughout Christendom. Cairns ended his paper with the missionary ideal as the means of spreading the kingdom. Faced with the enormity of the task of the expansion of the kingdom, he had found inspiration in the work of Kirkup, who had refused to believe that socialism was an impracticable and unattainable goal. Where Kirkup found his solution in the cooperative movement as a practicable way to turn vision into reality, Cairns saw the missionary movement of the church as the vehicle for realizing the kingdom.[91] A few days later Oldham asked him if he would contribute to a volume that the SCM was about to publish, with the comment that Cairns had been expressing the characteristic ideas of the movement in his lecture. Cairns was invited by the SCM to attend their annual summer conference, and so began his lifelong association with the movement. Oldham himself became one of Cairns's closest friends, and would play a significant role in his personal life over the next few years. In his later reflections on his period, Cairns recounted an episode that revealed the respect he showed for other points of view. When writing one of his articles for the *Contemporary Review*, he had been tempted to make what he called a "rather depreciatory reference" to the "enthusiasts" who believed that the world could be evangelized in a generation, but he erased it on the ground that it was not for him "to

89. Boyd, *Witness of the Student Christian Movement*, 4–9.

90. Clements recounts the story of Oldham's life and work in *Faith on the Frontier*.

91. Cairns, *Autobiography*, 150.

speak disparagingly of honest enthusiasm." Looking back, Cairns also took this as an example of Providence in operation. "And when I think how easily I might have missed the many contacts and opportunities which the S.C.M. gave, by allowing that rather disparaging passage to remain, instead of striking it out, I see another illustration of how very far-reaching consequences may depend on very small things."[92]

Returning Health

By the final years of the nineteenth century, Cairns had recovered a large measure of health: enough to make two trips to Switzerland in 1899 and 1900. From the middle of the century there had developed in Britain an interest in alpine climbing, particularly among the middle and professional classes. An English clergyman, Charles Hudson, had been in the party that made the first successful attempt to scale the Matterhorn (14 July 1865), al-though, tragically, he died in an accident during the descent. The incident was sensationalized in the English press to such an extent that Queen Victo-ria is reported to have considered banning mountaineering among her sub-jects.[93] Callum Brown describes the nineteenth-century struggle to construct a narrative of masculine morality at a time when many regarded piety as essentially effeminate. Involvement in sport was seen as a means of develop-ing "muscular Christianity," although for some evangelicals it was associated with "the sins of gambling, drinking and rough culture," and therefore un-desirable.[94] In a class-conscious society, mountaineering, requiring time and money to travel, and therefore out of reach of the laboring classes, may have provided a more acceptable form of sport, and an alternative means of es-tablishing a masculine Christianity. Both trips made by Cairns are recorded in letters to his sister Jessie.[95] On his first trip he had traveled from Paris to Zermatt, most likely by train through the Chamonix valley, where among the Mount Blanc massif he saw the spectacular needle-shaped Aiguille du Dru. Its wildness and grandeur so impressed him that he wrote, "The Power behind Nature speaks to you in a new language. The great rock Dagger seems to say, I have outlasted the ages, I am stronger than the wind and the ice and the lightning. I saw Calvin come and I have seen Calvin go, and I will see you

92. Cairns, *Autobiography*, 170

93. Truffer, *History of the Matterhorn*, 6–14.

94. Brown, *Death of Christian Britain*, 88, 96–98.

95. Box 1, MS3384/1/5, Aberdeen papers, two letters to Jessie from the small village of Leuk, one undated, the other dated 25 April 1899. A letter to Jessie from Grindelwald dated 12 April 1900.

out too. Then says I, no, my brother, you will not. I will see you out, easily, but for all that you are a great Act of God."

The latter part of his statement sounds whimsical, but the whole speaks of a new confidence, and ease with the idea of the changing nature of theology and doctrines. Not far from the Riffelhaus where he was lodged in Zermatt, the Matterhorn towered among the Pennine Alps. From there he went on to do the Gemmi Pass, connecting Leukerbad in the Canton of Valais with Kandersteg in the canton of Bern. He was fit enough to walk to the top of the pass. The following year, he returned to Switzerland, this time to Grindlewald and the Berner Alpen with the great peaks of the Jungfrau and the Eiger. There is no record of another return to Switzerland, but the majesty of the mountains stayed in his imagination, and fifty years later, at the very end of his life, he recalled his visit for his son David, also an academic theologian, using it as an analogy for the theological task.

> The next day I went up to Leuk, and walked up the Gemmi, arriving just as it got dark at the hostelry at the top of the pass. I remember I got some excellent *bouillon* there, and stayed the night. The next day I remember going over into that glorious rich sunny jingling country on the other side. All the way up the Gemmi you could see only as far as the next turn of the road, and it looked as if there were no possible way out, but when you got there you could always see another stretch ahead. You must think of things in that way.[96]

Whatever Cairns's motivation for the journeys to Switzerland, he showed a remarkable degree of determination and pluck. The sight of the Gemmi is formidable, with its pathways invisible from the starting point. The journey through the pass is steep and long, with an ascent of over three thousand feet (965 meters). Even with the present well-tended pathways it takes at least four hours to complete, and walking at height is a strenuous activity.[97]

Marriage

In his early years in Ayton, Cairns developed his relationship with a young woman who had been a family friend since childhood: Helen Wilson Craw of Foulden West Mains, just five miles south of Ayton. Six years after his induction to Ayton, in line with the common custom of the day

96. Cairns, *Autobiography*, 36–37.

97. Official website of Switzerland Tourism.

for house weddings, the pair were married in the Foulden drawing room, on 3 December 1901.[98] Helen's father, Henry Hewat Craw, was a noted naturalist and well-to-do farmer, and her mother, Alison Hogue, was the niece of Thomas Wilson who had so generously left to David Cairns senior the legacy that allowed him to educate his children. Lyn Irvine related how the two families remained close friends after Wilson's death, with mutual visits during which Cairns would play with the Craw children, taking them for walks and telling them stories.[99]

In her account, Irvine also describes the tragic childhood of Helen's father. Henry Craw's mother had died at an early age, after only eight years of marriage, leaving three children, Henry and his two sisters. Then the two girls contracted tuberculosis and died in their teens. Not surprisingly, when Henry had his own children, Helen and Barbara, he was very protective, treating them "like two royal princesses."[100] When they were old enough to go to school, the family moved to Edinburgh, where the sisters attended St. Margaret's school and had a live-in governess. By the time of her marriage to Cairns, Helen's father had died. According to Donald Baillie, her home had been one of "considerable breadth of culture" and her father's protective attitude had not prevented her from becoming "a woman of great vivacity and goodness, with plenty of wit and humour and plenty of serious thought," and even before they were engaged, Helen and David exchanged letters about the books they had been reading.[101] Despite a fourteen-year age gap, the marriage apparently produced a very happy home for them and their two children, Alison Hogue, born 18 October 1902, and David, born 11 June 1904. In his autobiography Cairns described his marriage to Helen as one of the very greatest of God's gifts to him.[102]

Reaching Out to a Wider Academic Public

In 1906, with some revision and additions, Hodder and Stoughton published the *Contemporary Review* articles as *Christianity in the Modern World: Studies in the Theology of the Kingdom of God*. In his first book, Cairns presented his readers with a model for developing a society based on the Christian concept of the kingdom of God, at the individual, national,

98. Cairns, "Memories of Lochten and Foulden" (an unpublished private memoir, 1987), and family marriage notice, *Berwickshire News*, December 3, 1901.

99. Irvine, *Alison Cairns*, 9–11.

100. Irvine, *Alison Cairns*, 10.

101. Baillie, prefatory memior in *David Cairns: An Autobiography*, 12–13.

102. Cairns, *Autobiography*, 178–79.

international, and global levels. He embraced historical forces in the sense
that he saw God's purpose in them. The title of his first chapter, "The Modern Praeparatio Evangelica," set the tone: he looked at the causes of skepticism in contemporary society (science, positive philosophy, and biblical
criticism), and showed that they are part of God's plan for human development. Apologetical, but not defensive, his book was in keeping with his
evolutionary approach to history. He began by declaring that the nineteenth
century had delivered for Christianity the severest intellectual strain since
the days of the first Christians, but rather than castigating those who had
expressed religious doubt, he cited the personal cost of some of those well-
known figures who had given up Christian faith only after great intellectual
struggle and sorrow. Among these were Thomas Carlyle, Matthew Arnold,
and George Eliot (Marian Evans). Cairns suggested that some intellectual
currents which others find threatening to faith, are all part of a "slow coming to life of a new and nobler world."

According to Cairns, the controversy between science and religion
was inevitable because Christian dogma had been formed in a very different intellectual medium, making its expression inadequate in a scientific
era. For him, believing God to be present in all the events of history meant
seeing God's providence even in a collision of worldviews, and the atten-
dant uncertainty, and he concluded that the perceived conflict between
science and religion would have a positive outcome. The present tension he
described as due to the scientific conception of the natural law as a system
of causes and effects. How might that be reconciled with the religious interpretation of the world, especially in relation to such concepts as the conviction of human freedom, the power of prayer, and the detailed providence
of God in the lives of individuals? In philosophy, thanks to Immanuel Kant
(1724–1804), the idea of human freedom had been preserved in the face of
the determinist theories that denied its existence. In Kant's concept of the
human person as a rational agent with "the moral law within," Cairns saw an
analysis that gave humanity freedom over the apparent tyranny of nature.
As for biblical criticism, it brought the personality of Jesus to a position of
prominence not seen since the first century; and not just among Christians,
but among others who admired Jesus as a supreme ethical, although purely
human leader. Cairns maintained that it was impossible to maintain reverence for Jesus without accepting the truth of his ideas, and he held out the
hope that by building on the current admiration for Jesus, the church could
win people to a living faith in him, so bringing "positive results of incalcu-
lable value for the world at the present crisis of its History."[103] He continued
by discussing these distinctive ideas of Jesus.

103. Cairns, *Christianity in the Modern World*, 3–6.

1. The Idea of the Fatherhood of God

For Cairns, any attempt to isolate the ethical teaching of Jesus from his religious teaching, failed to give an accurate account of the historical Jesus, and any account of the historical Jesus must take into consideration his teaching about his relationship to God and his self-declared role of Messiah. He declared that above all the Jesus of the gospels saw himself as the Son of the Father.[104] Cairns described the work of the liberal historian John Robert Seeley in *Ecce Homo* (1855) as portraying an incomplete picture of Jesus. Seeley took for granted that most people could agree with the Christian ethical standard, and in an attempt to save something of religion in the growing climate of unbelief, he interpreted Jesus' work as the moral reformation of humanity, and presented Jesus as the Ideal Man whose "enthusiasm for humanity" had the power to inspire passion in his followers.[105] Cairns agreed with Seeley on two points: first, that Jesus made a unique and powerful impression on his followers, and second, that Jesus was inspired by a love of humanity. However, for Cairns the impression that Jesus made on his followers was so powerful that they could not think of the son without thinking of God: because it was enthusiasm for God that dominated Jesus' mind, formed his character and shaped his behavior. "Everything in the character and teaching of Jesus is staked so absolutely on the Fatherhood of God, that if we cannot accept His first principle, His life must cease to be ideal for us; for a life so consistently grounded in a mistaken conviction can never be ideal for earnest men."[106]

Cairns was confident that the concept of the universal Fatherhood of God was basic to Jesus' teaching: in addressing God as Father, Jesus assumed the role of son, and called others into the same filial relationship with God. Cairns saw all the spiritual influences mediated through Jesus as having the power to develop in people the potential of this "son-life." For Cairns Christian morality was the practical expression of this idea of the filial relationship expressed perfectly in the life of Jesus.[107] Wherever people sought to live out this relationship, the spiritual kingdom was present.[108]

The ethical dimension was based on the Fatherhood of God, which revealed humanity as a brotherhood. What is less clear is what Cairns meant when he wrote of the mediating role in relation to Jesus. How did he see Jesus

104. Cairns, *Christianity in the Modern World*, 37–40.

105. Hutchison, "Growth of Liberal Theology," ch. 13 in Ward et al., *Cambridge History*, 12:28–30.

106. Cairns, *Christianity in the Modern World*, 47.

107. Cairns, *Christianity in the Modern World*, 66–67.

108. Cairns, *Christianity in the Modern World*, 73.

affecting the transformation of people's lives? For him it was much more than "by the magnetic spell of a great Personality who is merely human."[109] Cairns listed some of the aspects of the new son-life, which, according to him, were realized only through Jesus: knowledge of and confidence in God as a loving Father, a constant source of moral and spiritual energy, and hope to maintain the new life. It may be argued though, that these do not necessarily point to the divinity of Jesus.

2. Discussion of Theories about the Person of Jesus

Cairns proceeded to consider two main theories of the person of Jesus, which he described as the humanitarian and the transcendent theories, and which differed most strongly over the concept of Jesus as Messiah. Cairns set out to challenge the humanitarian view, particularly as it was expressed by the Unitarian minister, philosopher, and theologian James Martineau (1805–1900). Martineau admired Jesus, not as a "Messiah" or "Lord," but as an inspired man filled with the spirit of God. For Martineau, Jesus revealed a devotion to God that strengthened the conscience, keeping people in fellowship with God, making them into incarnations of God as well.[110] He asserted that while many of the sayings in the gospels implied an authority which was more than human, they were "read back into the life of Jesus by the disciples and Evangelists."[111] Cairns based much of his own argument for transcendence on scriptural texts and seemed to dismiss the humanitarian theory by remarking, "Plainly, the line of least resistance is to question the accuracy of the records."[112] However, the question of the authority and interpretation of Scripture lay at the heart of this debate, and it cannot be dismissed so easily. Ironically, earlier in the chapter, Cairns stated that the science of biblical criticism contributed much to the resurgence of interest in the historical Jesus, and that humanitarianism had played a part in this.[113]

In defending the transcendence view, Cairns challenged the views of Ralph Waldo Emerson (1803–1882), American essayist and poet. Emerson had criticized what he perceived as an over-intellectual approach of the church and its failure to touch peoples' hearts. He believed that the church had elevated Jesus to a status above the rest of humanity, creating a cult

109. Cairns, *Christianity in the Modern World*, 59.

110. Schulman, "James Martineau," *Dictionary of Unitarian and Universalist Biography*, uudb.org/articles/jamesmartineau.html.

111. Cairns, *Christianity in the Modern World*, 108.

112. Cairns, *Christianity in the Modern World*, 100.

113. Cairns, *Christianity in the Modern World*, 88.

of personality which Emerson called the "noxious exaggeration about the person of Jesus." He saw this as robbing humans of their natural divinity because it failed to present Jesus as the greatest example to which humans could aspire.[114] Opposing the humanitarian viewpoint Cairns declared that the great spiritual movement that developed after Jesus cannot be accounted for by enthusiasm for a merely human teacher.[115] However, in declaring that the spiritual influence of Jesus could develop humankind's potential for the son-life, he came very close to Emerson's idea of the natural divinity in humankind being developed to its full potential by the example of Jesus.

Cairns made several statements that left room for further exploration of the person and work of Jesus. While acknowledging that the disciples, as Jews, would not have seen the Messiah as equivalent to God Incarnate, he saw them as having a new spiritual consciousness of Jesus which was difficult to define. He questioned in what sense the disciples believed Jesus was divine. He described them as creating a new world of thought around the conviction that God had manifested Godself in a new way in Jesus.[116] Cairns suggested that in such a new world, language was inadequate.

"It is difficult to define and specify this first Christian consciousness. It is religion as yet and not Theology, and when we are dealing with religious intuitions we must use symbol and picture and analogy rather than definition."[117]

3. Reflection on the Kingdom of God

The messianic consciousness of Jesus was at the heart of his reflection on two diametrically opposed views, represented by the German biblical scholars Julius Wellhausen (1844–1918) and Johannes Weiss (1863–1914). Wellhausen represented the view that the messianic and apocalyptic elements were "a Jewish excrescence on the Gospels, or a Jewish survival in the Mind of Jesus," with no relevance for modern theology. On the other hand, Weiss represented those who saw the apocalyptic element as central and characteristic in Jesus' teaching. Cairns claimed that both views contained elements of truth, and both must be brought together and harmonized within an understanding of the kingdom of God.[118] Asking why the

114. Carreira, "Ralph Waldo Emerson, Spiritual but Not Religious," https://jeffcarreira.com/ralph-waldo-emerson-origins-spiritual-not-religious/.

115. Cairns, Christianity in the Modern World, 147.

116. Cairns, Christianity in the Modern World, 154–58.

117. Cairns, Christianity in the Modern World, 154.

118. Cairns, Christianity in the Modern World, 167–74.

apocalyptic element in the New Testament was so misunderstood, Cairns reflected that such misunderstanding was the result of a clash between literalism and modern science, neither of which was able to deal with the figurative character of the language.[119] Declaring that "it is as nearly historically certain as anything can be that Jesus claimed to be the Messiah."[120] Cairns went on to examine the apocalyptic statements in this regard, and in doing so answered the criticisms of the humanitarians and described something of the character of the kingdom of God, present and yet future. For him, the messianic claim that Jesus would come again was a symbolic way of saying that his physical departure was not a real departure. His spirit would continue to empower his followers, but Cairns questioned whether a literal physical reappearance of Jesus was intended. He did, however, see in the apocalyptic teaching the implied culmination of history: a view of the future that took Jesus' followers beyond individualism, requiring them to think out the meaning of history in the light of its great climax, and to ask how the kingdom could be served in the present.[121]

Turning his attention to the practical application of his theology, Cairns interpreted the book of Revelation as "the cry of the Christian heart, harassed and burdened and tortured by the pressure of the Pagan Empire, for a Christian environment."[122] He saw twentieth-century aspirations for a nobler society as the modern analogue of the longings expressed in the Christian apocalyptic literature.[123] In this he made an eloquent response to the criticisms that J. S. Mill (1806–1873), British philosopher and economist, had leveled at religion, when Mill had accused it of standing in the way of the critical evaluation of social norms and preventing action for improving the lot of humanity.[124] Cairns saw it as providential that the intellectual forces of the day had brought to prominence the kingdom teachings of Jesus, just at the moment when imperial power was at its height, and when a new global interconnection was offering many advantages, but also bringing new dangers through the abuse of power.[125] He wondered if the ruling powers of the Western nations had the moral force to resist the temptation to exploit the lands they had colonized, in the interests of their private and national ambitions.[126]

119. Cairns, *Christianity in the Modern World*, 225.

120. Cairns, *Christianity in the Modern World*, 170.

121. Cairns, *Christianity in the Modern World*, 206–9.

122. Cairns, *Christianity in the Modern World*, 217.

123. Cairns, *Christianity in the Modern World*, 227.

124. Wilson, "John Stuart Mill."

125. Cairns, *Christianity in the Modern World*, 251–53.

126. Cairns, *Christianity in the Modern World*, 254–56.

Cairns set out a practical program for the churches, with three main strands that exhibited a strong sense of the influence and authority of the churches in Western culture. First, the churches must set themselves to the task of the evangelization of the world, and build on the missionary activity which had already spread around the world. Second, they must move into the sociological phase of developing a Christian civilization; that is, an environment in which it would be easier to nurture converts and build Christian communities that would be "provinces of a world-wide Kingdom of God." Third, the churches must ensure that there was no exploitation of indigenous peoples, and that state policy was in line with Christian ideals, governing in the interests of the common good. He warned that exploitation of "weaker races" resulted eventually in the deterioration of the oppressor.[127] While Cairns accepted the teaching of Jesus on the infinite value of the human soul, he was nonetheless a man of his time, and his language displayed an acceptance of racial stereotypes. His writing was peppered with such phrases as: "backward nations," "peoples of a weaker, and often of a debased type," "heathen ideas," and revealed belief in a hierarchy of races.

The historian Brian Stanley has pointed out that such overidentification of Christianity with Western values and progress contained a risk which became apparent with the rise of nationalism throughout the British Empire, as Christianity came to be perceived by many as a tool of imperialism.[128] However, Cairns also saw religion as countercultural in the sense that he perceived its role as challenging political and economic institutions that were based on self-interest and national pride. He also applied this countercultural perspective in assessing the political situation in Britain. In his preface to the book, Cairns noted his indebtedness to his friend Kirkup, "from whom, of all modern authorities upon the Social question, I have learned most." Cairns accepted the view of the English economist Alfred Marshall (1842–1924) that religion and economics had been the two formative agencies in history. Writing at a time of growing struggle between the forces of labor and capital, and echoing the philosophy of Emerson, Cairns declared an urgent need for the "Idea of the Common Good." The unfettered competition of laissez faire economics had polarized society and created a large underclass, which was now struggling to survive. Cairns supported the idea of a cooperative commonwealth, but felt that the time was not right. People needed to be prepared for the self-sacrifice entailed in such a change. He saw it as the task for the churches to build up the moral life of individuals, who would express their Christian values through institutional, customary, and

127. Cairns, *Christianity in the Modern World*, 256–62.
128. Stanley, "Discerning the Future of World Christianity," 21.

legislative reform. Cairns declared the need for the churches to rise above their present divisions in order to tackle the great questions of the age.[129] His sociology reflected the influence of Ritschl's theology, in which the church's power lay in its ability to transform the public consciousness through love, and in embedding the principle of love in its public institutions.[130]

In the final pages of the book, Cairns turned his attention to the problem of militarism, which he perceived as preventing development at home and creating the potential for war "on an incredibly destructive scale." "The traveler through modern Europe finds the nations everywhere armed to the teeth."[131] As with industrial unrest at home, he saw the pursuit of self-interest as the cause of international conflict. Cairns echoes some of the criticisms articulated by the English economist and social theorist J. A. Hobson (1858–1940), in his 1902 critique of British imperialism. Describing imperialism as a perversion of nationalism, characterized by greed and self-aggrandizement at the expense of others, Hobson declared, "Not only does aggressive Imperialism defeat the movement towards internationalism by fostering animosities among competing empires: its attack upon the liberties and the existence of weaker or lower races stimulates in them a corresponding excess of national self-consciousness."[132]

Cairns called for a new interpretation of nationality in the light of the concept of the kingdom of God. Christianity could not give up its hopes for universal peace, because such pessimism would be a negation of the living God. He asserted the need for the churches to throw the weight of their influence behind the newly established Hague Tribunal (1899), in its efforts to establish a system of international arbitration and justice.[133] He closed by challenging the churches to become the means for realizing the kingdom of God on earth:

> What is needed to-day is a form of religion which will invest the common secular duties of life with sacredness and grandeur, which will bring the mighty sanctions of Eternity to bear upon modern industry and the home and foreign policy of nations, which will compel men to feel that human society itself is a sacred thing, that it is not the scaffolding, but the living rock, out of which God is Himself building His city. A religion of this type, I believe, you cannot get if you make the visible Church

129. Cairns, *Christianity in the Modern World*, 263–90.

130. Ritschl, *Christian Doctrine of Justification and Reconciliation*, 49:466.

131. Cairns, *Christianity in the Modern World*, 291.

132. Hobson, *Imperialism*, 9. http://archive.org/stream/imperialismastuoogoog.

133. Cairns, *Christianity in the Modern World*, 291–303.

the final end of creation; a religion of this type you do get if you make the Church, like the Family and the State, a means to the world-wide realization of the Kingdom of God.[134]

The book was widely read, and according to D. M. Baillie it "stood for something new in Scottish theology."[135] Baillie did not explain in what sense it was new, but he did record the long list of invitations that came to Cairns because of it, including offers of city churches and chairs in universities in America and Australia. The nineteenth century had seen many works of apologetics, which tried to defend Christianity in the face of skepticism, or to reconcile the religious and the scientific interpretations of the world. Gordon Booth has recorded William Robertson Smith's views on the apologetics of his day. Speaking to the Theological Society at New College in January 1869, Robertson Smith had declared that "all theology is running into apologetics," and he continued:

> No one seems to grudge learning, ability, or labour bestowed on the defence of Christianity against unbelievers. We do not seem much interested in the internal development of Christian science. We either acquiesce in the traditional solution of nice theological questions, or regard the solution of the questions either way as unimportant; but the outposts as it were of theology—all points that touch on science, history, criticism, and in so far, on philosophy—are guarded with restless jealousy.[136]

Reflecting on Robertson Smith's words, Booth concluded, "The result, in terms of apologetic writing, was often an unhappy, weakly-argued and grudging compromise, as Smith had foreseen would be the case."[137] At the beginning of a new century, Cairns's book was more than a work of apologetics, it was a rallying cry made in complete confidence in a world in which the sacred and secular, the personal and political, formed a unity in which God acted to fulfill a purpose for humankind. Such confidence was about to be tested in a very personal way, for near the end of the year in which Cairns published his first book, in the winter of 1906-7, Helen was diagnosed with Bright's Disease, a type of kidney disease for which there was, at the time, no cure. Lyn Irivine related how, in the fashion of those days, Helen was told immediately of the incurable nature of her illness, and "bore it with

134. Cairns, *Christianity in the Modern World*, 311.

135. Cairns, *Autobiography*, 14–15.

136. Black and Chrystal, *Life and Letters*, 109; cited by Booth, "William Robertson Smith," ch. 9.

137. Booth, "William Robertson Smith," ch. 9.

great fortitude."[138] Cairns had a very different reaction, which he recalled in his autobiography, referring to the help he received from his friend from student days, Ivor Roberton. "When in my Ayton ministry many years afterwards my wife was suddenly taken ill and my health threatened to give way under the strain, he took me into his house in Galashiels for a month, and so helped me through a difficult time again."[139]

There is no mention of Helen here, and whether or not she was included in the visit. It seems unlikely that if she and the two children had gone with Cairns that he would have remembered the experience in the singular. It does seem extraordinary that Cairns would leave her at such a time. The strain he was under led him to confide in another more recently-made friend, Joe Oldham, and their correspondence reveals that Helen's illness brought the two men into a closer relationship, with Oldham introducing Cairns to the ideas of Christian Science and spiritual healing.[140] Helen's illness and subsequent death were to focus Cairns even more sharply on the problems presented by the existence of disease, suffering, and death for belief in a providential God. In the years to come he would struggle to forge a theology which might accommodate this seeming paradox, but in the meantime, another significant change was to occur with his election to the chair of Dogmatics and Apologetics in the United Free Church College in Aberdeen. (At his ordination dinner in 1895, Cairns had spoken of his hopes for unity among the churches, and in 1900, as we have seen, the first major reunification took place when the United Presbyterian Church and the Free Church combined to form the United Free Church, of which he then became a minister, and later a professor.)

Conclusion

In the space of fourteen years, Cairns had gone from being a seemingly unsuccessful probationer who found it hard to get his own congregation, to being an apologist and a writer of some repute. His probationary years had allowed him to build up a variety of experiences and skills that benefited him in his ministerial role, for instance in his work with young people, and in his pastoral capacity. In the call to Ayton, he found a charge in a familiar area and near his family, but one that offered not just familiarity and security, but challenges in terms of preaching, uniting a fragmented congregation, and of

138. Irvine, *Alison Cairns*, 14.

139. Cairns, *Autobiography*, 111.

140. Box 1/4 Cairns Papers, two letters from Joe Oldham to D. S. 26 April (year unclear) and 20 September 1906.

engaging young people. From the start of his ministry, he tried to establish his own identity, independent of the expectations that had followed him on account of his family name, and especially due to the reputation of his uncle John; and in this he had the support and blessing of his father. Years of lone study on the subject of the kingdom of God, gave him the desire to share his thinking with others who, like himself, had struggled with the intellectual currents that seemed to deny the validity of Christian faith. The success of his early forays into publishing for the *Contemporary Review*, and speaking to university students, gave him the confidence to develop his apologetics for an academic audience. His years of reading and reflection culminated in publications that brought him into contact with Joe Oldham and with the Student Christian Movement, and both were to play highly significant roles in his life. Cairns now had a theology that was firmly centered on the kingdom of God. In his interpretation of it, he revealed his indebtedness to the Ritschlian school with its idea of a kingdom that was based on the evidence of the ideas in the gospels, and that was both present and future, task and gift. His first book displayed the comprehensive nature of the intellectual task he had undertaken, and spoke to a wide and appreciative audience, bringing him fame and accolades within Scotland and beyond.

During this period, his health had improved and allowed him to be more adventurous, for instance in traveling to Switzerland and enjoying hiking in the Alps. In an age when there was a focus on manliness, these experiences must have brought confidence to a young man who had for so long felt timid because he was anxious about his health. To crown it all, his long-standing relationship with Helen developed into love and marriage, and brought the birth of their two children. At the beginning of 1906, it seemed as if life was just beginning to bring fulfillment and opportunity; but then came the devastating news of Helen's illness. The tragedy did not shake his belief in God's providence, but served to drive him on to further reflection on the nature of the kingdom of God, and how individuals might appropriate the power of such a kingdom in the historical context.

Chapter 4 _____

Defending the Faith and Describing the Kingdom, 1907–1915

IN 1895, THE YEAR in which Cairns went to Ayton, Alexander Balmain Bruce, professor of apologetics and New Testament exegesis at the Free Church College in Glasgow, had published a book entitled *Apologetics; or, Christianity Defensively Stated.* (Bruce had already, in 1890, published a work of apologetics, *The Kingdom of God; or, Christ's Teaching according to the Synoptical Gospels.*) In the new publication, he described his conception of the task and method of the apologist in the contemporary situation, declaring that the primary task was to help honest doubters regain their faith by confronting the challenges arising from philosophy, science, history and criticism. "Apologetic, then, as I conceive it, is a preparer of the way of faith, an aid to faith against doubts whencesoever arising, especially such as are engendered by philosophy and science. Its specific aim is to help men of ingenuous spirit who, while assailed by such doubts, are morally in sympathy with believers."[1]

Bruce continued by suggesting that the apologist should not direct his writing at the convinced atheist, as it is futile to argue with dogmatic unbelief; but nor should the apologist side with the dogmatic beliefs of a particular Christian denomination. He should steer away from any of the internal controversies of the church, distinguishing between religion and theology, and between faith and opinion; he should not advocate any particular theological system, but aim to reach those with an open mind. To those who felt that this would narrow the limits of the apologist's sphere of influence, Bruce suggested that a wider definition of "honest doubters" would extend the task to a very large constituency, including many

---

1. Bruce, *Apologetics*, 37.

outside the church and outside Christendom. For him, such a constituency included "all in whom there is a sincere sympathy with the good,
an implicit rudimentary faith in God, a spiritual receptivity that would
readily respond to such teaching as that of Christ, a vague, restless longing
for light on the dark problems of life."[2]

Bruce was also convinced that a renewed focus on Jesus' life and teaching might win back those who had left the church because of its poor record
of dealing with social grievances.[3] Drawing on his knowledge of German
apologetics, he presented advice on the method of presentation. For Bruce,
the purpose of apologetics was practical rather than theoretical: dealing with
doubts that made faith difficult. Rather than simply reacting to current opposition, the apologist should set the parameters for discussion, avoiding the
traditional method of trying to justify individual doctrines by dealing with a
large variety of topics under two headings: "Evidences of Natural Religion"
(all that could be known from the natural world), and "Evidences of Revealed
Religion" (particularly those found in Scripture). For Bruce, this kind of selection of topics seemed arbitrary and removed from the burning issues of the
day, and the method was unsatisfactory. Instead, he advocated the construction of a system "aspiring to scientific form and completeness."[4]

Nowhere in his first publication does Cairns refer to Bruce, but it is
highly unlikely that he would not have read these two publications, focused
as they were on a theme that was central to his own study and aspirations.
Bruce was a well-known academic, having defended William Robertson
Smith in 1881, and having been called to account before the general assembly of the Free Church for one of his own publications, *The Kingdom of God*.
Cairns's own brief summary of his intentions shows that he had moved away
from the traditional framework to one that was similar to those described
by Bruce in his introduction to *Apologetics*.[5] A brief outline of Cairns's
method shows his systematic approach to the apologetical task. First, he
dealt with the intellectual threats to Christianity, showing them in the positive light of bringing the character of Jesus to prominence once more. Next,
he described the distinctive kingdom message of Jesus, emphasizing the
fatherhood of God and the brotherhood of man. Lastly, he applied these
principles of Jesus to the practical problems of the day. His hope of developing the "power to speak in the light what has been learned in the darkness"
would have found inspiration in Bruce's description of the apologetical task,

2. Bruce, *Apologetics*, 38.

3. Bruce, *Apologetics*, 43.

4. Bruce, *Apologetics*, 42.

5. Cairns, *Christianity in the Modern World*, 250, and Bruce, *Apologetics*, 40–45.

and the invitation to accept the chair of Dogmatics and Apologetics at the United Free Church College in Aberdeen must have seemed to offer a natural progression for him.

The Intellectual Milieu in Aberdeen

Although a large variety of offers of work had come to Cairns during his Ayton ministry, he had been hampered in considering them by his indecisiveness, and by his desire to maintain his scholarly pursuits. At the time of his move to Aberdeen, appointments to university chairs of the United Presbyterian Church colleges were made by the general assembly. For Cairns, nervous about making wrong choices, the selection process of the day brought relief from the responsibility of decision-making.[6] In 1907, at forty-four years of age, with a wife who was seriously ill, and two small children, aged three and five, he moved into rented accommodation in Rubislaw Terrace, an imposing Victorian crescent near the United Free College in Alford Place, in the west end of the city. According to the historians Fraser and Lee, during the 1880s and 1890s, while the established and Episcopal churches had concentrated on work with the poor of the city, the United Presbyterian Church had focused its mission on the middle classes, and had built two grand churches in the area—one in Union Grove and the other in Carden Place. In the latter, an organ replaced the traditional precentor, and the building's dominant spire earned it the nickname "the U. P. cathedral." This location reflected the growing prosperity and increasing segregation of the social classes, and Cairns's neighbors would have included those considered among the elite of Aberdeen society, including other professors at the United Free Church College.[7] In 1910, shortly before Helen's death, the family was to move again, to Hamilton Place, just a few streets away, in what had also become a prestigious address.[8]

In his autobiography, apart from one brief mention of the process of appointment to the chair, Cairns says nothing about his time in Aberdeen, although he was to remain there until 1937. The college began its life in 1843, when all the city ministers "went out" at the Disruption, and teaching of candidates for the Free Church ministry began in a room in South Silver Street.[9] Throughout the 1840s, the general assembly of the Free Church

6. Cairns, *Autobiography*, 177.

7. *Scottish Church and University Almanac 1917*, 161.

8. Fraser and Lee, *Aberdeen 1800–2000*, 355–56, 381–82.

9. Sefton, "Christ's College," *Divinity Alumni Association University of Aberdeen Newsletter* 22, Winter 2000–2001.

claimed that it could not support more than one good college, and tried to centralize its teaching in New College in Edinburgh, and to close the college in Aberdeen, but this was resisted by members in Aberdeen, who raised the funds for the erection of a new purpose-built college building in Alford Place. It was opened in 1850, although its future was not secured until 1853, when the general assembly of the United Free Church committed itself to support a professor of theology and a teaching assistant. Other chairs were established during the 1870s. In spite of fluctuating numbers of students in the late nineteenth century, the college survived, and when the Free Church united with the United Presbyterian Church in 1900, it was renamed the United Free Church College.

From 1907, Cairns was to make a significant impact in a number of ways. In a speech to mark his retirement in 1937, J. A. Robertson declared, "His way-going makes an irreparable blank in the life of the community." He described Cairns as a beloved colleague and comrade, whose wise counsel had steered the college through difficult times, and whose students had benefited from his gifts of exposition and accessibility as a counselor and friend. Also, according to Robertson, Cairns had represented the church and college on civic occasions "with dignity and distinction, nay more, with that grandeur of mien and diction which has so often characterised our national leaders of action and of thought."[10] The *Senatus*, too, paid tribute, reporting that Cairns had exercised "a wide and ever-growing influence on theological thought," gaining an international reputation through his work with the Student Christian Movement, and a high place in the councils of the church.[11]

There is evidence that Cairns's students endorsed these positive depictions of their professor. George Cameron, minister of Glenburn Parish Church in Paisley from 1958–69, had been a student of Cairns in the 1920s, and on reading Lyn Irvine's book about the family, wrote to endorse her admiration for him, commenting that Cairns had enlarged his thinking.[12] Praise came from other former students, who, on the occasion of his retirement to Edinburgh, invited him to a meal in Mackie's Restaurant in Princes Street, where they presented him with a note-filled wallet. In making the presentation, W. J. Manson of Belford Church in Edinburgh

10. Robertson, "Tribute," *Aberdeen University Review* 25 (1937–38) 126–28. Robertson's reference to difficult times most likely refers to the protracted negations that took place between the University of Aberdeen and the United Free College after the union of the churches in 1929.

11. *Senatus* "Tribute," *Aberdeen University Review* 25 (1937–38) 70–72.

12. Cameron to Lyn Irvine, 27 March 1967 in St. John's Library / papers of Newman L./Cameron G./1.

thanked Cairns for all he had done for them. Recalling their college days with fondness, Manson assured him that every passing year had revealed to them their great debt to him.[13]

Although far removed from Edinburgh and Glasgow, Aberdeen was no intellectual backwater, as it had within the academic community, including the University of Aberdeen, some eminent figures. It had seen its share of public theological controversy following the appointment of William Robertson Smith to the United Free Church College chair of Hebrew in 1870, and during the years of his heresy trial. In 1907, James Iverach was appointed principal of the college, having previously been professor of dogmatics. A Christian Darwinist, Iverach had published several works in which he tried to reconcile Christian teaching with the new philosophical and scientific ideas of the day.[14] Cairns was elected to Iverach's former chair, on the occasion of the latter's promotion, and was one of four professors.[15] James Stalker had occupied the chair of Church History and Christian Ethics since 1902. He had been invited, in the spring of 1891, to give the Yale Lectures on Preaching. In these lectures he made clear his views that it was the preacher's job to nurture in his congregation a sense of public spiritedness that would inspire church members to action for social reform, and such reform he linked to the idea of the kingdom of God.[16] John A. Selbie, appointed six years after Cairns, had the chair of Old Testament Language and Literature. By the time of his appointment, along with James Hastings, he had edited the *Bible Dictionary* (New York, 1909), incorporating the most up-to-date biblical scholarship. The academic staff appeared an outward-looking group, engaging with the intellectual and social challenges of the time.

The intellectual milieu of the city was enriched too by the contribution of academics at the University of Aberdeen.[17] In 1910, the renowned Semitic scholar and United Free Church minister George Adam Smith became principal. As we saw in the previous chapter, nearly twenty years before, when Cairns was a struggling probationer, he had found Smith's articles on the historical geography of the Holy Land a great asset as he studied the life of Jesus in the Synoptic Gospels. Among the university academic staff in divinity was William A. Curtis, professor of systematic theology from 1903–1915,

13. *Aberdeen University Review* 25 (1937–38) 274.

14. One example of such works was *Christianity and Evolution*, a text digitally reprinted by Cambridge University Press, considering it one of the landmark texts of the late Victorian period.

15. *Scottish Church and University Almanac 1917*, 161.

16. Stalker, *Preacher as Patriot*.

17. Simpson, *Fusion of 1860*, 151, 227–29, 234.

who while at Aberdeen published *A History of Creeds and Confessions of Faith in Christendom and Beyond* (Aberdeen, 1911), which was highly commended at the time. When Curtis moved to New College, Edinburgh, he was succeeded by William Fulton, whom Simpson describes as a "scholar among scholars," contributing to the *Expository Times* and to the *Encyclopaedia of Religion and Ethics*, also edited by Hastings and Selbie. The importance of the critical movement was kept alive by Thomas Nicol, professor of biblical criticism from 1899-1916. Other faculties contributed to the intellectual dynamics.[18] The professor of moral philosophy from 1902-24 was James Black Baillie, who came to lectures in a chauffeur-driven Rolls Royce. Along with John McTaggart of Cambridge, he was the leading interpreter of Hegel, producing major works of scholarship on the philosopher.[19] Baillie's encouragement of students to question and reflect on traditional beliefs, led him to be regarded by some as a dangerous influence on the young. Another long-standing member of staff, J. Arthur Thomson, was professor of natural history from 1899-1930. In his Gifford Lectures at St. Andrews in 1915-16, he warned of the limitations of science and of the need to consider the function of feeling as a pathway to reality. In discussing religious interpretation and scientific analysis as "equally natural and necessary expressions of the developing human spirit," Thomson described religion as belief in a higher or deeper order of reality that cannot be reached through the sense-experiences, and he quoted Cairns as an "authority."[20]

Helen's Illness and Death

The difficulty of the Cairns's home situation must have been compounded by the distance from family and the loss of support from familiar friends in the Borders. Family friend Lyn Irvine recalled that the children had "the look of little exiles" as they stood at the door of their new home in Rubislaw Terrace.[21] For Cairns there was a great struggle, as he tried to reconcile this experience with a worldview centered on a God of love. During the final stages of Helen's illness, a circle of close friends prayed for her recovery, including Oldham and his brother-in-law, Alexander Garden Fraser of Trinity College, Kandy, in Ceylon. Ever since Helen's diagnosis, Cairns had been in regular touch with Oldham about the situation, the effect of which was

18. Simpson, *Fusion of 1860*, 172-73, 289-93.

19. *Hegel's Logic* (1901), *The Idealistic Construction of Experience* (1906), and *Phenomenology of Mind* (1910).

20. Thomson, *System of Animate Nature*, 40.

21. Irvine, *Alison Cairns*, 14.

to bring the two men into a very close relationship. Oldham kept a book in which he recorded special experiences and subjects that he was praying for, and recorded the following comment: "The illness of Mrs. Cairns and the fellowship with Cairns to which it has led have in a mysterious way become the occasion through which God has opened up new truth."[22]

Oldham and his wife, Mary, had been missionaries in Lahore, India, from 1897–1901, during which time they had contracted typhoid. At one stage, Oldham was very near death, and the couple were afterwards convinced that their survival and recovery were due to the prayer of the Young Men's Christian Association members with whom they worked. On their return to Scotland, they continued to reflect on what they saw as the church's lost ministry of healing, and they explored the teaching of Mrs. Mary Baker Eddy (1821–1910), founder of the Church of Christ Scientist in Boston, Massachusetts, in 1879.[23] Focusing on the healing ministry of Jesus, as described in the New Testament, Eddy claimed to have discovered the science behind healing. She propounded the following ideas: mortal existence is a state of self-deception; illness has its origin in the mind and can be cured by the divine mind;[24] the miracles of Jesus were not supernatural events, but were the natural outcome of his trust in the divine love or mind of God. This same love "crowned the demonstrations of Jesus with unsurpassed love and power," so that he was able to heal the sick.[25]

Right at the start of Helen's illness, Oldham had referred Cairns to a Christian Science contact, Mrs. Whyte. Oldham declared that he had never been able to believe that the healing ministry of Jesus was an isolated, unique, unaccountable miraculous phenomenon, but rather it had been an indication of the higher possibilities of human experience. He saw this as an area that the church had been too faithless and timid to explore, but wondered now if God was leading them, or Cairns alone, to take on the role of shaping the corporate will of the church in this respect.[26] In the last months of Helen's illness, and just before the World Missionary Conference, in reply to a query from Cairns about the wisdom of contacting a Christian Scientist, Dr. Riley, Oldham encouraged him to go ahead with the "special treatment." Cairns seemed to fear being seen to endorse such a controversial movement, but Oldham related that the more he read Mrs. Eddy, the more

22. Oldham, personal notebook entry for 23 October 1906, Box 1/4 Cairns Papers.

23. Eddy, *Science and Health*. This, her primary text, can be read online at http://christianscience.com/read-online/science-and-health. See also Eddy, *Christian Healing*.

24. Eddy, *Science and Health*, 394–422.

25. Eddy, *Science and Health*, 243.

26. Oldham to Cairns, 20 September 1906, Box 1/4 (10) Cairns Papers.

he thought that she had had a genuine Christian experience. He admitted that she expressed herself in a crude and mistaken way, but that he had frequently had recourse to spiritual healing and had found that it strengthened his faith as nothing else did.[27] In the same letter, Oldham reassured Cairns that it was unlikely that his action would become known, but reiterated his opinion that the church needed those with the courage to experiment and try new paths.[28] It seems strange that something so close to Cairns's heart and mind should be a cause for reticence, but at the time he was working on the Commission IV report, in which he was to make a plea for a return to what he described as the "radical supernaturalism" of the early church, and perhaps, not knowing how that would be received, he did not want to add any further controversy, or to compromise his standing within the ecclesiastical mainstream. Focus on the supernatural element in Christianity was becoming a central component of Cairns's theology, and one that would be developed most fully in *The Faith That Rebels*, 1928.

In describing the phenomenon of the rapid development of Christian Science, the historian and author William Henry Withrow described Eddy's theory: "The principle feature of her theory seems to be that 'mind is all and matter is naught,' that 'flesh is an illusion' and 'pain is an imagination,' that disease can be cured by believing its non-existence."[29] Withrow was ready to believe that nervous conditions might be cured by spiritual healing, and admitted that some of the devout and religious principles which Christian Science advocated made it attractive to many thinking people. In his desperation to help his wife, Cairns was among that number. It would seem that at the time, there were enough people in Scotland who were sympathetic to the cause of Christian Science, as in 1910 the church was able to afford to employ the distinguished Edinburgh architect Ramsay Traquair to design a church building next door to the Women's Missionary College. The imposing Church of Christ Scientist at 18 Inverleith Terrace, Edinburgh, was completed in 1911.

In his Gifford Lectures in Edinburgh in 1901–1902, William James, the American psychologist and philosopher, had delivered a positive verdict on Christian Science, seeing it as one of the groups in what he called the "Mind-cure movement." He admired the optimistic nature of the movement, and the remarkable results it had achieved; it was attracting many followers, and beginning to influence the medical and clerical professions in America. He admitted that there were failures, too, but that failure was

27. Oldham to Cairns, 26 April 1910, Box1/4 (2) Cairns Papers.
28. Oldham to Cairns, 26 April 1910, Box1/4 (2) Cairns Papers.
29. Withrow, *Religious Progress in the Century*, 287.

an inevitable part of any human project.[30] In his defence of the movement, James cited the work of H. H. Goddard, of Clark University, who in his thesis *The Effects of Mind on Body as Evidenced by Faith Cures*, concluded: "We do find sufficient evidence to convince us that the proper reform in mental attitude would relieve many a sufferer of ills that the ordinary physician cannot touch; would even delay the approach of death to many a victim beyond the power of absolute cure, and the faithful adherence to a truer philosophy of life will keep many a man well, and give the doctor time to devote to alleviating ills that are unpreventable."[31]

In the month before Helen died, the family had moved to Hamilton Place, and according to the local doctor (Christie), Helen had been none the worse for the move, and was even considering going south (presumably for a family visit). However, in a letter to his brother-in-law, James Hewat Craw, Cairns warned him that he should be prepared to see his sister look "pale and weak . . . more so than for a good long time."

On 3 May, Cairns sent a telegram to his brother-in-law, informing him that Helen was very ill, although not in pain, and suggesting that James make an immediate visit. In the last days of Helen's life, she spent prolonged hours in prayer with Mrs. Whyte, during which they felt assured that their prayers had been answered. Aged only thirty-three, Helen died on 5 May 1910. Several touching letters, particularly to her brother, depict her last days and hours, and her death in the arms of her husband. They reveal a great outpouring of emotion, including shock and grief, but in spite of the apparent failure of prayers for healing, Cairns found in Helen's experience a note of victory. May there have been in his reaction an echo of the opinions of Goddard? Dr. Christie had conveyed the opinion that Helen's health during the last three years had been "nothing short of a miracle" in view of her condition, and Cairns, admitting that they hadn't won all they had been fighting for, took this as confirmation that in some sense their prayers had been answered. Writing to James on the day after her death he stated, "Nellie herself won her battle and proved our case for us. For if her faith and love did this thing, what is the limit? . . . I feel that our darling has won a great victory, and that it must be ours to make that plain."[32]

Cairns chose to have the burial in Aberdeen, rather than at a site near Helen's family in West Foulden, because Aberdeen was where she had "fought and won her battle."[33] Among the letters of appreciation for her, one

---

30. James, *Varieties of Religious Experience*, 94–96.

31. Goddard, quoted in James, *Varieties of Religious Experience*, 96–97n2.

32. Letter to James Hewat Craw, 6 May 1910, Box 1/4 Cairns Papers.

33. Letter to James Hewat Craw, 6 May 1910, Box 1/4 Cairns Papers.

came from his former parishioners in Ayton. In replying, Cairns declared that he was glad they had appreciated Helen's life and work, and acknowledged her great influence on him. He told them that Helen had been happy during her last few months, and although very frail, she had remained active. "Although she has been early promoted to the higher and happier life I feel that she has won a great victory over all the powers of sin and death by faith and by love, and that the future will make this plain."[34]

When Cairns later came to write his memoir, only one paragraph was devoted to Helen, but it revealed the significance of their relationship. In it he included the following declaration: "We were very happy together during the eight years of our united life. I have never lost the confident expectation of reunion. That has been one of the things that has made the interval of nearly thirty years that have passed since she went forward worth living."[35] An obituary in the *Berwickshire News* recalled her fine intellect and love of the poets, especially Browning. The writer concluded, "All who knew her well rejoiced when Miss Craw found a life companion in Professor Cairns, one who could so well estimate and delight in the best that was in her, and when the dark shadow of grievous illness, which has cut short this fine life, fell on their married happiness, the way in which it was borne by both husband and wife was a revelation of heroic faith."[36]

As Cairns faced the future, he believed that Helen was now meant to help from "the other side," and that he had to have his heart and mind in tune with her—"a loyal and loving ally there."[37] The spiritual struggle produced by her illness and death continued, and it was to be nearly twenty years before he worked out, in *The Faith That Rebels* (1928), a distinctive theology that spoke to the questions it raised. On a very practical level, though, his emotional struggle to cope with the loss was revealed by his daughter many years later, in a letter to Willa Muir: "I remember my father once saying that after my mother's death one thought had helped him to bear it was that he was bearing it for her, because if he had died she would be having the unhappiness that was at that time his."[38]

34. Letter to Ayton congregation, 20 May 1910, Box 1/4 Cairns Papers.
35. Cairns, *Autobiography*, 178–79.
36. *Berwickshire News*, 10 May 1910.
37. Letter to James Hewat Craw, 18 May 1910, Box 1/4 Cairns Papers.
38. Irvine, *Alison Cairns*, 142.

Chairing Commission IV, Edinburgh, 1910

During the second half of the nineteenth century, a series of international conferences was held to promote the work of Protestant missions. At the time of the New York conference in 1900, the American Methodist layman John Raleigh Mott, national secretary of the Intercollegiate Young Men's Christian Association of America and Canada, and founding member and general secretary of the World Student Christian Federation, had published *The Evangelism of the World in This Generation*, drawing attention to the fact that virtually the whole earth was now known and ready to receive the gospel. He argued that "with literal truth it may be said that ours is an age of unparalleled opportunity."[39] By 1908, when planning began for a world mission conference to be held in Edinburgh, an atmosphere of anticipation had been built up. Mott was appointed to oversee the event, and Oldham became conference secretary. The focus was on the experience of missionaries and the difficulties they encountered in the field, and how this might impact on the church's theology and its training of missionaries. Eight representative international commissions of around twenty members were set up to investigate the most pressing problems facing Christian missions.[40] Each commission was to devise questionnaires to elicit the relevant information from missionary organizations, and from missionaries and indigenous people of the mission fields, who would be corresponding members. A list of topics on which to base questions was provided, and the chairman of each commission was to produce a draft with "findings" by December 1909, so that final copies of the reports could be made by 1 May 1910.[41] The historian Brian Stanley relates that among the most thoughtful of the advocates of missionary endeavor there was the belief that "rigorous methods of modern social science" must be applied to the task, and that Oldham in particular insisted that action must be based on the "ascertained and sifted facts."[42]

Commission IV was to deal with "The Missionary Message in Relation to the Non-Christian Religions," and Cairns committed himself to chairing it in 1908, shortly after going to Aberdeen. The fact that he was willing to undertake such a huge task at a time when he had to cope with adjustment to academic life, and the strain of Helen's illness, reveals the significance of the task for Cairns. Between Helen's death and the opening of the missionary conference there were just five weeks. During that time Cairns's father

39. Mott, *Evangelism of the World in this Generation*, quoted in Rowdon, "Edinburgh 1910," 49–71.

40. Mott, *Decisive Hour of Christian Missions*, vii.

41. Stanley, *World Missionary Conference*, 34.

42. Stanley, *World Missionary Conference*, 4–5.

also died, on 25 May. A letter to his brother-in-law, some weeks before the conference, revealed the pressure that Cairns was under, both at home and in terms of getting approval for the contents of the report. He thanked James for his support in his "hour of terrible strain," and doubted if he could have got through mentally or physically without his help.[43]

The conference began on 14 June 1910, with an opening address by Randall Davidson, the Archbishop of Canterbury. Donald Baillie recorded that Commission IV was perhaps the most important of the eight commissions,[44] an opinion shared by William Henry Temple Gairdner, a Church Missionary Society missionary in Cairo from 1899–1928. Temple Gairdner, on leave to attend the conference, wrote the official account of the proceedings, in which he averred that Cairns's report was "one of the most remarkable, perhaps the most remarkable of a whole series."[45] Stanley points out that Commission IV has received "more recent scholarly attention than all the others put together."[46] He has also suggested that Cairns owed his role at the conference to his friendship with Oldham.[47] While this may be the case, Cairns had also had a life-long interest in missionary work through the influence of his family, and he had seen something of it at first hand during his months in Cairo. When he was still a probationer in Selkirk in 1894, his reading of the report of the 1888 Missionary Conference in London had convinced him of the potential of the missionary movement in delivering the kingdom of God throughout the world. His involvement with the Student Christian Movement was directly related to the missionary movement; but above all, his publication *Christianity in the Modern World* had set out a practical program for the evangelization of the world based on the paradigm of the kingdom of God. The Church of Scotland minister and writer, Kenneth Ross, agrees with Kenneth Cracknell's suggestion that rather than looking for a missionary leader for Commission IV, Mott and Oldham were looking for someone who would give an intellectual grounding to the report, and not just provide a survey of the world's religions.[48] Ross points out that Cairns

43. Cairns to James Craw, 18 April 1910, Box 1/6 Cairns Papers.

44. Baillie, in Cairns, *Autobiography*, 15.

45. Gairdner, *Edinburgh 1910*, quoted in Ramachandra, "Missionary Message." This paper was prepared for discussion during the centenary celebrations in Edinburgh in 2012, www.towards2010.org/downloads/t2010paper04ramachandra.pdf.

46. Stanley, *World Missionary Conference*, 205-8, gives some examples of such debate.

47. Stanley, *World Missionary Conference*, 208-11.

48. Ross, "Edinburgh 1910," cites Cracknell, *Justice, Courtesy and Love*, 187. See also Sharpe, *Not to Destroy but to Fulfil*, 277.

had proven his capability in his 1906 publication and had also been a significant influence in the development of the theology of the missionary A. G. Hogg, one of the carefully chosen corresponding members.

The Work of Commission IV

The work of Commission IV was divided into five areas—Animism, Chinese religion, Japanese religion, Islam and Hinduism—each with its own subcommittee.

Replies related to the five areas were drafted by the chairmen of the subcommittees, and formed the bulk of the report, followed by a long chapter entitled "General Conclusions," written by Cairns, including his interpretation of the evidence as it pertained to the theology of the church and to the training of missionaries. This material was sent out to those who would attend, so that the limited time of the conference might be used for discussion of the contents. Cairns had also devised the eleven questions that were sent to the corresponding members, and these certainly reflected some of his interests. Several of the questions provided scope for the development of an apologetical response to the findings. For instance, question 3 asked, "What do you consider to be the chief moral, intellectual, and social hindrances in the way of full acceptance of Christ?" Another question (9) asked about the influence of higher criticism on missionary work. Altogether, the questions revealed a fulfillment theology, which encouraged the search for "points of contact" or similarities among religions, that might be used to prepare people to receive the message of the Christian gospel.

Cairns's individual contribution to the report was seen most clearly in his "General Conclusions." Here he compared the situation of contemporary missionaries with that of the members of the early church as they struggled to maintain the church's identity, while trying to accept what was true in Hellenistic culture. He declared, "They, too, were in the heart of a great battle between the living forces of Christianity and the death and life forces of the non-Christian religions of their day."[49]

He reassured his readers that it was out of this great struggle that the early Christians had shaped doctrines to meet the needs of their day. The question now was "how can the living forces of Christianity be strengthened by Christian thought and by Christian statesmanship?" He suggested that each of the great mission fields had a contribution to make based on reflection on their encounters with the world religions. While these religions fell short of the Christian revelation, there were elements in them which

49. Cairns, *Missionary Message*, 214.

provoked thought. For instance, animistic religions were very aware of the power of the unseen world, although its forces were hostile. On conversion to Christianity, their followers retained this awareness of the power of the unseen, transferring it to faith in a loving God who was ready to help them. For Cairns, this simple faith of theirs seemed much more like the Old Testament conception of the living God than might be found in contemporary Christianity.[50] It also seemed to him to be more like the conception of God and prayer that underlay Christ's teaching, as he summoned people to a life of peace and freedom from fear and care. He asked,

> Is the ordinary theological view of nature as a closed system, sporadically broken on rare historic occasions, really philosophically sound or religiously sufficient? Is there no better way of formulating the relations between God and man and the world, which will at once do justice to the scientific and the religious view of nature, than that which prevails at present in Christian theology? Does the working compromise which we have between science and faith which we have inherited from the apologists of the eighteenth century give room for the full religious conception of the world which underlies all Christian morality, and which is essential for the vitality of Christian faith?[51]

Evident in Cairns's stance is the influence of the Ritschlian school, which had refused to adopt what they saw as the premature synthesis of science and religion. For Cairns, Christianity had become tinged with the prevailing naturalism of the West and had lost something of the sense of the sovereignty of God. He wondered if the modern Christian really believed that God was free to act in the world. Some tried to make room for God by saying that he had made a closed system which he would one day bring to an end. In the meantime the outer world was determined while freedom was found in the inner life. Cairns saw this as unsatisfactory for science or religion, leaving no room for Providence or prayer, conserving the freedom of neither God nor man. He compared this apparent impotence with the vital faith of the early church, and asked whether or not his readers believed that God could still be a creative presence in the world. Was the church admitting to being under a more limited dispensation?

Recognizing the intellectual difficulty of whole-hearted belief in the supernatural in a world of law and order, he went on to point out that a contraction in the spiritual environment had led to a contraction in the

50. Cairns, *Missionary Message*, 219.
51. Cairns, *Missionary Message*, 220–21.

missionary vision, emphasizing that the missionary movement depended on its idea of God. He asked on what grounds they might expect great things of God. If there were none, why should they try to achieve the great things that were being proposed? If they believed that the spiritual environment was the same as in New Testament times, then they must show that it was grounded, not in isolated verses of Scripture, but in the essential Christian revelation, and they must renew their conceptions of prayer, faith, and miracle.[52] In a reference to Mott's writings on the opportunities for world evangelism, Cairns suggested that the success of the enterprise did not depend solely or ultimately on numbers, wealth, or organization, but required above all a living faith expressed by a living theology.[53] Here he was touching on the subject that had been dominating his own theological quest, and was to continue to do so for the rest of his life. Underlying the whole report were questions about the kind of God the church believed in, and a call for a new theology to replace the conventional one which, for Cairns, had become effete. His sense of urgency regarding this aspect of the missionary agenda was indicated in a letter to his brother-in-law, written shortly before Helen died.

> If we get it through it will go all over the world, to innumerable brave and good men who are fighting a desperate battle with darkness, and if it helps them, we shall surely be well repaid. Of course I have not been able to say all I would like, but all our message is in principle there, and if men think it out, as they will, they will be led to very different conclusions about God and His love to men, and the possibilities of human life. We have abundant ground for gratitude and for fuller faith and more thorough thought that we may lay firm hold on those things, which as yet we are only thinking.[54]

No individual attributions were made regarding the contents of the report, but according to Eric Sharpe, it was Cairns alone who drafted it, although it had to be approved by his vice-chair, Robert Speer.[55] Cairns did submit his report to at least one other member of the commission, Principal A. E. Garvie of New College, London, recording that Garvie had been one of the men he had been most doubtful about. However, Garvie had "approved its main drift."[56] The chapter certainly reflects Cairns's main theo-

---

52. Cairns, *Missionary Message*, 253–65.
53. Cairns, *Missionary Message*, 217–18.
54. Cairns to James Hewat Craw, 18 April 1910, Box 1/6 (21) Cairns Papers.
55. Sharpe, *Not to Destroy but to Fulfil*, 276n6.
56. Cairns to James Hewat Craw, 18 April 1910, Cairns Papers, Box 1/6 (21).

logical preoccupation at the time. He saw the fight against Helen's disease, and the struggle to extend the boundaries of the kingdom of God in the mission field, as part of the same struggle to overcome evil and suffering in the world, and as one that required belief in a God who was able to act on the side of good in the world. That theological perspective found a central place in the general conclusions of the report.

The Acceptance of Fulfillment Theory as an Approach to the Other World Religions

In fulfillment theory, Christianity is regarded as the highest religion, in which the other religions are able to find the fulfillment of their search for truth and salvation. The Finnish systematic theologian Veli-Matti Kark-kainen points out that most of the missionaries who responded to the questionnaire sent out by Cairns, replied in terms of fulfillment theory, and that Edinburgh 1910 was the apotheosis of this idea.[57] Karkkainen says this was the case in spite of the fact that the conference was dominated by the ideas of absoluteness and superiority of Christianity over other re-ligions. The fulfillment approach had been in development for decades. From the middle of the nineteenth century, there had been the beginnings of a movement away from the traditional evangelical missionary approach, which was based on a paradigm that divided existence into two realms, the realm of God, life and light, over against the realm of Satan, darkness and death. The traditionalists saw all non-Christian religions as "heathen," be-longing to the latter realm, and their followers in need of the salvation of-fered by Christ, if they were not to be doomed to eternal punishment.[58] In reaching their conclusions about Hinduism, Eric J. Sharpe writes that most of the evangelical missionaries working in India up to the 1850s, compared the least favorable aspects of Hinduism with the best of Christianity, and that attempts to describe Hinduism in more favorable terms were not wel-come.[59] Clearly, there were important exceptions to the majority view.[60] Annie H. Small, missionary in India, and principal of the United Free Church's Women's Missionary Training College in Edinburgh, was a prime example of such openness, an approach learned from her father, John, in

57. Veli-Matti, *Introduction to the Theology of Religions*, 104, cites Cracknell, *Justice, Courtesy and Love*, 221.

58. Sharpe, *Not to Destroy but to Fulfil*, 25, 317.

59. Sharpe, *Not to Destroy but to Fulfil*, 28.

60. Sharpe, *Not to Destroy but to Fulfil*, 37.

his missionary work among the Hindu intelligentsia in Poona where he worked from 1863 until his death in 1899.

J. N. Farquhar, A. G. Hogg, and Nicol Macnicol were correspondents of Commission IV, and so the experiences and ideas of these influential missionaries fed into Cairns's report. Many of these ideas would not have been entirely new to Cairns, for as far back as 1847, his favorite English theologian, F. D. Maurice, had argued for the presence of God in the great religions of the world, in his *The Religions of the World and Their Relations to Christianity*. By the time of Edinburgh 1910 the attitudes of many missionaries had changed, and according to Sharpe, more and more missionaries were coming to regard sympathy, "points of contact," and in some cases "fulfillment," as standard items of their equipment.[61]

With regard to the commission's approach to the world religions, the report concluded that the evidence pointed to two main things. First, the attitude of missionaries should be one of understanding and, if possible, sympathy. They should seek out the nobler elements of the different religions, and use them as steps to higher things. "All these religions without exception disclose elemental needs of the human soul which Christianity alone can satisfy, and that in their higher forms they plainly manifest the working of the Spirit of God. On all hands the merely iconoclastic attitude is condemned as radically unwise and unjust."[62]

Second, it reinforced the church's emphatic witness to the uniqueness of Christianity. The report made clear the commission's view that Christianity was not just one religion among others, but rather that the Christian faith was absolute. Cairns admitted that critics thought it incompatible to believe in such absoluteness while accepting that there may be truth or light in different religions, but he declared that the witnesses (missionaries) disagree.

In the general conclusions of the report, Cairns focused on what church leaders could do. Among the suggestions for action were the following:

People who offer for missionary service need a thorough knowledge of the religions which they will encounter, as lack of knowledge had led to insensitivity in the past, so knowledge of comparative religion should be provided in all colleges and training institutes prior to missionaries taking up posts. Missionaries should also be trained in the art of teaching—an art based on finding a point of contact with the hearer. People working in the field should produce monographs setting out points of contact and contrast

---

61. Sharpe, *Not to Destroy but to Fulfil*, 236.

62. Cairns, *Missionary Message*, 267.

in the religions with which they are familiar, as these will benefit other missionaries newly arrived in the field.[63]

In a concluding note, written after the conference, responding to claims that he had neglected the negative in the religions, Cairns agreed that he had emphasized the positive, mainly ignoring the ignoble aspects, but he justified this by saying that he was trying to find a way to use knowledge of the non-Christian religions to bring to light the "latent riches of the absolute religion"—meaning perhaps that by reflecting on another's spiritual practice, one may recover and appreciate some undervalued riches in one's own—an effect to which many people engaged in contemporary interfaith dialogue would testify. He suggested that no one could successfully attack the evils of Hinduism unless he had a "true and sympathetic view of its nobler thought and life, so being able to build up as well as destroy."[64]

In his closing remarks to the conference, Robert E. Speer, vice-chair of Commission IV, condensed the material into a few points around which he felt there was a consensus. The main thrust of his remarks endorsed Christianity as the absolute and final religion, and suggested that as such, it could take a generous and fearless road in its attitude to the different religions. The commission had not been looking for truths that were not already in Christianity, but no one had the whole truth, and the church could learn from listening to what others thought of its understanding of itself, and perhaps recover latent or lost aspects of its own life. He agreed that the commission had dwelt on the positive aspects of the religions, and that in a more comprehensive presentation they could have looked at the best and worst aspects, but that this would have had to include the shortcomings of Christianity too. He reported that the commission had chosen to use as its operating principle "do as you would be done by." (In this they also adhered to an important principle of modern interfaith dialogue, in comparing like with like, and not the ideal in one religion with the worst in another.) Speer concluded with recognition of the need for an immense deepening of life at home before the enormous project of world mission could be undertaken.[65]

Reflections on Commission IV

Stewart J. Brown, while agreeing that the conference was dominated by the big British and North American missionary societies, suggests that the delegates tried to distance the missionary movement from Western

63. Cairns, *Missionary Message*, 268–73.
64. Cairns, *Missionary Message*, 279.
65. Cairns, *Missionary Message*, 324–26.

imperialism, and to separate the message of Christianity from Western culture. He describes the approach of the delegates as one of respect for the different world religions, noting that Commission IV produced one of the most sensitive and perceptive reports. Brown concludes, "For the British churches, it also contributed to the movement away from Victorian notions of the elect nation and the providential empire."[66] The closing lines of the Commission IV report provide room for reflection and debate in relation to Brown's perspective on the commission's work.

> The spectacle of the advance of the Christian Church along many lines of action to the conquest of the five great religions of the modern world is one of singular interest and grandeur. *Vexilla Regis prodeunt!* [Abroad the regal banners fly!] But at least as remarkable as that spectacle of the outward advance of the Church is that which has also been revealed to us of the inward transformations that are in process in the mind of the missionary, the changes of perspective, the softening of wrong antagonisms, the centralising and deepening of faith in the Lord Jesus Christ, the growth of the spirit of love to the brethren and to the world. Once again the Church is facing its duty, and therefore once more the ancient guiding fires begin to burn and shine.[67]

The use of military metaphor in the first few lines, might on its own contradict Brown's idea that the commission was moving away from its identification with imperialism and triumphalism, but as Ramachandra points out, these three lines are most often quoted in isolation, suggesting a traditionally orthodox interpretation of the theology of the commission. He suggests that the overwhelming impression from the correspondents was one of deep understanding, sympathy, and respect for the different religions, which posed a powerful challenge to Western Christianity.[68] Set alongside the militaristic imagery, is the longer following passage describing a different sort of relationship with people of different religions, which is "at least as remarkable" as the other vision. As far as notions of an elect nation or providential empire were concerned, the report's findings on China revealed that these concepts were being challenged by the Commission, who declared that the policy of Christendom toward China had not been "inspired by faith working through love." Rather, Christianity had been apprehended by the Chinese as the religion of

66. Brown, *Providence and Empire*, 438–40.
67. D. S. Cairns, *Missionary Message*, 273–74.
68. Ramachandra, "Missionary Message," 2–3.

those who had insulted and injured China, through land-grabbing and war, and by flooding the country with opium.[69]

In his reflection on Commission IV, Ramachandra points out, "The Report writers and respondents were overwhelmingly of the stock of white Western males who dominated the ecclesiastical and missionary centers of power. No African spoke for African Christianity, nor were there any representatives from indigenous churches outside the European world. It is Western Christendom that informs their conversation and constitutes its background."[70]

It is certainly true that of the almost two hundred correspondents, only seven were women. There was one female member, the prominent Anglo-Catholic Mrs. Ethel Romanes. At the planning stage in 1908, it had been decided to have women's help on all of the commissions,[71] and Annie H. Small, regarded as a pioneer in missionary training, was appointed a member of the Conference Preparatory Committee.[72] Small, as much as anyone, had contributed significantly to the growing attitude of respect for what she called the "living religions," rather than Non-Christian religions, and for the longing for God or an ultimate reality that was expressed in the faith of their devotees. For some years before 1910, she had been implementing some of the educational ideas put forward by Commission IV. As well as teaching about Islam, Buddhism and Hinduism, she tried to create empathy in her missionary students by using hymns from the different religions, allowing them to see into the inner lives and yearnings of those they went to evangelize. Minister and church musician, Douglas Galbraith, concludes that Small was regarded as "a little too much at times" by the "clerical gentlemen" who ran things.[73] However, her book, *Missionary College Hymns*, was launched at the Conference,[74] and when one of the choirs failed to turn up, she and some of her students sang Indian and Chinese hymns from the gallery.[75]

Small had published works on Buddhism, Islam and Hinduism, in which she tried to create understanding of these religions, and point to what might be learned from them in order to enrich the Christian experience.[76]

69. D. S. Cairns, *Missionary Message*, 48, 228.

70. Ramachandra, "Missionary Message." Stanley, *Bible and the Flag*, 134–46, describes the missionary enterprise in China then.

71. Stanley, *World Missionary Conference*, 313.

72. Stewart, *Training in Mission*, 8.

73. Galbraith, "Annie Hunter Small," paper delivered to the Edinburgh Ecumenical Group, 11 November 2010.

74. Small, *Missionary College Hymns*.

75. Stewart, *Training in Mission*, 8.

76. Small, *Islam*; Small, *Buddhism*; and Small, *Yeshudas*.

Views that may have appeared radical to many at the Conference in 1910, had for some years been the operating principles among missionaries and others like Annie H. Small.

The United Free Church was not the only well of radical thinking in terms of mission. The established church minister, Norman Macleod (1812–72), minister of the Barony in Glasgow from 1851–72 and chaplain to Queen Victoria, visited India for about six months in 1867. He was asked to address the general assembly about the conduct of mission there, having been involved in the management of Indian missions for some years. On his return, he appealed to the church for a "generous and self-forgetful policy towards India."[77] He wondered if people realized the enormity of what they were asking Indians to do when they tried to evangelize them.

> They were asking Hindoos [sic], men of flesh and blood like themselves, and far more sensitive than Scotchmen, of great intelligence and culture, to give up hoary traditions, to cut down the tree of that religion under which they and their fathers had sat for teeming centuries, and to accept the religion of a people whose very touch was pollution. They were asking these men in many cases to give up father and mother, and brother and sister, and were much astonished that they did not make the sacrifice![78]

To those who judged missions by the number of converts and found them wanting, he suggested that they should think about the number of conversions in their own parishes, and try to convert an honest seeker after truth (a man of science) and see how hard it is to convert an educated man. Macleod also raised the issue of the export of ecclesiastical differences, wondering if this was the right way to present the gospel, considering it monstrous to expect Indian Christians to sign up to the Westminster Confession of Faith or other particular denominational creeds.[79] Before delivering his report, Macleod was reported to be nervous that people would not support him, fearing accusations against them of latitudinarianism, but when he rose to his feet he urged, "You must take care that your Cairns do not stand so near as to shut out Calcutta, and the Watchword make you so tremble for petty consequences at home that all India is forgotten by you."[80]

Macleod was referring to the fact that Principal John Cairns and others had been attacking the established church for her latitudinarianism—

77. Macleod, *Memoir of Norman Macleod*, 2:369.

78. Macleod, *Memoir of Norman Macleod*, 2:370.

79. Macleod, *Memoir of Norman Macleod*, 2:370–71.

80. Macleod, *Memoir of Norman Macleod*, 2:373.

presumably the watchword—and that this had resulted in people being over cautious, not wanting to be so labeled. As a result, Macleod felt the assembly had been the most reactionary he had ever seen. For his part, if latitudinarianism meant not believing that God will save some only from "excruciating torments in soul and body for all eternity" then he was a latitudinarian.[81] Macleod spoke of the old forms as effete, and of the need to consider the different meaning for Hindus of terms like sin, salvation, regeneration, holiness, atonement, and incarnation: missionaries needed to know more about the beliefs of those they went to evangelize.[82] It is likely that Cairns, in his work for Commission IV, was influenced by Small and Macleod. At the very least, they were kindred spirits.

Involvement in the Student Christian Movement

Cairns's role in Commission IV brought him into an ever-widening circle of contacts, and resulted in several significant invitations. Among these was a call to St. George's church in Edinburgh, where J. H. Oldham was on the selection committee. Writing to his mother about the call, Cairns said it was not for him.[83] Another invitation was more significant, asking him to address the Scottish Students' Conference in Edinburgh on 23 March 1911. This was to be the beginning of over two decades of service to the Student Christian Movement, involvement with which was very much in keeping with his developing theological vision. His lecture, later published by the Movement, was entitled "The Vocation of Scotland in View of Her Religious Heritage." In it Cairns located the movement firmly within the church context, and set out a vision for its future work as it encountered social grievances at home and the spread of secularism in India and the Far East. Decrying ecclesiastical divisions as the result of a lack of love, he reminded the students of the three great ideals in the religious history of Scotland: the kingdom of God; the vital importance of the church; and the need for a strong theology. He saw and admired the embodiment of the concept of the kingdom in the practical program of the movement, and like them did not think that religion should be concerned only with the relation of the soul to God in terms of justification and sanctification.

> The Student Christian Movement has a practical ideal, the Christian World Society. It aims at the Evangelization of the

81. Macleod, *Memoir of Norman Macleod*, 2:381.

82. Macleod, *Memoir of Norman Macleod*, 2:413–22.

83. Cairns to his mother, 2 March 1911, Box 2/2 Cairns Papers.

world in this generation, but it aims also at the Christianization of the entire structure of Society. It seeks to attain a legislative and economic order of Society which shall be in accordance with the mind of Christ. It has become increasingly interested as the years have gone on in the Social Problem, and in the moralization not only of social but of international relations.[84]

He praised the loyalty of the movement to the church, and impressed on them the need to have a clear and reasoned faith, with a theology expressed in the terms of their day. No return to Calvinism could be made, but there was a need to recapture something of its idea of the sovereignty of God, if Christian faith was to have the vitality to counter naturalism and humanism. "It is here that our modern religious thought is weak. It adopts all manner of compromises. It deifies the system of nature. It is afraid of the supernatural. It is tending to lose faith in the power of Prayer."[85]

He told them that a new theology could be developed by working together, facing and sharing intellectual problems, in fellowship with each other and with Christ. He ended with three suggestions for practical action, very similar to the program he had set out in *Christianity and the Modern World*, but with an enlarged view of mission that included the home front. First, they must expand the Christian unions in the universities, as the church looked to them to bring on the next generation. Second, he called for "a steady stream of missionaries for the heathen abroad and for the heathen at home," urging those who accepted the call to ministry at home to work through the great working-class churches and the country congregations, and not just in the prosperous suburban churches which were often seen as "prizes."[86] Finally, he reminded them that the ministry was only one divine calling among others equally divine. He spoke of other professions and of the life of the home, emphasizing that the task would not be achieved by a purely clerical movement; they needed people who were in the thick of life's practical everyday business and who had the confidence of others.[87]

The following month, April 1911, saw Cairns accompany Tissington Tatlow, general secretary of the Student Movement in Britain, to a conference in Constantinople, where in a crowded fortnight he addressed seven meetings. His stay included the first anniversary of Helen's death, and he wrote to reassure the family; to let them know that he was thinking of them and that he was sure Nellie wanted them to think happily of her. In a moving

84. Cairns, *Vocation of Scotland*, 22.
85. Cairns, *Vocation of Scotland*, 41.
86. Cairns, *Vocation of Scotland*, 48–53.
87. Cairns, *Vocation of Scotland*, 57–59.

letter to his mother he confessed, "Today the thought of her sweet and loving ways have come to me most vividly—I have her Bible with me and take
it to every place where I have to speak 'to keep me right.' But some small
article she wore had slipped in among mine in packing, and the sight of it
brought her presence to me with peculiar vividness. With all the shock of it
it came like a healing presence too."[88]

Later on in November 1911, Cairns attended the Student Conference
in Kephissia, near Athens, and from there he wrote another letter to his
mother, indicating how much it meant to him to be involved with the
Movement, and how he saw in it many possibilities for "world changes in
the future towards a happier and better state of things."[89] He had already
confessed to Tatlow that it was one of the greatest privileges of his life to be
involved in the work of the movement, enjoying friendship and common
work with him and his colleagues.[90] Cairns and Tatlow had known each
other since their involvement in the 1910 World Missionary Conference,
by which time the Student Movement had been established internationally as the World Student Christian Federation. Correspondence between
the two men during 1911–12 reveals the extent of Cairns's involvement
and influence as the British section of the movement reflected on its basis
of membership. The Matlock Conference of 1901 had accepted the following basis and aim:

> I desire in joining this Union to declare my faith in Jesus Christ
> as my Saviour, my Lord, and my God. Any student in becoming a
> voting member of an affiliated Union, or signing the declaration
> of the Student Volunteer Missionary Union shall be understood
> thereby to express his acceptance of the above. . . . The object
> of the Union shall be to lead the students of British universities
> and colleges to become disciples of Jesus Christ; to unite them
> in seeking a fuller spiritual life; and to enlist them in the work of
> extending Christ's Kingdom throughout the world.[91]

Throughout the remaining years of the decade, staff and students and
some leading theologians, for instance E. S. Talbot, bishop of Winchester,
and Professor H. R. Mackintosh of Edinburgh, tried to work out a new basis
that would describe the movement in more detail.[92] Cairns was anxious that
the basis would not be too prescriptive in terms of its Christology, and while

---

88. Cairns to his mother, 5 May 1911, Box 2/1 Cairns Papers.
89. Cairns to his mother, 6 November 1911, Box 2/1 Cairns Papers.
90. Cairns to Tatlow, 31 July 1911, Box 2/3 Cairns Papers.
91. Boyd, *Witness of the Student Christian Movement*, 10.
92. Boyd, *Witness of the Student Christian Movement*, 10–11.

he had been sympathetic with the conservative members of the movement who feared that it would become a "nondescript horde of students without any definite faith and without spiritual power," he had not agreed with their proposed method of making the basis more specific in terms of a commitment to overseas missionary work. He did not want to be a party to urging men and women to make declarations when they may not have had enough experience on which to base their decisions. Tatlow wondered if Cairns's position might not imply a lack of confidence in God's ability to reveal the divine will to a student. Both men were at the time preparing for a large Student Conference in Liverpool in 1912, and Cairns replied that he felt there would be people in the Liverpool audience who might be of more real service through tackling social problems in Dundee or problems of truth in London, than by active service in Moukden, China.[93]

As the discussions about the basis continued, Cairns wrote again to Tatlow, from Washington, where he had gone on a lecture tour with J. R. Mott. The committee working on the basis had asked Cairns to write a memorandum on the subject, which he sent in his letter. Commenting on the basis in use, he pointed out that it was inadequate as it had nothing in it about the divine Father, nor anything about the Holy Spirit. The committee also needed to recognize the reality that there were many among the students who did not see Jesus as God, although they were truer disciples than some who found his divinity easy to believe in. His students in Aberdeen had signed the existing basis, but "winked at" members who did great work but were "doctrinally shaky." Cairns went along with this approach, but admitted that it put them in a false position. He pointed out that the early Christians had had an undeveloped Christology, and as far as he was concerned, what was good enough for the apostolic church should be good enough for the Student Christian Movement. Cairns felt that what the movement should aim at was winning the hearts and consciences of the students, trusting that their theology would develop as they matured in the Christian life. As they could not all agree on what was normative for faith, he advised keeping the text of the basis simple, requiring only profession of faith in Jesus as Lord and Savior, and put forward a possible formula: "I believe in God through Jesus Christ, His only Son our Lord." In his characteristically generous style, he admitted that his contribution was more polemical than it would have been if delivered in person, and he left it to the committee to correct his one-sided-ness.

93. Cairns to Tatlow, 3 and 15 November and 13 and 16 December 1911, Box 2/2 Cairns Papers.

When the statement of the aims of the movement and its basis were finally adopted in 1913, Cairns's influence is clear to see. The personal declaration of membership was concise: "In joining this Union I declare my faith in God through Jesus Christ, whom as Saviour and Lord I desire to serve." Thus was left open a way to include members with varying theological perspectives, and with the freedom to choose their particular path of service. The aim was stated in terms which reflected strongly Cairns's appeal in his "Vocation of Scotland" address

> The Aim of this Movement is to lead students in British universities and colleges into full acceptance of the Christian Faith in God—Father, Son and Holy Spirit; to promote among them regular habits of prayer and Bible study; to keep before them the urgency of the evangelization of the world, the Christian solution of social problems, and the permeation of public life with Christian ideals; and to lead them into the fellowship and service of the Christian Church. Any Christian Union becoming affiliated shall incorporate in its Constitution the following clause: "The corporate activities of this Christian Union shall be in harmony with the Aim of the Student Christian Movement."[94]

In 1913 he went on a six-week lecture and preaching tour in America, during which he stayed with J. R. Mott in his family home.[95] The lecture tour was successful enough to bring an invitation for a further American visit, this time from the Christian Socialist, Walter Rauschenbusch, who wanted his seminary students to hear Cairns.[96] More importantly, the visit saw the beginning of a significant friendship between Cairns and Mott, which was evidenced by an affectionate and mutually enriching correspondence that lasted for the next thirty years.[97] Mott had read Cairns's "Vocation of Scotland" address and in one letter declared it one of the finest addresses ever given at a Student Conference. He expressed the wish that someone of "like imagination and grasp" would speak at each of the national student gatherings.[98] In keeping with this opinion, Mott invited Cairns, in the same year, to go to Japan on behalf of the movement, an invitation which Cairns declined, mainly for the sake of his children. Mott admitted to "coveting" Cairns for the cause, because he was so deeply interested in the work he was

94. Boyd, *Witness of the Student Christian Movement*, 11.

95. Cairns to Glover, 12 April 1915, Glover Papers 5/2/13, St. John's Library Cambridge.

96. Rauschenbusch to Cairns, 23 July 1913, Box 3/3 Cairns Papers.

97. Mott Papers, RG 45, Box 13, Folders 244–45, Yale Divinity School Library.

98. Mott to Cairns, 23 September 1911, Box 3/4 Cairns Papers.

doing.[99] He issued another invitation to go to Japan in 1915, but by then World War I had begun, and once more, for quite different reasons, Cairns found it impossible to accept. It was not until much later, when Cairns was in his sixties, that he was able to visit the Far East, but in the intervening years, he maintained his contacts with the movement, corresponding with its leading figures, and becoming a well-known speaker at Student Conferences in Britain, Europe and America.

Mott's respect for Cairns found its deepest expression in a personal request made in 1915. His son, Johnny, was about to graduate from Princeton, and had become a Student Volunteer with the idea of entering the service of the Student Movement in China. Mott and his wife wanted Johnny to spend one of his three years of theological training in Aberdeen, where he would be able to spend a lot of time with Cairns and "come under such of the other minds as you would think best."[100] They also wanted him to stay in a good home which Cairns might choose for him, although they would prefer it if Johnny stayed with the Cairns household if at all practicable. In Cairns's reply to Mott, he described the prospect of having Johnny with his family in Aberdeen as something that gave him great pleasure, but he wondered if the young man might not be better off in Glasgow or Edinburgh, as they "are much more in the full tide of life of Scotland than is our northern capital," and had a number of American students, whereas Aberdeen had only one. In spite of this advice, Johnny Mott went to live with the Cairns family for a year, from October 1915, and he and Cairns developed a very close relationship. Some years later, while on active service, Johnny wrote an emotional letter to Cairns, recalling all that his older friend had done for him, and declaring that any study after his year with him would be an anticlimax.[101]

Among Cairns's other close friends who were involved in the Student Movement, was the Cambridge historian Terrot Reavely Glover, whose father had served with Cairns on Commission IV. Their correspondence portrayed a relationship of deep mutual affection and admiration.[102] In January 1912, still using the black-bordered notepaper which was customary for those recently bereaved, Cairns wrote to accept an invitation from Glover to give the Christian Evidence Society lectures to students at Cambridge. For some unexplained reason, he later withdrew his acceptance. However, in Cambridge at the time was the Scottish systematic theologian

99. Mott to Cairns, 14 December 1913, Box 3/4 Cairns Papers.

100. Mott to Cairns, 25 March 1915, Mott papers, RG 45, 13/244, Yale.

101. Private John Mott to Cairns, 10 July 1918, Box 3/8 Cairns Papers.

102. Cairns to Glover, 16 January 1912, 6 May 1913, and 27 May 1920, Glover Papers, St. John's Library Cambridge, Boxes 4/6/3, 4/7/12, 6/2/168, respectively.

John Oman (1860–1939), professor at Westminster College. Oman had grown up in the United Presbyterian Church in Orkney and attended the church's theological hall in Edinburgh, but then had joined the English Presbyterian Church. He and Cairns had been friends for many years, and had been writing to each other on theological matters since Oman had his first charge in Alnwick, Northumberland. On hearing of Cairns's doubts about speaking in Cambridge, he wrote asking him to revise his decision to decline, even if it meant asking the general assembly for permission. He declared, "The mere fact of asking you is one of the most amazing ecclesiastical phenomena since Charles II." He went on to comment on how few people there were who could present religion in a way that was persuasive to open and inquiring minds. It needed someone who had already overcome the prejudices of the students, and Oman was sure that Cairns was in such a position, presumably because he was known to them through the Student Christian Movement. Not only that but Oman was convinced that not another non-Anglican enjoyed that advantage.[103] Cairns took up the challenge and agreed to deliver the lectures, which were later published as his second book, *The Reasonableness of the Christian Faith* (1918), in which he focused on three main themes: faith, revelation, and the finality and absoluteness of Christianity.

Christianity—a Reasonable Faith?

Cairns had been asked to speak about Christian certainty, and, in tune with the scientific temper of the day, he began by warning about the hard work involved in finding such certainty. Intellectual rigour had to be applied if they were to be sure that the Christianity they accepted or rejected was the real Christianity, and not one based on false assumptions or ignorance.[104] "If you wish to have a faith that you will not need to carry, because it carries you, you must not seek certainty, you must seek truth. Having begun that inquiry, moreover, you must carry it through. Truth and certainty as to truth lie on the other side of such honest labour of the mind."[105]

In the first lecture he broached the subject that he had introduced in the report on Commission IV, and which was now the central theme of his theological quest—the reality and power of the unseen world. Influenced by the findings of the discipline of comparative religion, and by what he saw as its scientific methodology, Cairns stated that Christianity must be seen in

103. Oman to Cairns, 20 February 1913, Cairns Papers, Box 3/4.
104. Cairns, *Reasonableness of the Christian Faith* (5th ed. [1924]), 6–7.
105. Cairns, *Reasonableness*, 5.

the wider context of religion, which was an age-old and universal feature of human life. Rather than seeing religion as "wishful thinking," it seemed that humankind was by its very nature religious—it had a religious consciousness. Faced with the mystery of suffering and death, "the riddle of the world," and of its own powerlessness, humankind had responded with faith in an unseen ruling world, greater than nature, and whose power could be accessed on their behalf. Religion, in its attempt to unite the human with the divine or ultimate reality, was a response to this riddle, which everyone had to face. The fact that millions of people, all over the world, and throughout history, had responded to the riddle in this way suggested to him that there must be some "deep and imperious instinct" which leads to such a persistent universal conviction.[106] "Think of the intimidating power of Nature—earthquake, thunder, and tempest, and you will realize the wonder of the undying and universal conviction that, in spite of all appearances, the real power lies in the Invisible, that the Unseen is absolutely sovereign over it all. Is this a delusion? Surely if it is a delusion there is no instinct that we can trust."[107]

In the following lecture, Cairns turned his attention to two questions: first does such a greater spiritual order actually exist or is it simply a hypothesis—is there a living God with whom humankind can establish a relationship?[108] Second, if such an order exists can its character be known— does humankind possess the capacity to apprehend such a world?[109] "For if religion be more than a subjective illusion, if there really be such a vast and omnipotent spiritual world transcending and interpenetrating our life of sense and time, then the power in us of discerning that world, whether we call it instinct, sense, consciousness or intuition, is a very wonderful thing. It must, indeed, be the greatest endowment of human nature."[110]

Cairns declared that belief in a supreme living God had developed first in the Hebrew people, who had not reached it through dialectical reasoning but through faith and revelation; two channels which he believed were still open to contemporary believers. While he did not want to disparage what may be for some people helpful findings of theology or metaphysical speculation, such conclusions were secondary, having been built on the primary apprehension of faith in response to revelation. His thinking echoed Schleiermacher's theology, which Macquarrie described as having repudiated scholastic orthodox theology and the dry conceptualism of the rationalists

106. Cairns, *Reasonableness*, 8–28.
107. Cairns, *Reasonableness*, 8–28.
108. Cairns, *Reasonableness*, 43.
109. Cairns, *Reasonableness*, 42.
110. Cairns, *Reasonableness*, 43.

of the Enlightenment, in an attempt to speak of the living reality of religion. Schleiermacher went behind the creeds to the experiences out of which they had come, and in which God was first felt or intuited wordlessly. Only when reflected on, was this apprehension put into words and creeds. Macquarrie emphasized that for Schleiermacher, faith was not reliant on what might be dismissed as purely subjective experience: "Feelings do not arise in our minds at random, out of our own subjectivity. They are aroused in us by the impinging upon us of particular events and situations."[111]

Such religious feeling Schleiermacher defined as a "sense and taste for the infinite" and a "feeling of absolute dependence."[112] In answer to the second question, therefore, does humankind possess the capacity to apprehend the unseen world, Cairns believed with Schleiermacher, that the human mind had an innate capacity which allowed it to experience God or Ultimate Reality. Cairns realized that the contradictions exhibited in the different religions might argue against the validity of the faculty of faith, but stated that the constants among the religions were the supremely significant factors, for example the belief that the power of the unseen world might be accessed on behalf of believers.[113]

Returning to the contribution of the Hebrew people to the idea of a living God, and to questions about the character of the unseen world, Cairns said that the Hebrews had identified the one God with goodness, and this intuition had led them to unite religion with morality. In doing so, had they made a great error, or had they had a profound intuition of reality? He advised his listeners, "You will never face a greater question than this, though you live to all eternity. It is really the question as to whether Force or Right is the ultimate thing in the universe, and that in the end of the day is the question as to whether in the end humanity will exterminate itself, or climb to undreamed-of heights of nobility and joy."[114]

Henry Calderwood, professor of moral philosophy at the University of Edinburgh in Cairns's undergraduate period, had taught that the principles of morality are intuitive and self-evident, and that Kant's categorical imperative had the force of universal law.[115] For Cairns, the acceptance of Kant's idea of the moral imperative led to the conviction that the universe itself is fundamentally moral, existing for moral and spiritual ends. Conscience revealed the existence of an ideal world with absolute standards whose pursuit

111. Macquarrie, *Jesus Christ in Modern Thought*, 195.
112. Macquarrie, *Jesus Christ in Modern Thought*, 197.
113. Cairns, *Reasonableness*, 48.
114. Cairns, *Reasonableness*, 52–53.
115. McKimmon, "John Oman," 56–57.

is imperative on all humankind.[116] He realized that some would find the leap from the inner spiritual world to its identification with the character of the universe too great.[117] In a compelling personal statement he admitted,

> We who believe in Him know that there is a Living God. If you ask us how we know, we say, "Because He haunts us, because we cannot get away from Him; because we would not if we could: because we feel Him, know Him, see Him." It is an immediate consciousness, which may fluctuate and waver in a man because of his own want of prayer and obedience, but if he follow his highest and fights the world instead of yielding to it, more and more God possesses him, and he becomes broader and broader awake as the years go on.[118]

To those who found his thinking too emotional and too imaginative, and who wanted scientific proof, he pointed out that the distinction between passionless science and emotional and imaginative faith had been grossly overdone. Referring to T. H. Huxley's belief that yielding to emotion in the search for truth was immoral, he pointed out the role of courage and faith in the scientific process of forming hypotheses, of the scientist's need sometimes to take a leap in the dark because of a conviction or intuition. In a similar way, religious faith might be seen as a kind of genius, leading people into a very different kind of unknown territory. The intuitions of scientists may be verified through the scientific processes, and the intuitions of religion find verification in the experiences of believers. Only a lack of faith, lack of courage to live in complete dependence on God, made it difficult for people to discover the truth of the claims of Christianity.[119]

In the third lecture Cairns turned to the subject of revelation. He referred to the common practice of the religious thinking of the day to talk about the divine immanence in all things. For him, the important question was whether God was equally immanent in all things. Were all things equally revelatory of their Creator? On a humorous note he wondered, "Is there as much of Him in the Standard Oil Trust as in the Student Christian Movement?" replying that the idea was monstrous. In developing his argument, Cairns cited *Appearance and Reality* (1893), the work of the British idealist philosopher Francis Herbert Bradley, who held that the absolute is more fully present in some things than in others.[120] Cairns agreed, and

116. Cairns, *Reasonableness*, 64.
117. Cairns, *Reasonableness*, 64.
118. Cairns, *Reasonableness*, 75.
119. Cairns, *Reasonableness*, 75–86.
120. Cairns, *Reasonableness*, 96.

went on to say that if you admit that God is more present in some elements than in others, you have practically admitted the existence of revelation and even of "special revelation."[121] Next he considered the forms in which the supreme Reality might reveal itself. The order and beauty of nature revealed a certain amount, but the appearance of the human personality in the evolution of the cosmos revealed "a new depth of reality in the arena of Nature." Humankind came out of nature but was greater than nature in being free to think and act in accordance with its moral consciousness, reflecting the moral character and purpose of the Ultimate Reality. Beauty and order were not enough of themselves. For Cairns, "the whole of the beauty and order which are in Nature become sacramental when I look at them in the light of justice, truth, and love. If nothing spiritual had come out of this long travail, the beauty of the world would grate upon me as does the association of a beautiful face with a false and malicious heart. I could feel no joy in Nature if the soul of things were indifferent or evil."[122]

He then turned to the Christian revelation. Expressing gratitude for the preoccupation of modern scholarship with the humanity of Jesus, he urged his hearers, out of duty to God, to themselves and to humanity, to study the revelation in the gospel narratives so that they could make up their own minds about the Jesus of history. His own living faith had come through such a study, and he appealed to them to find out for themselves what kind of person Jesus was, and what he thought of God and of human life and duty. They should begin as they would with any great character of history, and they should not avoid difficulties.

> When we come to real difficulties as we shall in all probability do, places where our consciences do not at once recognize what He says as the highest, or places which the critical intellect fails to explain, we must not gloss them over, or content ourselves with superficial explanations. In such cases we must frankly admit them, and say, "This is a real difficulty. I do not understand here, but I will go on and understand as much as I can."[123]

Cairns confessed that there was no advice that he could give them that "lies nearer my own heart, that springs more immediately out of my own experience."[124] Such an approach to his own study of the gospels was described in his autobiography and to it he credited a major contribution

---

121. Cairns, *Reasonableness*, 96.
122. Cairns, *Reasonableness*, 100–101.
123. Cairns, *Reasonableness*, 107–8.
124. Cairns, *Reasonableness*, 106.

to his restoration to faith.[125] He was confident that they would similarly discover the personality of Jesus and his defining characteristic: an "enthusiasm for God," or a confidence in God, unmatched in human history. This confidence was in the power and love of God, and in God's liberty to help humankind, and it was so profound and extensive in its application that Jesus was, for Cairns, "unintelligible without God."

In his fourth and final lecture, Cairns asked whether or not this revelation of God in the life of Jesus was relative or absolute. He introduced this section of his argument, by describing the vitality introduced into the world by the emergence of the new religion of Christianity, contrasting its lively faith and hope with the noble endurance of Stoicism and the pessimism of Hebrew spirituality, both of which had been dominant worldviews in the Greco-Roman world at the time. The New Testament, he said, described the radical faith of the new community. It told of their love for others and hope for the future, based on a confident faith in God, and how this faith had driven them out into the world to share the good news of God.[126] Cairns affirmed that the underlying conviction of the New Testament was that in the life and death of Jesus lay the ultimate revelation of God, and that it provided the answer to the riddle of the world.

He concluded that Christianity was not just one religion among others, as it bestowed the gift of union with the divine through the presence and operation of the Holy Spirit. Such a gift had not been withdrawn, but Christianity had lacked the faith to appropriate its power as the first century Christians had done. Belief was hindered by doubts about the supernatural or miraculous elements in Christianity, because these seemed to clash with the scientific view of the uniformity of the natural law. He pointed out that the uniformity of the natural law was not an axiom but a postulate, used for practical purposes, and that it was wrong to turn a working hypothesis into a self-evident truth. He also wondered if it was possible to hold that nature is a closed system along with belief in human freedom. Cairns declared that Jesus and his disciples had been conscious of Jesus' sinlessness, and that this characteristic made him unique among humankind. He asked, "What if perfect nearness to the Great Author and Sustainer of all should give a man power over all the tragic forces of Nature and time?"[127] He maintained that scientific facts were constantly being reviewed in the light of new knowledge, and that old theories which had held sway in the past were being scrapped and new ones formed to include new discoveries. To him,

125. Cairns, *Autobiography*, 120–21.

126. Cairns, *Reasonableness*, 134.

127. Cairns, *Reasonableness*, 154.

the practice of trial and error was in line with the true scientific temper and he urged them to apply it to Christianity. To those who argued that the evolutionary principle precluded the idea of an absolute manifestation of God in the unfinished development of history, Cairns simply pointed to what he accepted as Jesus' own claims about himself.[128] For instance, according to Cairns, "It is luminously clear that He always said that He was Saviour and Lord, and that He was the final manifestation of God. It is, for instance, certain historically that He said He was the Messiah."[129]

For Cairns, Jesus had to be more than just another founder of a religion: it was not enough to think of him as the best of these. If people were to be sure of God's will, then they must have an absolute revelation on which they could depend, and which would not be superseded. Cairns closed the series of lectures with an appeal to the students to gamble on God and give the Eternal World the opportunity to verify itself in their experience. For him, this was the greatest trust that could be given to humanity.

> To take this heritage of human life that is ours and to make it luminous with the glory of God, to begin each day with the confession, "I believe in God the Father Almighty, Maker of Heaven and Earth," and to go out into the world to prove its truth by faith and love and hope, and so add our part to the growing demonstration of His nature and purpose, and the final solution to the riddle of the world, is surely a vocation great enough to make us glad that ever we were born.[130]

Summary and Reflection on the Text

For Cairns, the future of the world depended on the young and whether they would be able to act in accordance with the true nature of the universe. This true nature had been revealed to some extent in the orderliness and beauty of nature, but nature also had a darker side that brought suffering and death. Opposing the purely naturalistic worldview, Cairns averred that humankind did not inhabit a closed physical system in which people were powerless and at the mercy of fixed laws. The appearance of the human personality in the evolutionary process, pointed to a moral aspect and purpose in creation. Man's moral consciousness indicated the moral nature of Ultimate Reality.

128. One who held such a viewpoint was his friend John Oman, who had been among those Cairns thanked for their help with his production of the lectures. See preface to Cairns, *Reasonableness*, xiii, and McKimmon, "John Oman," 4.

129. Cairns, *Reasonableness*, 165.

130. Cairns, *Reasonableness*, 182–83

Religion had been shown to be a universal feature of human experience, which pointed to the reasonableness of having a religious faith, as it was unlikely that millions of people throughout history had acted under a delusion. Religious faith was a valid capacity of human nature. So far, Cairns had shown that theism was a reasonable, or at least not unreasonable, position to hold. His arguments were eloquent and convincing, appealing not only to the intellect, but to the imagination and emotions. Among his many personal anecdotes, stands out one about the tragic death by drowning of one of his students, named only as Maclean. Cairns also showed evidence of reading in a variety of disciplines, and when he included the opinions of those with whom he disagreed, for instance T. H. Huxley, he did it in a respectful way, and not aggressively or defensively.

It was when he moved to speak about Christianity as the absolute revelation, that his arguments appeared more tenuous, and his hermeneutics more opaque. In the effort to convince his hearers of the finality of Christianity, he declared, "If human religion is, as scholars in the science of religion tell us, a prayer for life, then Christianity, as the New Testament shows, is the decisive gift of life. It is the supreme proof in history that God hears prayer."[131]

Here the argument had the appearance of deductive reasoning, but was unreasonable in the sense that while religion may have been shown to be "a prayer for life," it did not follow logically that only one religion, Christianity, was the answer. Christianity could not therefore be the "supreme proof" that Cairns claimed for it in terms of an answer to the riddle of the world. Proof was a term rarely used in his apologetics, and in using it here, Cairns weakened the whole argument of his last lecture. It is clear that he welcomed the findings of biblical criticism, yet he was able to assert that certain claims by Jesus about his messiahship were historically certain. At the same time, displaying the influence of the Ritschlian school, he admitted that he was content to rest his own response to Jesus on "a simple judgment of value." This seems to ignore the idea that the writers of the gospels might similarly have based their recollections on value judgments, and that the words ascribed to Jesus were added by them, after theological reflection on their experiences with him. When asked about his belief in the miracles of Jesus, and why people should believe them, he suggested that the answer was clear. "Just because He was Jesus, do we believe them." Such circularity of thought may have been hard to contradict, but it was equally unlikely to have convinced his hearers. In spite of such weaknesses, the otherwise thoughtfully reasoned lectures, with their recourse to anecdotal

131. Cairns, *Reasonableness*, 137–38.

recollections and to personal testimony which was sometimes passionate, interspersed with a wide selection of scholarly references, must have had a strong appeal to the listeners. Certainly the published version of the lectures was very popular, going into five editions between 1918 and 1924.

Home Life

From his autobiography, it is clear that Cairns regarded his relationships with his children as close, "closer than in most families."[132] Evidence from the correspondence and from Lyn Irvine's book on Alison bears this out.[133] Nonetheless, the time following Helen's death was very difficult for the family. While Cairns fulfilled his academic and church commitments, the children were first looked after by a cousin of friends, whom Irvine describes as "an anxious little spinster of forty, with no experience of small children," and who was "simply a dragon."[134] According to Irvine, the children drew closer to one another for self-protection, and lived for their visits to family in the Borders. As far as schooling was concerned, they had both started at a small school run by three unmarried women, the Misses Knowles. The school was conducted in their house in Carden Place, just a few streets away from the first two Cairns homes in Rubislaw Terrace or Hamilton Place.[135] Later, Alison went to the prestigious Albyn Place Ladies School.[136] Although there is no record of what happened to David's schooling at the time, presumably he attended a similar institution for boys. In 1912, a Parisian governess came to live with them for a year, allowing them to acquire a considerable knowledge of French. Both children became very fond of Madamoiselle Germaine Pire.[137] By 1914 both of Cairns's parents had died, and his sister, Jessie, who had lived with them in Edinburgh since David Sr.'s retirement, came to stay in Hamilton Place to help with the children. Irvine describes Jessie as tall, plain, and angular, and someone who preferred reading books and writing letters to housekeeping. In the custom of the period, she accepted her role in helping out in times of family need, while maintaining a kindly manner and a sense of humor.[138]

132. Cairns, *Autobiography*, 179.

133. Irvine, *Alison Cairns*, esp 94–97, 105–7.

134. Irvine, *Alison Cairns*, 15.

135. Interview with Margaret Agnes Stephen, for the Oral History Archive, MS 3620/1/15, Aberdeen Special Libraries and Archives.

136. See the "Short History" page on the school's website, www.albynschool.co.uk.

137. Cairns, "Memories of Lochton and Foulden."

138. Irvine, *Alison Cairns*, 19.

In 1916, when Cairns was invited to lecture to the troops in France, under the auspices of the Young Men's Christian Association, David and Alison went to live with their aunt Jessie in her home at Braidburn Crescent in Edinburgh. Their uncle William Cairns, minister of Davidson Church, Eyre Place, and his wife, Christina, also lived in the city, at Howard Place, and David and Alison used to spend Sundays with them. David went to Merchiston Castle School, and Alison to St. George's. After their secondary education they went on to university, Alison to Girton College, Cambridge, and David to Aberdeen and then Balliol College, Oxford. David was to follow in his father's footsteps, being ordained and then becoming an academic. Alison, for most of her life, rejected Christianity, although her relationship with her father remained very close. For many years of her adult life, amid a variety of other jobs, she lived with him, organized his mail, accompanied him on his travels, and acted as the unofficial secretary without whom it is unlikely some of his publications would have made it into print.[139] Irvine comments that it would be hard to say which of the two gained most from the relationship. "The wisdom of the age never grew stagnant with D. S. Cairns; Alison kept it in healthy and vigorous movement."[140] While Cairns had dedicated his first book to his parents and his wife, his second was dedicated to his sister, Jessie, doubtless in recognition for all the support she had given him and the children since Helen died, without which it would have been impossible for him to continue his work.

Conclusion

Cairns's new style of apologetics had led him into academic life in Aberdeen, and the family moved into the affluent west end. For three years he continued to hope for Helen's recovery, and his reflection on the situation led him to investigate spiritual healing and the Christian Science movement, from which they sought help. In this time of trouble he and Helen were also supported, through prayer and correspondence, by Oldham and Fraser, both of whom were also involved with him in the World Missionary Conference. In terms of Helen's illness, and of the work of Commission IV, a vital element was the struggle of faith to conquer suffering and death in the cause of the kingdom. Helen's death brought this into much sharper and more urgent focus, and Cairns would spend the next twenty years trying to work out a theology which addressed it. Commission IV introduced Cairns to a wider circle of church activists and theologians, especially from England and

139. Irvine, *Alison Cairns*, 41, 45, 49, 51–52.
140. Irvine, *Alison Cairns*, 100.

America. Many of these were heavily involved in the student movement, for example J. R. Mott, T. R. Glover, and Tissington Tatlow, and enabled Cairns to continue and develop his own involvement with the movement. The theological views described in his report for Commission IV spoke of a fulfillment theory in which Christianity was seen as the absolute and ultimate revelation of God, but also of the opportunity of realizing or recovering aspects of revelation through contact with the different world religions. Recognizing the existence of truth outside Christendom, the commission had begun to distance itself from Christianity's identification with imperialism. The main contribution of the report was its call for a more sensitive approach to the different religions, and an openness to learning about them and from them. It was entirely in keeping with the three-stranded practical program for the churches, set out by Cairns in *Christianity and the Modern World*, especially as it related to his suggested second phase, in which the churches needed to create an environment in which it would be easier to nurture converts.

With regard to the content of his Cambridge lectures, Cairns's comments on the insights of the different religions reinforced the fulfillment theology that informed his contribution to Commission IV. While he was able to praise the various founders for the truths revealed to them, he referred to the religions as "broken lights," a term which jars with the contemporary consciousness.[41] However, Cairns chose his words very carefully, and the metaphor of "broken lights" would have been familiar to him and to his audience, from Tennyson's reference to the fragmented Christian denominations:

> Our little systems have their day,
> They have their day and cease to be:
> They are but broken lights of Thee,
> And Thou, O Christ, art more than they.[142]

His evolutionary approach to the religions, described by him in his lectures as a series of revelations, each displacing the inadequate truth of the former, begs the question about the problem of the chronology of the arrival of Islam, and about the continued existence of each of the different types of religion.

From the time of Helen's death, Cairns had had to organize the care of Alison and David, and this he was able to do with the help of family and

141. Cairns, *Reasonableness*, 130.

142. Tennyson, "In Memoriam A.H.H.," in *Poetical Works of Alfred, Lord Tennyson*, 378–79. (A.H.H. refers to Arthur Henry Hallam.)

friends, and so was able to sustain his academic life and the other significant commitments that he undertook.

His work at the university brought him both affection and respect from his students and colleagues, and growing admiration for the work that he was doing there.

During this period, recognition of the power of his apologetics brought him opportunities to continue to share his ideas on an international level, and his links with the student movement strengthened. For some years he had been motivated by the desire to engage with young people who like himself had been shaken by doubt. It was perhaps such a strong feeling of empathy with them that made *The Reasonableness of the Christian Faith* one of his most eloquent and passionate texts.

Chapter 5

Conflict, Power, and Kingdom, 1916–1923

IN HIS 1906 PUBLICATION, Cairns had identified a symbiosis between evangelization and training in Christian civilization in the missionary enterprise. He felt that if new converts were to maintain Christian faith, missionaries had also to create societies "imbued with the spirit of Christ." The churches had to evangelize and 'moralize" those whom he described as the "lower races." By moralizing he meant creating an environment in which indigenous customs, which were believed to have an immoral effect, such as polygamy, were abolished and where people were offered the perceived benefits of a Western education in order to make it easier to accept the Christian message and to live a Christian life. Such a view echoed the belief of his early spiritual guide, F. D. Maurice, who saw the church as the great instrument for education, preparing people for the knowledge and love of God.[1] Stanley suggests that this shift of focus to the Christianization of the fabric of national life tended to idealize the values of Anglo-Saxon Protestant civilization as the imagined solution to non-Western "backwardness."[2] However, this confidence in the achievements and potential of Western civilization and its relation to the Christian gospel were challenged by the catastrophic events of the First World War, 1914–18. During the war years and throughout the 1920s, Cairns would deepen his friendship with John R. Mott, and indeed would strengthen his association with the World Student Movement, becoming one of its significant figures. The period was also productive in terms of his writing, and he continued to publish, especially in relation to the Great War.

1. Higham, *Frederick Denison Maurice*, 46.
2. Stanley, *The Bible and the Flag*, 134.

143

The Escalation of Western Militarism

The English historian J. P. T. Bury pointed out that by 1900 international relations had become world relations to a degree unknown before in history.[3] Nationalism and industrialism had altered the balance of power in the world, and the great powers of Europe, as they extended their territories to other continents, were engaged in an intensified rivalry. Germany had become the strongest state on the European mainland, with the second largest population, the strongest army, and great industrial potential. As far back as his student days in Marburg, Cairns had noted the growing emphasis on national self-interest in the West, and found it challenging to his Christian faith. On the one hand was the idea of the sovereignty of the kingdom of God, while on the other these nations seemed to enjoy success through policies of self-aggrandizement. The Germany of the day seemed particularly prosperous, comfortable, and cultured.[4] For nearly a decade before the outbreak of the Great War, Cairns had been one of those who had issued warnings about the dangers of militarism, and had called for a new basis in international relations. The European powers were divided into two armed camps, with the Triple Alliance of Germany, Austria, and Italy on one side, and (from 1906) the Triple Entente of France, Russia, and Britain on the other. The situation had become increasingly unstable following the accession in 1888 of the German emperor Kaiser Wilhelm II. The Kaiser's naval ambitions and aggressive colonial expansion were seen as a source of threat, particularly by Britain, and international insecurity was increased by an arms race among the European nations. In an effort to stem the armaments build-up, the first Hague Peace Conference was held in May–July 1899. While the conference failed in this objective, it did establish a permanent court of arbitration.[5] Eight years before World War I broke out, while reflecting on the state of Europe, Cairns had declared,

> The Great Powers are one and all groaning under the burden of militarism. In the time of peace they are hampered in their moralization and political evolution alike by their unproductive outlays and by the necessary stiffening of the national framework which militarism entails, and besides this there is the constant danger of war on an incredibly destructive scale. The systems of alliance which have sprung up have only warded off danger at the expense of aggravating its threatening horrors.

3. Bury, "International Relations, 1900–12," 300–301.

4. Cairns, *Autobiography*, 137.

5. Cairns, *Autobiography*, 308–9.

The nightmare of a general war makes the peace of Europe but a troubled slumber.[6]

To those who argued that war was an inevitable aspect of human existence, Cairns's reply was that hope for peace depended on a person's worldview. For him, such pessimism was a negation of God, and he described the path that he felt the churches should take.[7] Just as the laissez-faire approach had failed at the national level, so it was now failing at the international level. Unless Christianity wished to abandon its claim to be a universal religion, it must believe in the idea of a universal good. Nationalism was a barrier to human solidarity. According to Cairns, "the eight great powers of Christendom treat one another like ruffians in an East End slum or a mining camp rather than like Christians or even gentlemen. They swagger and boast, they glory in one another's disasters and are full of the meanest envy and detraction when any one of them is successful."[8]

He believed that in order to move toward a more peaceful and just society, the international institutions needed to recognize a system of international justice. Selfishness and materialism needed to be transformed into a quest for the common good, and a stronger power was needed to achieve this. The task was that of overcoming the world, and bringing about the worldwide realization of the kingdom of God, through faith in Jesus as the Son of God. The spirit of peacemaking was already at work in various sections of the British churches. In 1910 "The Associated Councils of the Churches in the British and German Empires for Fostering Friendly Relations between the Two Peoples" was inaugurated by two members of Parliament, the Quaker J. Allen Baker and the Anglican W. H. Dickinson. Their aim was to work for peace in and through the churches. In 1914, just before the outbreak of war, this organization became known as the "World Alliance for Promoting International Friendship through the Churches." Just days after its inaugural conference in Germany, war was declared in response to the invasion of Belgium.

The Churches' Reactions to the War

According to S. J. Brown, the outbreak of the Great War came as a shock to the churches, although there had been concern over "military alliances, the arms race, imperial rivalries, and bellicose nationalism." With the outbreak

6. Cairns, *Christianity in the Modern World*, 291–92.
7. Cairns, *Christianity in the Modern World*, 293–314.
8. Cairns, *Christianity in the Modern World*, 300.

of war, a wave of patriotic fervor swept Britain, embracing the clergy of the major denominations, who saw the conflict as a moral crusade, and as an opportunity to revive the influence and authority of the churches.[9] At the general assembly of the Church of Scotland in 1914, chaplains were encouraged to "continue to exert a beneficent influence in promoting the union of patriotism and religion," and young men were exhorted to offer themselves in the cause of national defence.[10] By 1915, over two hundred parish ministers had offered their services as chaplains at the front.[11] In his moderatorial address to the United Free Church, in May 1915, Alexander R. MacEwen declared his support for the Allied armies, and called on parents to respond to the call to sacrifice. "May sorrowing parents not here only but throughout the Church be guided to make the sacrifice to which they have been called in the spirit of the 'Father of the faithful,' and hear the Divine word; 'Surely blessing, I will bless thee because thou hast not withheld thine only son.'"[12]

The United Free Church had about four hundred of its younger ministers "in the field" by the beginning of 1917, most as chaplains and hut workers (described in the following pages), but a few as combatants.[13] One small section of the Scottish Church, the Free Presbyterians, saw the conflict as the "just vengeance" of God for the sins of the Western nations, including Britain, and called for national repentance.[14] Nonetheless, they too felt it was their duty to support the nation: Britain's sinfulness may have called down divine judgment, but in defending Belgium's freedom, the country was playing an honorable role. "Personally we regard Great Britain as the representative of Christ, the righteous, the Prince of Peace, and Germany as the representative of Satan, the unholy prince of darkness, in the present Armageddon."[15]

Callum Brown has observed that the war intensified reflection on male piety. Many clergy felt that the Christian ideal had been misrepresented during the Victorian period in being regarded as "the apex of human goodness"; that respectability had been too highly prized, and the Christian life too narrowly associated with feminine qualities.[16] When thousands of young

9. Brown, *Providence and Empire*, 452.

10. "Report of the Committee on Army and Navy Chaplains," *General Assembly Reports on the Schemes of the Church of Scotland* (1914), 555, 557.

11. "Report of the Committee on Army and Navy Chaplains" (1915), 535.

12. Cairns, *Life and Times of Alexander Robertson MacEwen*, 285–86.

13. Cairns to Mott, 23 January 1917, Mott Papers, RG 45, 13/244, Yale.

14. MacLeod, "Mighty Hand of God," 22, cites Brown, "Solemn Purification," 97–99.

15. MacLeod, "Mighty Hand of God," cites Sinclair, "Moral and Religious Aspects of the War," *Free Presbyterian Magazine* 19 (1914) 246.

16. Brown, *Death of Christian Britain*, 104.

men rushed to enlist, many felt that this new generation was setting aside the materialism of the past decades, choosing the path of self-sacrifice that represented Christian values.[17] Although there had been attempts to create a peaceful outcome to the hostile relations between Germany and Britain, the majority felt that military preparation was the correct response. For instance, the University of Glasgow responded by setting up, in 1910, an Officers' Training Corps, recruiting four hundred men, who were among the first to be mobilized when war broke out. Even before compulsory conscription was introduced in January 1916, the Senate had urged all students who were fit to consider recruitment, and all lecturers and assistants of military age, except qualified medical practitioners, were expected to offer themselves.[18] Half the male students in the University of Aberdeen had enlisted by October 1914, in response to Kitchener's appeal, "Your Country Needs You," and his call for thousands of recruits to support the regular army. The new recruits formed the battalions of the "New Armies."[19] By the spring of 1915, Cairns informed Mott that his college's numbers were sadly depleted due to the high proportion of students who had volunteered. So many students left the university and the college that the two theological departments in Aberdeen merged for the duration of the war.[20]

A variety of Christian bodies set out to create social, spiritual, and physical support systems in temporary accommodation (huts, tents or marquees) in the areas of conflict English historian Michael Snape describes the mixed motives of these groups as "a conflation of missionary, paternalistic, philanthropic, prudential and patriotic concerns."[21] American historian Jeffrey S. Reznick records that such facilities had been established by the Young Men's Christian Association at British military garrisons around the world, since the 1890s, in an effort to halt what was seen as "social decay" among working class men and women. In a home-like atmosphere, the volunteers who ran the centers hoped to provide an alternative to the attraction of alcohol, gambling, and prostitutes. In 1914, in contrast to the red lamps of the prostitutes, the huts of the YMCA began to display an alternative "red," the distinctive red triangle that stood for care of mind, body, and spirit.[22]

17. Brown, *Providence and Empire*, 452.

18. "University of Glasgow Story," http://www.universitystory.gla.ac.uk/ww1 -background.

19. Holmes, *Western Front*, 52.

20. Cairns to Mott, 4 November 1919, Mott Papers, RG 45, 13/244, Yale.

21. Snape, *God and the British Soldier*, 206.

22. Reznick, *Healing the Nation*, 19–21.

Snape attributes the use of the "triangle" to Sir Arthur Yapp, the national secretary of the British YMCA.[23]

Under the auspices of the Scottish Churches Huts Joint Committee, the Church of Scotland and the United Free Church combined their efforts to support the forces at home and in France after 1916. Support was geared primarily to "buttressing faith," although some recreational facilities were provided too.[24] The delay in making this contribution was attributed to a lack of funds, but by 1918, the committee had thirty-four centers and over three hundred workers in France. No such lack affected the YMCA, which within ten days of the war beginning had over two hundred and fifty recreational centers in Britain, and developed in France over three hundred centers in camps, hospitals, railway stations, and areas of military action. According to Snape, of all the philanthropic and religious groups, the YMCA was the largest and the best organized, while the YMCA's Yapp was the principal architect of its wartime mission.[25] The organization concentrated first on the physical needs of the men, providing food, entertainment, and writing facilities so that they could keep in touch with loved ones at home, but lectures and services of worship also featured in their programs. They also provided accommodation and care for family members who wished to visit injured soldiers.

Cairns's Theological Response to War

In 1914, at fifty-one years of age, Cairns had been exempt from military service on three counts: his age (over forty-one), being a widower with children (then ten and twelve), and being a minister of religion. The war gave his apologetics a particular focus and purpose, and provided an opportunity to reflect on the churches' failure to engage the hearts and minds of large sections of the population, particularly among young men. He continued in his academic post in Aberdeen, and three months after the start of the war he was invited to contribute to a series of pamphlets, "Papers for War Time." The authors of these pamphlets represented a spectrum of political and denominational opinion on the challenge represented to the church by the war, and included ecclesiastical, academic and literary figures. In the "Explanatory Note" included in each booklet, the editors suggested that a failure to understand and put into practice Christian principles lay at the root of the violence between so-called Christian nations. The pamphlets

23. Snape, *God and the British Soldier.*
24. Reznick, *Healing the Nation,* 211–12.
25. Reznick, *Healing the Nation,* 206–8.

were an attempt to find a truer understanding of Christianity and its mission. Cairns's pamphlet, *An Answer to Bernhardi*, was in response to a 1911 publication, *Germany and the Next War*, by the Prussian military writer General Friedrich von Bernhardi.[26] Cairns set out to challenge his main ideas: the biological necessity of war; the duty of self-assertion; and negotiation as a sign of weakness.

While recognizing the national popularity of Bernhardi's ideas in Germany, Cairns suggested that they were not the ideas of the leading thinkers of the country, many of whom were familiar to him. According to Cairns, Bernhardi's central premise was that war is and always will be a necessity and it is our duty to recognize this and give it due honor. For Bernhardi, the survival of the fittest and the struggle for existence were the fundamental laws of life, and thus part of God's purpose. He viewed the moral law as secondary to the law of survival applying only within the boundaries of the state for the purpose of enhancing its efficiency in the struggle for national survival, which was best achieved through supremacy over other nations. There could be no agreed international morality, as this would necessitate negotiation with other states and the suspension of the struggle for supremacy. For Cairns, on the other hand, the very acknowledgment of God of itself "universalized human rights."[27] If moral law operated only within state boundaries, and did not apply to foreign policy, it gave statesmen the right to lie to each other and to go back on their word. He declared that Bernhardi's position, which was shared by much of the German high command, would lead to consequences "revolting to the conscience of mankind."[28] He described the brutal effects of war on the civilian population—things which he "understood to be approved and instigated by the militarism for which Bernhardi speaks."

> A man and his wife are sitting peacefully talking together in Antwerp in the quiet of an autumn night. No formal investment or warning of bombardment has been given. A Zeppelin sails in in the darkness, drops its bomb beside them, and all that is left of them is a falling drizzle of blood. Beside them hundreds are maimed or slain. Again, in a great French city, far from the battle-field, a little girl is playing beside her nurse. A "Dove" sails in overhead, there is a loud explosion, and what remains is a dead woman and a little wailing heap of crippled humanity.

26. Cairns's 1914 publication was no. 12 in the series, published by Oxford University Press. Other writers included William Temple (later Archbishop of Canterbury), the biblical scholar Burnett Hillman Streeter, J. H. Oldham, and Percy Dearmer.

27. Cairns, *Answer to Bernhardi*, 12.

28. Cairns, *Answer to Bernhardi*, 5.

The do-er of this deed, a strong and bold youth, sails away in triumph to receive military honours and the plaudits of an admiring people. Had that people been in its senses it would have hanged him, and repented in anguish and tears the deed that had stained the honour of a great nation.[29]

For Cairns, atheism was a nobler thing than a religion that saw such actions as part of God's plan for the world, and he averred that "if our country is going to do such things and make us complicit in them, then shall we renounce our country and seek admission to some nobler State."[30]

As well as the bombing of civilians, Cairns saw as intrinsically reprehensible the practice of espionage, trading as it did on betraying the trust of others.[31] For Cairns, war was an aberration from God's will by one or more parties. Christians who believed that it was inevitable because of sin, indulged in a self-fulfilling prophecy that was tantamount to saying that God must accept the defeat of his kingdom in this world. Because sin endured in the world, it did not mean that war was inevitable. He reminded his readers that at one time slavery had seemed a necessity. In the case of war, people needed to understand that "there is something ignominious and brutal in its very essence."[32] In questioning the militaristic nature of German patriotism, Cairns admitted its "gleams of nobility": love of country, willingness to endure hardship, toil, and sacrifice.[33] He concluded by calling on the church to preserve what was noble in patriotism, and to provide a "moral equivalent for war" in promoting the struggle to establish the kingdom of God.[34] War was a failure to live up to the Christian ideal, and the answer to militarism would only be found in the active embracing of the values of the kingdom of God, which transcended all national boundaries, and provided the basis for all human morality. The quest for world peace as obedience to kingdom values was now firmly established in the social dimension of his theology. For him, the end did not justify the means, and the bombing of civilians and the practice of espionage were intrinsically reprehensible practices. Cairns was not, however, a pacifist. When Mott came under the influence of Henry T. Hodgkin, Quaker and founder of the pacifist British Fellowship of Reconciliation [FOR], he invited Hodgkin to America in 1915, and a branch was formed there. The FOR saw pacifism as a Christian

29. Cairns, *Answer to Bernhardi*, 9.
30. Cairns, *Answer to Bernhardi*, 9–10.
31. Cairns, *Answer to Bernhardi*, 10.
32. Cairns, *Answer to Bernhardi*, 15.
33. Cairns, *Answer to Bernhardi*, 15.
34. Cairns, *Answer to Bernhardi*, 16.

duty, based on the concept that love prohibited war. Both Oldham and Cairns wrote to Mott, expressing their dissent from the Quaker view. For Oldham, pacifism represented a minority Christian view in which peace was sought at any price, against the real interests of humanity.[35] For Cairns, the Quaker view was one in which he saw no "light or hope" but one that just made things worse.[36] Repeating this view in a letter to Mott in 1919, he elaborated: "My complaint with the mere Pacifists is that they do not go nearly deep enough, or that when they do go deep enough, as in the case of Tolstoy, they teach a wholly impracticable and usually unattractive view of life. We must find a place for nationality and for an associated humanity, and these must be won for and baptized into Christ."[37]

True to the views he expressed in his reply to Bernhardi, when the British government wanted to introduce a policy of reprisal bombings in 1917, Cairns was among those who protested publicly by writing to the *Scotsman* newspaper, and by setting out a manifesto against the campaign. Among those who supported him was Charles Gore, bishop of Oxford, who wrote to say that he had signed Cairns's manifesto, and that he also had written to the *Times*, in the hope of influencing the forthcoming parliamentary debate. The two men carried on correspondence on the subject between April and October 1917.[38] Neither public opinion nor the British Press, however, were on their side. When Cairns wrote to Gore to let him know that the *Scotsman* had agreed to print his letter, he added that he would probably be allowed no more than the right to reply, that the paper had led with an article in support of reprisals, and had suppressed a letter from Oldham. Considering the weight of public opinion in favor of reprisal raids, Cairns's position required courage to stand out against the majority. An article in the *Dundee Courier* declared, "It is no exaggeration to say that the manifesto which has been signed by the Bishop of Oxford and other prominent personages is a most deplorable step in a dangerous and pernicious campaign."[39]

The item went on to accuse the signatories of being "guilty of a serious disservice to their fellow-countrymen" and of "encouraging the enemy to persist in his vile practices." The Bristol-based *Western Daily Press* aired the views of other influential voices, which were to win the day. Lord Rothermere, the Air Minister, asserted, "We are determined that whatever outrages

35. Hopkins, *John R. Mott, a Biography*, 470.

36. Cairns to Mott, 14 October 1916, Mott Papers, RG 45, 13/244, Yale.

37. Cairns to Mott, 1 August 1919, Mott Papers, RG 45, 13/244, Yale.

38. Cairns to Gore, 24 April 1917, Gore to Cairns, 2 May 1917 and Gore to Cairns, 15 October 1917 in Box 3/4 Cairns Papers.

39. *Dundee Courier*, "If You Want to Impress," 29 May 1917.

are committed on the civilian population of this country will be met by similar treatment of the German people."[40]

Also quoted in the article was Sir Arthur Conan Doyle, who urged, "Let us pay no attention to platitudinous Bishops or gloomy Deans, or any other superior people who preach against retaliation, or whole-hearted warfare."

Within the United Free Church there was ambivalence over the matter. The *Dundee Courier*, reporting on the general assembly of May 1917, recorded that a recent air raid on Freiburg had formed the chief subject of debate, which included an overture describing the raid as giving the sanction of the government to the policy of reprisals on noncombatants, and protesting at such a policy. The overture was received, but was neither sustained nor rejected.[41]

Leaving Home

Conscription was introduced in 1916, with the upper age limit set at fifty-one. In the same year, Cairns was given permission by the United Free Church to work for three years with the YMCA among soldiers, while the church continued to pay his salary.[42] During this time he made several visits to France, to the base camps at Le Havre and Rouen, where he lectured and presided at services of worship. Before he left for France for the first visit, he wrote a ten-page letter to his children, who were then ten and twelve.[43] Its composition took several days to complete, and revealed something of the emotional depth of family relations and the strain he felt in leaving Alison and David. The bulk of the letter was taken up with discharging the duty of telling them how they might live as good Christian disciples, but it began with a moving admission:

> My Dear Children,
>
> As I am going away for a while, and am alone in the house here tonight, I want to write you a letter instead of having a quiet talk with you by the fire like those we have often had at home. I wish you were here with me instead of being nearly a hundred and twenty miles away, but I will try to do my best. . . . Looking back, I see what dear kind children you have been both of you,

40. *Western Daily Press*, "Beginning of Reprisals," 27 December 1917.
41. *Dundee Courier*, "U. F. Church and War Reprisals," 28 May 1917.
42. Cairns to Mott, 4 November 1919, Mott Papers, RG 45, 13/244, Yale.
43. Cairns to Alison and David, 4–9 April 1916, Box 2/1 Cairns Papers.

who have given me as you gave your dear mother, much ground
for gratitude to God and for hope that some day you will be a
good and useful man and woman. It is to help you with this that
I write this letter. I want you to think often and seriously about
it all. The thing that I want most of all for you both is that you
should be good disciples and friends of the Lord Jesus Christ.
If anything should take me away from you to the greater and
happier world where your dear mother is, I want you both above
all things to live so as to join us there and take up the old happy
family life there together in our Father's good time.

He told them that their mother had told him that the last three years of
her life were her happiest, and he tried to reassure them by saying, "I believe
that she is not far from us now, and that God will use her to help and guide
us." He reminded them that they had a source of friendship and support
in their extended family, and a unique family inheritance: they had a rich
possession in the names they bore and must "do everything to be worthy of
those names and nothing to make people think less of them, and everything
you can to make them even nobler and richer."

Working with the Young Men's Christian Association

Cairns was already familiar with the YMCA's day-to-day work in its thriving Aberdeen branch. In 1908, just a year after Cairns's arrival in the city,
the first British Conference of YMCAs had been held there, attracting notable speakers such as Professor Marcus Dods and the well-known Baptist
preacher William Landels, who had had such a formative influence on
Cairns in his youth. The branch provided healthy recreational activities
catering for the intellectual, social, and physical needs of young men, and
by the beginning of the twentieth century, it had already produced a number of foreign missionaries.[44] When the war began in 1914, the Aberdeen
branch catered for soldiers in transit, providing canteen, laundry, banking,
and postal facilities, as well as entertainment and religious services. Similar
provision was made in the YMCA huts in France. Although Cairns never
held an official role in the Aberdeen YMCA, he identified with it during
his many years at the university there, particularly through his involvement
in study circles. This lay movement, with its aim of "fostering of Christian
manhood," fitted with Cairns's own social theology.

In terms of the war effort, according to Snape, the YMCA was the largest and best organized of the religious groups, but it had something more

44. Gammie, *Aberdeen Y.M.C.A.*

that attracted volunteers—its inter-denominational nature, which "proved a great draw for many liberal-minded Free Church clergymen who were unable or disinclined to take a chaplain's commission."[45] For Cairns, there was the added factor of his admiration for Mott, who, while continuing to serve as chair of the North American Council of Student Movements and as secretary of the World Student Christian Foundation, had in 1915 become general secretary of the International Committee of the YMCA. In accepting this latter position Mott had made it clear that the association was not a substitute for the churches.[46] Hopkins points out that the lack of any clear definition of the relationship between the association and the churches had led to misunderstandings and rivalry.[47] Rivalry was most pronounced between the Church Army (Anglican) and the association, although it did exist in relation to the Scottish churches. There was interdenominational rivalry too, seen mainly in the competition for representation by chaplains, or in the allocation of rank. Some felt that allocations of both were not always done on a fair basis, and that this would disadvantage their denomination after the war, but when the winter of 1916–17 brought a chronic shortage of clerical manpower, the association had to approach the principle denominations in England and Scotland to secure ministers for service in the huts in France.[48] Snape describes a sympathetic response, especially in Scotland, when the United Free Church produced over a hundred volunteers, with money to release them for service. Along with an otherwise unidentified Mr. Hall, Cairns had co-convened the group responsible for the recruitment of chaplains.[49] According to E. C. Carter (European director of the YMCA), without Cairns's help it would have been impossible to secure the "magnificent response" of the Scottish churches.[50] Cairns himself was convinced of the role of the YMCA, not as a competitor, but as the forward movement of the churches through its young people, much as he regarded the SCM. Contributing to the YMCA handbook of 1919 he wrote, "It is contrary to the whole purpose of the YMCA that the Association should become a substitute for the worship and corporate life of any Church or denomination."[51]

45. Snape, *God and the British Soldier*, 209.

46. Hopkins, *John R. Mott*, 455.

47. Hopkins, *John R. Mott*, 525.

48. This shortage was the result of the introduction of conscription in January 1916.

49. Cairns to Mott, 23 January 1917, Mott Papers, RG 45, 13/244, Yale.

50. Snape, *Back Parts of War*, 88, cites YMCA, K27 YMCA War Work No. 14 France. E. C. Carter to O. McCowen, 24 January 1917.

51. Snape, *God and the British Soldier*, 210, cites Cairns in YMCA handbook 1919, appendix 2, 451.

Cairns was convinced that the cooperation of the churches with the YMCA augured well for postwar relations.[52] Since 1916, he had been helping the YMCA with its war work in the new Armies, and had an advisory role in devising policy for the future.[53] By this time, as well as wanting to provide immediate help to the fighting men, the major denominations were also looking beyond the war to the period of reconstruction that would follow. One outcome of this was the publication by the United Presbyterian Church of a series of twenty-four tracts, the aim of which was "to promote the growth in our own branch of the Church of an impulse to self-examination, and of a quickened sense of the great tasks opening before us, and the resources of Faith through which alone they may be accomplished."[54]

Possibly to set the tone for the series, Cairns was invited to write the first tract, *The Call of God in the Present Crisis*. Reiterating some of the ideas in his 1906 publication, he spoke of the need to repent of the lack of faith in God, which had been replaced by materialism and the desire for power and wealth. The nation had become involved in a system that ignored God, and the result had been that social relations at domestic and on the international level had degenerated. A renewal of hope in God was needed if they were to build a new world; and a return to faith in the assurance that "God is infinitely greater, more loving, freer and readier to help than Humanity ever knows, that all the tragedy of human life springs from its obsession of doubt and fear about Him, and all its enduring victory and courage from opening its eyes and taking hold of what has been waiting all the time."[55]

While Cairns saw the war as the result of the failure of the churches to live up to the Christian ideal, as the Free Presbyterians had stated, he never accepted the view of the war as punishment from God. Such a view would have been anathema to him. He finished his tract on a hopeful note: "It is impossible for the man who believes in God not to rejoice. Though the whole world fall to pieces around him, the ruin will strike him undismayed."[56]

52. Cairns to Mott, 23 January 1917. Mott Papers, RG 45, 13/244, Yale.

53. Cairns to Mott, 14 October 1916, Mott Papers, RG 45, 13/244, Yale.

54. Prefatory note in the tracts, which had been supervised by a committee of the general assembly of the United Free Church (Edinburgh, 1917). The tracts appeared in the series The Church and the War Tracts for Today.

55. Cairns, *Call of God*, 7.

56. Cairns, *Call of God*.

The Need for an Inquiry

As leaders within the educational, industrial, commercial, and political institutions sought to help plan for the country's postwar future, so too did
leaders within the churches.[57] The United Free Church and the Church of
Scotland appointed commissions to work among the Scottish forces to explore the moral and spiritual meaning of the conflict. In 1916, the Church
of England had instituted a National Mission focused on repentance and
hope, and in connection with this, a private inquiry, led by John Maud, the
bishop of Kensington and the theologian George K. A. Bell, had been carried out among some one hundred Anglican chaplains.[58] The YMCA agreed
to fund a larger scale inquiry among the English forces, and cover the cost
of the publication of the results. The combined findings of the Scottish and
English inquiries were published in 1919 as *The Army and Religion: An Inquiry and Its Bearing upon the Religious Life*. The project was overseen by a
committee which appears to have developed organically out of the experiences in France of one man, unnamed, who then gathered around him a
small group of like-minded people equally concerned to interpret the experience of the war for the church's future life. The group decided to expand
its numbers in order to be more representative. From among its members,
Cairns and Edward S. Talbot, the bishop of Winchester, were appointed
co-conveners of this larger committee, which spanned the denominations,
including the Quakers, represented by Dr. H. T. Hodgkin of London. The
SCM and the YMCA had representatives, and there were a number of well-
known academics. Among its members were several friends of Cairns: J.
H. Oldham, Professor Oman of Westminster College, Cambridge, A. A.
David, the headmaster of Rugby, and Tissington Tatlow, secretary of the
SCM. Talbot was also well known to Cairns, who had been friends with his
son Neville for almost a decade. There was one representative from Wales,
Professor David Williams, of the Theological College in Aberystwyth.
Only two women were committee members, including Zoe Fairfield, assistant secretary of the SCM. While all the committee members were from
the Protestant denominations, Roman Catholic evidence was sought, and
several Roman Catholic chaplains contributed by responding to the questionnaires.[59] Baron Friedrich von Hügel, the scholar of mysticism, had been
invited to join the committee, but declined to be an official member or to
sign the report. In spite of this, he attended meetings of the committee, took

57. Cairns, *Army and Religion Report*, 7.

58. Cairns, *Army and Religion Report*, 3, and appendix 1, 208–9.

59. Cairns, *Army and Religion*, 1–4.

a leading part in discussions, and carried on a detailed correspondence with Cairns, making "valuable suggestions and criticisms," and according to the Talbot, "no member of our body contributed more to its work, or was a more hearty comrade in its conduct."[60]

As well as his administrative tasks, Cairns took an active role in the process of investigation, going out to the base camps in France several times. In 1916, Yapp reported a visit to a camp in Rouen, where Cairns led between six and seven hundred men in worship in a weeknight service, and then spoke to several individuals who stayed behind to talk privately with him. In the following year E. C. Carter reported that Cairns had asked permission to go to France for six weeks to "visit our workers and a few of the chaplains in, say, three different bases, and in, say, two of the armies."[61] In his account of the work in the base camps in France, Sherwood Eddy, YMCA secretary for Asia, described how distinguished scholars lectured to the soldiers on a variety of topics. Writing of Cairns he said, "Principal D. S. Cairns, of Aberdeen, has had crowded meetings night after night for his apologetic lectures, and the questions raised in the open discussions would make one think he was in a theological seminary."[62]

When the *Army and Religion* report was published in 1919, its preface stated opaquely that the idea for an inquiry "suggested itself first to one of our company," but it is clear that Cairns was its chief architect, and the driving force behind it. He had already mentioned the possibility of an inquiry to Mott in the autumn of 1916, and informed him that he had introduced to Yapp and Carter the idea of utilizing the opportunity in the camps to produce a report on the thinking of the youth of the nation about religion and the churches.[63] In another letter to Mott at the beginning of 1917, he had described in more detail the opportunity that such an investigation offered.

> I am going up to London tomorrow for a month to lend a hand in various ways: in particular, to see if an inquiry into the religious outlook of the entire army, through the Y.M.C.A., is practicable, after that, I hope to get across to France again. I cannot help feeling that the right preliminary to the work of the next twenty-five years among the youth of the country is a searching

60. Cairns, *Army and Religion*, 4.

61. Snape, *Back Parts of War*, cites YMCA, K27 YMCA War Work No. 14. France. E. C. Carter to O. McCowen, 24 January 1917.

62. Eddy, *With Our Soldiers in France*, ch. 5.

63. Cairns to Mott, 14 October 1916, Mott Papers, RG 45, 13/244, Yale.

inquiry as to where they really stand to-day in matters of religious and moral outlook.[64]

Cairns had looked ahead to the postwar period, and imagined that
things would be very different. He relayed to Mott his hope in the returning
armies, who would have a new way of looking at things, shaped by their
experiences. He had concluded from his impressions among them that they,
especially the younger men, put up with the war but hated it, and had a
"deep and stern determination" that their children should not endure such a
thing.[65] He also expressed his hope and gratitude for the Student Federation,
presumably referring to its ability to provide an international structure for
the work that would need to be done. He included with the letter a memorandum that he had written for the Scottish churches, which were already
considering such an inquiry.[66] In it he reiterated the desirability of such an
inquiry as an unprecedented opportunity to get to know the real mind of
the youth of the nation. The war had drawn the youth of all classes together,
and in every regiment there were chaplains and "earnestly religious men"
who "can be appealed to, to give their impressions as to the prevailing tone
of matters of religion and morality." The inquiry would also provide a way of
testing the churches' educational and religious work of the last twenty-five
years. Cairns was convinced that the outcome would call for a complete
reorganization of church life: "its services, its type of preaching and theological training, its constitution and its spirit." The inquiry should study
the deep changes that must be working in the men, as they were "passing
through the most poignant and novel trials." It should try to discover which
aspects of Christian truth appealed most to them, as this would be valuable
knowledge for those who would later work with them. For his part, his experiences in France had told him that the men were interested in "God and
Immortality, and the reality of the Unseen world, and the power of prayer."
He speculated on the findings of the inquiry and suggested that if his own
findings were proved to be general, then that should have an impact on the
preaching ministry of the future. He observed that a large number of men in
the armies belonged to the lapsed classes, and that here was an opportunity
to find out what kept them from the churches, noting that at least part of the
blame must lie with the churches themselves. Cairns suggested a method
for the inquiry based on his experiences as chair of Commission IV at the
World Missionary Conference. He emphasized that the inquiry would need

64. Cairns to Mott, 23 January 1917, Mott Papers, RG 45, 13/244, Yale.

65. Cairns to Mott, 14 October 1916, Mott Papers, RG 45, 13/244, Yale.

66. The five-page memorandum, "On Enquiry into Moral and Religious Outlook
of men in Scottish Forces." Included at the end of the aforementioned letter.

to be "thorough and exhaustive," in terms of the kinds of regiments it covered. A strong subcommittee would be needed, capable of scrutinizing and selecting the evidence, and made up of people who were sharing the daily life of the men. Care would have to be taken drawing up the questions, and it would be useful to obtain from the respondents "the numerical proportion of men vitally connected with the Churches."

The Report

In his preface to the report, the bishop of Winchester explained its organization.[67] The first step was to prepare and send questionnaires to individuals and groups who were willing to participate, and around three hundred replies were obtained. Committees at the great bases had collected this evidence, which came from men of all ranks, and chaplains, doctors, nurses, hut leaders, and workers. Copies were made and sent to the Report Committee, which met several times during 1917 and 1918, sometimes for a few days at a time. During the first gathering, a four-day meeting in August 1917, at the Marquis of Salisbury's Hatfield estate, the committee considered the evidence and decided on their approach. Faced with such an enormous task, Cairns was "unhesitatingly and unitedly" asked to be the draftsman, as it was felt that a single author would give the text coherence while still expressing the corporate viewpoint. Talbot wrote later:

> The Committee cannot acknowledge too cordially the unwearied patience, diligence, and courtesy with which Dr. Cairns throughout discharged his task. They desire to pay him an affectionate tribute of gratitude and admiration; but they believe that their draftsman's best reward will be found in the public sense that he has done a great service to the Church and to all who desire, in the Lord's Name, to face frankly, humbly, and teachably the situation here described.[68]

Talbot also acknowledged that Cairns had entrusted the chapter on education to Dr. A. A. David, headmaster of Rugby School, and that he had special assistance from Fr. Frere of the Anglo-Catholic Community of the Resurrection at Mirfield and A. Herbert Gray, minister, marriage guidance counsellor and author of *As Tommy Sees Us* (London, 1919), on the chapter on morals and morale. Talbot pointed out that the inquiry was limited to England and Scotland, and expressed gratitude for the use of evidence

67. Cairns, *Army and Religion*, 1–3.
68. Cairns, *Army and Religion*, 2.

from inquiries by the Church of Scotland, the United Free Church, and the Anglican Church.

In the introduction, Cairns explained the thinking behind the report.[69] As the churches faced the future, they would need to harness the idealism of the youth of the nation in an effort to change society for the better. To achieve this, they needed to know what the young men were thinking, and the inquiry provided an opportunity for that. The questionnaire had been devised in three main sections, to elicit the following information: the first section comprised questions about the men's thoughts on religion, morality, and society. The second comprised questions about the impact of the war on how the men thought about certain issues. The third section included questions about the men's relation to the churches. The subsequent report was organized in two parts: part one included considerable quotation from the responses to the questionnaire, and provided an analysis of the situation based on their responses; and the second part was an attempt at larger interpretation, and at suggesting a way forward. Quoting Neville Talbot, his friend and military chaplain, Cairns observed that "the soldier has got religion, I am not sure that he has got Christianity."[70] The report concluded that while it seemed as if many had rejected Christianity, it was not the true Christianity that they rejected, but a version maintained by churches that had been seduced by naturalism and materialism.[71] From the replies to the questionnaire, it was deduced that four-fifths of the young male population were no longer associated with churches in any vital way, and this was blamed on ecclesiastical divisions, on the churches' failure to meet the social and physical needs caused by the Industrial Revolution, and on the decay of faith which resulted from the materialism of Church members.[72] In response to this situation, the churches had to present the kingdom of God as an alternative basis for international relations: they had to show that the appeal to force as the final authority is a denial of God, and to win youth over to that ideal. In looking for grounds of hope for the future, the report pointed first to the inexhaustible power and love of God and of God's liberty to help humankind. The second ground of hope was the "self-revelation" of the men:

> Placed suddenly in these terrible and abnormal conditions, with so poor an outfit of education and spiritual knowledge as our country has been able to give most of them, coming in the main

69. Cairns, *Army and Religion*, 5–10.

70. Cairns, *Army and Religion*, 13.

71. Cairns, *Army and Religion*, 121.

72. Cairns, *Army and Religion*, 116–26.

from economic conditions which were fitted to depress and dis-
courage the best in them and foster the evil, what an imperish-
able witness they have given to the good that is in man, to the
heroic in the commonplace, to the deep founts of courage and
loyalty and sacrifice and affection!

And if the manhood of our nation can get so far with such a
vague and meagre gospel, to what heights might it not rise if it
were fully won for the God and Father of our Lord Jesus Christ
and for the service of His world-wide Kingdom?[73]

A third ground of hope rested paradoxically in the very misunderstanding of Christianity. What was needed now was more than an evangelical campaign; the church needed to widen and deepen its outlook. It had
taught its doctrines without relating them to life. It had taught them "in a
foreign tongue which has been learned by rote but never understood" and
when the "great convulsion" of the war came, Christian "truth" had been
dropped as something useless and irrelevant.[74] The church needed a "vital-
izing of theology," so that it could restate the faith in terms that the men
could understand.[75] Many of the men in the camps had spoken of experiencing a spiritual struggle, and in doing that they had shown themselves to
be "fellow investigators" of the age-long dilemma concerning the presence
of evil and suffering in the world.[76] However, in the process, their literalist
approach to the Bible had revealed a shocking ignorance of Scripture and
how it should be regarded and interpreted. The report concluded that the
men's views had been untouched by seventy years of gospel scholarship, and
that "there must have been a grave want of candor [sic] and courage in the
teaching of the Church for this to be possible."[77]

Turning to the solution to the problem, the report suggested some
ways forward. Two of the report's findings provided the starting place for
the church to take up the challenge: first, the inquiry had found that most
of the men professed to a belief in God, albeit often a vague Theism; and
second, the men almost all professed to having a respect for the person of
Jesus Christ. Its task was to build on these; first by making believable to
thoughtful people the Christian doctrine of God, and then by clarifying

73. Cairns, *Army and Religion*, 126.

74. Cairns, *Army and Religion*, 129.

75. Cairns, *Army and Religion*, 128–42, provides details about the revitalizing of
theology.

76. Cairns, *Army and Religion*, 131.

77. Cairns, *Army and Religion*, 13.

the personality and teaching of Christ, and his teachings regarding evil and suffering.[78]

Taking the idea of the kingdom of God seriously meant considering how it might become a reality, and the universal nature of the church made it the obvious international force—a supranational league of the kingdom—which might exist alongside the League of Nations. There had been much criticism of the church, particularly in its identification with the governing classes, but the report asserted its potential role in building the kingdom of God, despite it past failures.[79] Following on from this theme, and closely related to it, was the report's comment on the church and society. There followed a debate on whether or not the church had a social mission.[80] The report concluded that it had, as Jesus had given his followers a social ideal in the kingdom of God, and a social law in the law of love. Jesus' teaching about the Fatherhood of God had implied that human beings were akin to the divine, and therefore sacred. "Hence everything whatever, custom, tradition, institution, and law, that does violence to the sacredness of personality is condemned by essential Christianity. This is the basis of the social mission of the Christian Church."[81]

According to the report, the great immediate moral problem that faced the world was its attitude to war and peace, and the church must take the lead in the pursuit of peace. The evidence of the inquiry showed that the men blamed the churches for not having done more to prevent the war.[82] The report noted an awakening of conscience throughout Christendom, in which attitudes to war were changing, partly due to the scale and horror of the recent conflict, but also because of "a deepening sense of individual freedom, of the rights of human personality" and to the idea that these will prove to be incompatible with militarism.[83] "The whole structure of world society has become so interwoven that world war is an anachronism. Mankind cannot face the repetition of such things unless it is prepared to face dissolution. The men who used to think that world peace is an impracticable ideal are beginning to see that the alternative way is impracticable also.[84]

The church's task was to recover the ideal of the kingdom and make its teaching clear to those both outside and within. It must reexamine its

---

78. Cairns, *Army and Religion*, 135.

79. Cairns, *Army and Religion*, 141–45.

80. Cairns, *Army and Religion*, 145–58.

81. Cairns, *Army and Religion*, 148.

82. Cairns, *Army and Religion*, 158.

83. Cairns, *Army and Religion*, 159.

84. Cairns, *Army and Religion*, 160.

teaching methods and organization. In a short section on morale and morals, the major topic was sexual behavior, and in particular the use of prostitutes. The section began with the heroic and self-sacrificing virtues of the men, perhaps in an effort to prepare the way for the frank discussion that was to follow. The virtues of the men were lauded, which raised the question of the source of such virtues. "They have shown a courage, a self-sacrifice, and a cheerful endurance that, as one of our witnesses has said, make our civilian loyalties look mean. Now we must ask the question, 'Has Christianity had anything to do with their splendid manifestation of great qualities?'"[85]

The report concluded that the "military virtues" of courage and endurance might be exhibited by any group when put to the test, but there were other virtues displayed by the troops, which must be attributed to the influence of Christian homes and teaching, and to the fact that most of the men had been baptized and educated, even if imperfectly, in the Christian faith. Among these virtues were "generosity to the vanquished, unselfishness, half-humorous humility, and chivalry," which if they were not Christian virtues, were "astonishingly like them." The report admitted that the men themselves did not associate these virtues with Christianity.[86] With regard to the question of sexual morality, while not minimizing the "evil," the report took a sympathetic and pragmatic view, taking into account a variety of abnormal circumstances and experiences which included the intense emotional strain of warfare, the segregation of the sexes, the tedium of the camps, and the necessarily strict discipline. The problem was one that also affected the nation at home, and a variety of suggestions were put forward to deal with it in a positive rather than recriminatory way. While lack of self-control and the use of alcohol were seen as causes of social problems, the report included among other contributory causes the lack of decent housing, ignorance of the facts of life, poor wages and employment systems that made it hard for young people to start out on family life. The church had been complacent about social evils, and now it was time to take action to remedy the situation by working for better housing and wages, and for the provision of sporting and leisure facilities for the young.[87] In relation to prostitution, the report advised against its regulation, as that seemed "a tacit assent to laxity." It also rejected the imposing of legal penalties on prostitutes, seeing that way as a "really unchristian method" that had already been tried without success. The law should not discriminate unfairly against women in this regard, and for the church to support this would be to "fight for purity upon an un-

85. Cairns, *Army and Religion*, 171.

86. Cairns, *Army and Religion*, 171–73.

87. Cairns, *Army and Religion*, 174–80.

sound basis." Finally, the report declared that the church must adopt a more positive approach to the whole question of sexuality. "But if the Christian Church is to expect virtue it must do something more than denounce vice and be scandalized at sinners. It must inspire the world with an ideal of the nobility and sacredness of married life in all its range, physical, mental, and spiritual. It must exalt true love and pure passion to that position which is theirs of right, in the great sacrament of human life."[88]

In terms of the broader agenda, the report emphasized the social mission of the churches, who, in light of the law of love and the ideal of the kingdom of God, were bound to work for the transformation of the existing social order, which was based on self-interest and the pursuit of wealth.[89] The churches must prove by deeds their belief in the value of human personality, and they must do so, not with the aim of winning members, but out of the same spontaneous love shown by Jesus.[90] The committee agreed with the estimate that 29 percent of the population still lived "beneath the line of wages on which a physically wholesome life is possible," and stated that as the "socially disinherited" had served the nation in the war, the churches owed them a debt of spiritual honor.[91] The task was so huge that cooperation was vital, and it was suggested that the time had come to move from the "undenominational" approach to cooperation, to the "interdenominational" one.[92] The undenominational approach had been applied at Edinburgh 1910, when the churches focused on the things that they agreed on, while accepting that they would ignore their differences. It was built on the principle that what united the churches were "the only matters of primary importance, the distinctive tenets being secondary."[93] The report pointed out the limitations of such an approach, comparing it to a friendship in which the friends kept silence on the matters on which they feel deeply. Such a position was unsatisfactory. Interdenominational-ism was founded on a very different basis:

---

88. Cairns, *Army and Religion*, 180.

89. Cairns, *Army and Religion*, 180–89.

90. Cairns, *Army and Religion*, 180.

91. Cairns, *Army and Religion*, 181–82. Cairns does not attribute this precise statistic to any particular research. The committee may have made the estimation based on Army Medical Department Returns, in which the men were described in terms of class and economic status; or the estimation may have been based on statistics from the Royal Commission on the Poor Laws and Relief of Distress, which operated between 1905 and 1909.

92. Cairns, *Army and Religion*, 183–89.

93. Cairns, *Army and Religion*, 183.

> Each of the denominations has in it something vital and pecu-
> liar to itself which it cannot wholly abandon without denying
> its history and compromising something peculiar to its life, and
> that, therefore, it should not be asked to abnegate its peculiar
> standpoint as an initial condition of cooperation. It is rather
> invited to make its own contribution to the common service of
> the Kingdom of God. What that contribution may ultimately be
> is left to the future to determine. Meantime, freedom of expres-
> sion is accorded to all parties assenting to the concordat, and
> labouring together for Christ's Kingdom.[94]

The committee recognized that this was a more risky option, but considered it bolder and potentially richer. It also removed an obstacle to cooperation in that no one had to sacrifice any principle or feel disloyal to past traditions or antecedents in the faith. The greatest difficulty was felt to be on the practical level of organization, but the committee pointed to the missionary movement, the Young Men's and Women's Christian Associa-tions, and the Student Christian Movement, as examples of the success of this approach. The churches had to move forward on the lines of social Christianity; the interdenominational principle must be the basis for such an enterprise, and the YMCA could provide them with a platform for an-nouncing such a program. Under its auspices the churches had cooperated during the war, and this was an opportunity to make such cooperation per-manent. The association already had plans to develop institutes throughout the country, based on the huts in the camps. Rather than seeing this as a threat, the churches should welcome the initiative, as one in which they and the association might share their experiences and skills. They were reminded that both belonged together. Referring to the association the report declared, "Its function is to be that of an exploring, pioneering body moving on in advance of the main body of the Church army, while working in close touch with it."[95] There were two main tasks ahead, evangelism and education. There was widespread misunderstanding about Christianity because the churches had failed in two major ways. They had used un-suitable methods of teaching and there had been a "coldness in our own life," both of which might be remedied. "The primary necessity is that the Church throughout all the range of its activities should learn itself to seek first the noblest of all ideals, 'the Kingdom of God,' and draw to itself as a spiritual home all generous, humble, and earnest hearts. Christian witness is cumulative. If the life of the community be warm, consistent, heroic, and

94. Cairns, *Army and Religion*. 183.
95. Cairns, *Army and Religion*, 188.

full of the spirit of prayer and brotherhood, the task of the evangelist is immeasurably simplified."[96]

The report urged that evangelism must be rooted firmly in teaching about the kingdom, so that when people are confronted by the claims of Christ, they knew what Christ really stood for. The churches must also take into account points of contact with the men, the first of these points of contact being the universal belief in God. Second was the widespread belief that the good life is impracticable, and third was the deepening sense of the prevailing moral injustice in society.[97] The gospel of the kingdom of God and that of personal salvation must work in sympathy with each other, and the report put forward the example of the SCM as an organization that had already achieved this.[98]

The war had revealed a capacity for service and suffering which the church must now enlist in the service of the kingdom. In his reflection on the huge challenge which that presented, Cairns, for the first and only time in the report, adopted the first person singular: "How can this be? Would that I had no uncertain answer to utter! I fling these lines out to comrades in the Lord that we may provoke one another to find the answer."[99]

The closing section of the report called for a new and greater vision of God.[100] The nations were planning reconstruction, but it must be undergirded by a rebirth of the spiritual life essential for moral regeneration. The churches needed to grasp the opportunity that the crisis of war had offered by harnessing the love and optimism of Jesus, which was based on his idea of God. They needed to return to Christ, in the sense of reexamining his teaching about God, humankind and the future. Modern Christianity, as a whole, did not expect great spiritual victories, because it differed from the belief of Christ and the first apostles in that it thinks evil is stronger and God weaker, and therefore lacked hope. Its lack of the spirit of love and brotherhood had driven the men from the church, and its faith had been too weak to face up to the central problems of the day, based as it was on too narrow a view of God. The revival of faith must begin in the church, and the call to faith was based on the belief that "God Almighty is incomparably mightier, nearer, more loving and ready to help than any human being, save Jesus Christ, has ever known."[101]

96. Cairns, *Army and Religion*, 190.

97. Cairns, *Army and Religion*, 191–94.

98. Cairns, *Army and Religion*, 195.

99. Cairns, *Army and Religion*, 197.

100. Cairns, *Army and Religion*, 201–8.

101. Cairns, *Army and Religion*, 207.

Sin and tragedy, we are sure, have no rights in His world, and they are here not to be endured but to be cast out and destroyed. When we come out as disciples into the presence of Christ, prepared to take Him as more modern than any teacher of to-day, we enter, therefore, a world of new discovery of God and Man immeasurably more wonderful and beautiful than we have ever known. If we believe that He is here disclosing to us the very roots of the universe and the deepest nature of the men and women around us, the impression that so easily besets us when we think of past failure and of the wreck of these last years will melt and vanish. Depression in His presence is impossible. The future is lit up with promise. In the wreck of the old order we divine the beginning of the new.[102]

In spite of the hopeful note of the report, its production had taken a lot out of Cairns. His daughter, Alison, remembered the day it was finished, when she walked with her father to the Post Office in Edinburgh, Cairns carrying the manuscript in a parcel. She recorded in her diary, "It seems a weight off his chest."[103]

Criticism of the Army and Religion Report

In his memoir of Cairns, Donald Baillie described the report as having "great influence and importance."[104] Baillie regarded it as a "classic of its kind, as a document of religious history." While the report described its committee as practically unanimous as to the facts and their main causes, and the broad outlines of the solution, there was evidence of serious division at one point. This was revealed in correspondence between Cairns and committee member T. H. Hodgkin, who was secretary of the Friends' Foreign Missionary Society. It would seem that there was an element on the committee which had little hope that the churches could contribute to a new social order, and which felt that it would be better to rely on the labor movement. Cairns referred to a "complainers' group" and their "futile and acrimonious grousing." In an untypical tirade, he accused them of aimlessness and having no practical suggestions; of having no real understanding of the church; and of being devoid of firsthand experience and knowledge. He felt that he had plenty of experience on which to draw, based on his own, his family's and his friends' work within the church. Contradicting his previous comment, he

102. Cairns, *Army and Religion*, 208.
103. Irvine, *Alison Cairns*, 52.
104. In Cairns, *Autobiography*, 20–21.

liked their practical suggestion of getting in touch with alienated labor folk, but he felt that this must go hand in hand with maintaining a church connection. Explaining his position, he wrote: "To me the Church is a big unwieldy organism, always slow to move, and often failing, and sometimes filling one almost with despair, and yet steadily doing an enormous amount of good, 'Struggling on towards heaven against storm and wind and time' and with all its failings sustaining the whole future of the human race."[105]

Historically they owed the church everything and it was indispensable in winning the world for Christ—they needed the "loyalty and love of the great slow-moving blundering irritating organism." The subject of the letter was of such importance to Cairns that he felt he had to speak out, but its uncharacteristically polemical and censorious nature is surely the reason why he requested Hodgkin not to circulate it.

In more recent times there have been comments on and criticisms of the report. Michael Snape has suggested that while the inspiration of the report was to give the churches information about the army's attitude to religion, and to communicate the gospel effectively to the troops, and while it purported to be an objective investigation, the nub of it was a manifesto for far-reaching change in the postwar churches. It was, he insisted, "a manifesto that included the reinterpretation of Christian doctrine, the 'Christianizing' of the social order, the democratization of church government and an emphatic commitment to the cause of international peace."[106]

Snape concludes that the report was deeply flawed in that the co-conveners were "hand-in-glove"; that Cairns had admired Talbot since the publication of Lux Mundi in 1889 and was a close friend of his son Neville, a "fellow luminary" of the Student Christian Movement. Snape suggests that Cairns had been given carte blanche to recruit members to the committee. Out of a committee of around thirty members, there was, to be sure, only a small number of his friends, but they were people of general high standing in terms of experience and intellectual capacity, such as Oldham, Tatlow, and Oman. In spite of Talbot having lost his younger son in the war, Cairns was able to say that it was the bishop's wisdom and courage that pulled them through the process of getting the report out.[107]

Callum Brown points out that the call for reconstruction on a social gospel basis was received coolly by the churches; a fact he attributes to the post war conservative leadership of John White and Alexander Martin—of

105. Cairns to Hodgkin, 5 July 1917, Box 2/1 Cairns Papers. Cairns made a similar defence of the church in the Army Report, 145.

106. Snape, Back Parts of War, 87.

107. Cairns to Mott, 30 November 1918, Mott Papers, RG 45, 13/244, Yale.

the Church of Scotland and United Free Church respectively. As principal of New College, Martin had actually served on the report committee. Brown explains that social and economic unrest, especially as manifested in Glasgow during the war years, and in the rent strikes there, and the rise of Bolshevism in Russia, had resulted in hostility to any program that seemed to contain socialist ideas.[108] However, lack of progress on the social front may have been due as much to depleted emotional and financial resources following such a period of sustained violence, rather than outright rejection of its social agenda, or to the fact that the energies of the two major churches went into the drive for union throughout the 1920s, culminating in the reunion of the Church of Scotland and the United Free Church in 1929. The report had emphasized the need for Christian unity in the face of so much social need, so in this respect it could be said to have contributed to a satisfactory outcome. It had also anticipated the likelihood of a negative reception by the churches:

> Is it possible in such a time of social tension as assuredly lies before us courageously to teach the Christian view of society, without rending into fragments the unity of the Church? That it will be difficult is certain, and the temptation will always be to rule such themes out of court or to say as little about them as possible. The inevitable effect of that will be to spread the impression that Christianity has no social Gospel at all, and to leave thinking men and women without help from the Church in problems which are likely more and more to engross their thoughts.[109]

Others, including Callum Brown, questioned the methodology of the report.[110] The historian Peter Howson reminds us that "this apparently impressive study" was based on the responses of "only some three hundred people." He points out that the report was based on only one of a number of inquiries, referring to those of the Church of Scotland and the United Free Church, and contrasting it with the Church of Scotland's less pessimistic report.[111] The *Army and Religion Report* itself owns its gratitude to these inquiries and refers to its inclusion of their findings in its own inquiry. Regarding the report's methodology, far more than three hundred views were collected. Three hundred people volunteered to help collect the evidence, but they produced memoranda based on the replies of the many contacts

108. Brown, *Religion and Society*, 140.
109. Cairns, *Army and Religion*, 157.
110. Cairns, *Army and Religion*, 139.
111. Howson, *Muddling Through*, 96.

they made.[112] Michael Snape, too, challenges Cairns's methodology and his conclusion that about four-fifths of the men had no vital relationship with the churches. He records that Cairns was only able to reach such a conclusion after he had "shrugged off" the evidence of the War Roll, dismissing it as the product of "the stress of abnormal conditions." Snape goes on to say that the origins and content of the report show how much its conclusions were predetermined by Cairns, citing a letter from E. C. Carter of the YMCA to Oliver McCowen about Cairns's anxiety over the loss of so many young men from the churches. Apparently urging McCowen to "indulge" Cairns because of his role in recruiting so many volunteers for the association, Carter explained his position: "Professor Cairns has had heavily laid upon him the conviction that the YMCA ought to make a very serious and searching enquiry with reference to the attitude of the men in the armies, to Christ and to the Christian Church. . . . He desires to mass the evidence from responsible sources, in order to enable the YMCA to issue a masterly book which shall arrest the thought of the nation, and lay the lines for the work and thinking of the Church, for the next twenty years."[113]

Given this mass of contradictory evidence, Snape suggests, the committee was too disposed to take a pessimistic view of British society and soldiers in particular; that they "were not slow to expand upon depressing aspects of the soldier's religion and moral condition."[114] While it was true that the report dealt at some length with problems relating to the abuse of alcohol and sex, its approach was not narrowly moralizing, and took into consideration a number of social factors, like low wages and poor housing, as aggravating circumstances. It also referred to such activity as "blots on a humanity mainly noble."[115] Rather than dwelling on the negative, the report found that its investigations demonstrated "that there is in vast numbers of men an unimagined capacity for sheer self-forgetfulness and self-dedication to a great cause," and regretted that religion had not been able to appeal to the heroic in man.[116] The report's positive attitude to the men was seen in its discovery that those who worked most closely with the armies found that their judgment of human nature rose greatly as a consequence. Its view of the men was expressed most poignantly in the following two excerpts: first, "We know now . . . what we ought to have

112. Cairns, *Autobiography*, 21, and *Army and Religion*, 2.

113. Snape, *Back Parts of War*, cites YMCA, K27YMCA War Work No. 14. France. E. C. Carter to O. McCowen, 24 January 1917.

114. Snape, *God and the British Soldier*, 39, 57.

115. Cairns, *Army and Relgion*, 171.

116. Cairns, *Army and Religion*, 196.

known long ago, that immeasurable moral forces are lying in the youth of our country, awaiting only the summons to life and power."[117] Second, "As a nation we are far richer in manhood than we knew. But we cannot stop there. Why did we underestimate them? We could not have underestimated them if we truly loved them."[118]

Perhaps a more telling response to Snape's criticism of the report is a comment on it in the memoirs of Barclay Baron, an Anglican layman and Oxford graduate who was a key figure in social work among young people before the war, and a leading figure in Toc H after it. When, in the 1960s he reminisced on his time in France and his meeting with Cairns, he wrote: "This was sober, painstaking work by a very wise man and his general conclusions were, I think, too sombre for the vague optimists. We greatly enjoyed his company at our headquarters as he sat talking gravely, humbly, humorously at the supper table; he was a man to be revered, listened to and loved."[119]

In the late 1930s, J. A. Robertson, professor of New Testament at the United Free Church College in Aberdeen, observed of the report that "it evoked a good deal of criticism for its somewhat pessimistic view, but on the whole it held its own among those best qualified to judge."[120]

Another wartime publication, based on a completely different methodology, made many similar points to the report. *God and the Soldier*, by Norman Maclean and John Robert Paterson Sclater, was based on a series of lectures given weekly to chaplains in one of the base camps in France. The lectures were intended to inspire discussion of the problems confronting the soldiers, and were led by Maclean and Sclater. In a chapter entitled "The Unending War," they linked selfishness and lack of Christian love to the causes of the war, and also to social problems at home, claiming that it was more dangerous to be a child in the slums of London or Glasgow than to be a soldier in the trenches in Flanders.[121] In another chapter on "The Church," they described criticisms from all classes and ranks of soldiers about the ineffectiveness of the churches in dealing with social inequalities. The lecture also spoke of denominationalism as having had its day, and urged the churches to accept the help of the interdenominational YMCA. Blaming a

117. Cairns, *Army and Religion*, 155.

118. Cairns, *Army and Religion*, 205.

119. Snape, *Back Parts of War*, 130.

120. Robertson, tribute to Cairns, *Aberdeen University Review* 25 (1937–38) 127.

121. Maclean and Sclater, *God and the Soldier*, 72.

lack of spirituality for their failure to exert social power, the lecture urged the churches to unity to give greater strength for the work ahead.[122]

Just one month after the war ended, Cairns published *The Reasonableness of the Christian Faith*, dedicated to his sister Jessie, perhaps in gratitude for her role in parenting Alison and David while he was absent from home. Since delivering the lectures in Cambridge, he had used them with soldier audiences in the base camps at Rouen and Le Havre. In a newly added epilogue, he reiterated the opinion that the war had brought home to all the awful reality of sin, and that the churches, with their lack of faith, had offered no solution to the ancient riddle of the presence of evil in the world. It was time to recover the basic principles of the Christian revelation, which, for him, included the following concepts: God as the Universal Father, Creator of all things, and the Almighty Sovereign of the world; human freedom as the corollary of God's self-limitation; divine omnipotence exercised through the education of experience within a moral order; the role of vicarious suffering; the kingdom of God as the working out of God's purposes; and faith in immortality.[123]

Cairns produced another pamphlet in the same year. *Christianity and Macht-Politik* (Power Politics), was published in New York, with its main focus on the need for a way ahead for international relations that did not rest on the authority of force. The war had brought to the fore issues that concerned the whole future of the human race.[124] In his views on the "sordid and even odious" nature of international politics, Cairns admitted the influence of Sir Edward Grey, a liberal politician and former foreign secretary.[125] Cairns concluded that war was becoming a "moral anachronism" because scientific knowledge had made the potential for destruction too great and now threatened human survival. The world was growing into an economic whole, which, combined with the opportunities for mass conscription and the forming of huge alliances, presented the potential for dragging many countries into conflict.[126]

He repeated his view that it was not good enough to say that war was inevitable because of human weakness, and declared that the peace of the world had to be founded on the ideas of the sacredness of personality and life as a trust from Almighty God. For Cairns, those who exercised power

122. Maclean and Sclater, *God and the Soldier*, 223–66.

123. Cairns, *Reasonableness*, 202–20.

124. Cairns, *Christianity and Macht-Politik*, 1–2.

125. Cairns, *Reasonableness*, 201–11, cites Gilbert Murray, *Foreign Policy of Sir Edward Grey 1906–15* (Oxford, 1915).

126. Cairns, *Christianity and Match-Politik*, 3–4.

politics denied the existence of an absolute moral law in the sphere of international relationships. The League of Nations recognized a humanity above
the nations, and the churches must support it. Rejecting the way of violence,
the churches must nurture the freedom to follow the moral law—the law of
God.[127] In such a world men's energies would turn "to the war with the dark
powers of disease and death and ignorance and vice and poverty, and all the
tragic element in human life, and to the winning of all the nations into the
ever-growing, ever-coming Kingdom of God."[128]

The passion of this pamphlet echoed the feeling and content of *An
Answer to Bernhardi*. Its eloquence was marred, however, by the inclusion
of the following racist comment: "Moreover the economic and political
conquest of well-nigh the whole earth by the Western races has brought
into their military reserves great numbers of war-like peoples at a lower
stage of culture."[129]

Cairns followed by suggesting that these peoples would be conscripted
and add new "abominations." In the light of the past four years of conflict,
in which the Western powers had developed their weapons and tactics
to achieve ever greater levels of destruction, it is difficult to begin to understand such a comment. In spite of this, the bulk of Cairns's published
work during the war period set out a vision for a future in which all nations
would strive to set aside national interests and to seek the common good in
a peaceful future for humankind.

For his wartime work Cairns was awarded an OBE. Possibly because
he contrasted his achievements with the far greater sacrifice of the men,
his attitude to this was one of humorous irreverence, displayed in a letter
to his friend Glover on the occasion of Glover's receipt of a similar distinction: "I imagine you will feel as I did when they gave me the Royal distinction of Order Before Everything, that something especially irrelevant had
befallen me."[130]

Beyond the War

When Cairns had gone to France, the family home in Hamilton Place, Aberdeen, was sublet, and Alison and David had gone to live with his sister,
their Aunt Jessie, at 20 Braidburn Crescent in Edinburgh. The extended

127. Cairns, *Christianity and Match-Politik*, 6–19.

128. Cairns, *Christianity and Match-Politik*, 22.

129. Cairns, *Christianity and Match-Politik*, 4.

130. Cairns to Glover, 2 June 1921, Glover Papers 6/3/27, St. John's Library,
Cambridge.

family on both sides provided them with care and affection in their father's absence. William, Cairns's younger brother, was minister of Davidson Church in Eyre Place in Edinburgh. Alison and David spent Sundays in the manse at Howard Place with William and his wife, Christina, their much-loved Aunt Kirsty.[131] Holidays were spent with their mother's family in Lochton, near Coldstream, in the home of her sister Barbara and her husband, John Aitchison; times later described in loving detail in a memoir by David.[132] In Edinburgh, David attended Merchiston Castle School and Alison went to St. George's, although she moved to a Quaker boarding school—the Mount—in York, in September 1918. After the war, Cairns returned to Aberdeen to live in lodgings at 51 Carlton Place, and Alison joined him there in 1920, while she waited to go to Girton College, Cambridge, in the autumn of 1921. Much of her time was taken up filing her father's papers.[133] Around this time Cairns suffered the loss of his brother John, who had died unmarried at the age of sixty-five. Cairns described his reaction to John's death in a letter to his close friend Neville Talbot: "Since I last wrote I have been through the shadows again, and am still in the skirts of the cloud. My dear older brother has gone on ahead, and with him a great wealth of truth and strength and kindness."[134]

After Alison's graduation in 1924, she and her father shared a house he had bought at 139 Desswood Place, not far from their previous home in Hamilton Place, but smaller and according to Alison a "rather horrid little house" that was damp and chilly with a "skimpy front garden."[135] Based there for the remainder of his time in Aberdeen, Cairns continued to lecture and write, and to travel to Student Christian Movement meetings in Britain, Europe and America. In this period he contributed a chapter to *Religion and Life: The Foundations of Personal Religion*, six sermons delivered first to students at Oxford, and then published in the hope of reaching a wider audience. The authors, mainly Anglican clergy, included two friends who had worked on the Army report, W. H. Frere of Mirfield and Neville Talbot, by this time bishop of Pretoria in South Africa, and also William Ralph Inge, dean of St. Paul's Cathedral. The one lay author was William Brown, psychologist and reader in mental philosophy at Oxford, who had served

131. Irvine, *Alison Cairns*, 19–20.

132. Cairns, "Memories of Lochton and Foulden."

133. Alison to her brother David, 26 January 1921, Cairns Papers Acc. 6786/3, National Library of Scotland archive.

134. Cairns to Neville Talbot, 22 July 1922, Box 2/6 Cairns Papers.

135. Irvine, *Alison Cairns*, 34.

as a neurologist to the Fourth Army in France.[136] The lectures were an attempt by the writers to make clear some of the basic Christian teachings, and to provide a sure foundation on which a personal faith could be built. The men worked closely together to make sure that their lectures built on one another to form a coherent and comprehensive picture of the basic principles of Christianity. Cairns raised again the question that dominated his personal theological quest—the riddle of the world: "Why should God have made so sacred the things of human life, and then, having made so divine a thing, have put it at the mercy of the great brute forces of the world?"[137]

The answer involved deciding what kind of God had been revealed by Christ, and whether or not this was a God in whom they could place their trust. Was it possible to have a relationship with God, in which they could cast all their cares on him? Jesus had exhibited such faith. Cairns believed that the world was a training ground for developing the divine heredity: the divine spark of the Creator in humankind. Declaring that a man's idea of God determined what kind of character he would develop, he urged them to follow Jesus' example of complete trust in God as loving Father of all. Looking outwards and toward the future, Cairns concluded that Europe and humanity needed such faith in the living God if the selfishness and fear that dominated international relations were to be abolished.[138]

Cairns's final publication of this period was his biography of family friend Alexander Robertson MacEwen. The book took nine years to bring to completion and among the many acknowledgments of help was one for Alison's help in compiling the index. Cairns's brother William had also helped with revision of the proofs, as he had done with the *Army and Religion* report. The biography lacked the passion and eloquence of Cairns's apologetic works, but provides an important account of the struggle toward church unity, as this was an area in which MacEwen had had a passionate interest. J. A. Robertson of Aberdeen described it as "a work of piety and devotion to a beloved memory."[139] The hectic nature of Cairns's working life at this period was revealed in a letter to Neville Talbot. Writing to Talbot he confessed that he had been taken up with the business of the end of a session, and that in a period of thirty-five days he had given twenty-six lectures, addresses, and sermons to very varied audiences.[140] Throughout

136. Burt, (1952) Dr. William Brown (obituary), *British Journal of Psychology*, Statistical section 5, 137–38.

137. Cairns, "The Father," in Irge and Cairns, *Religion and Life*, 35.

138. Cairns, "The Father," 27–41.

139. Robertson, *Aberdeen University Review* 25 (1937–38) 127.

140. Cairns to Neville Talbot, 2 May 1923, Box 2/6 Cairns Papers.

the war Cairns had kept up his contact with the Student Christian Movement, attending conferences at Swanwick and elsewhere, and in 1921, with C. W. G. Taylor, he represented the Scottish universities and colleges in the largest ever British SCM conference in Glasgow. Thirty-five nations were represented at the conference, which took for its theme "Christ and Human Need," and focused on international and missionary questions, following the war and its lessons. Charles E. Raven was in attendance and gave his impressions of the conference.[141] He described how the students had laid in front of them the failings of the churches, and how they were encouraged to acknowledge their own responsibility in the matter, their failure to live out in practice the Christian ideal. With the call to repentance came the call to courage for the adventure of following Christ in the difficulties that lay ahead. Those who had faced the summons to sacrifice in war were invited to respond to the needs of the world. One of the speakers, Lord Grey, warned that along with external change had to go a change of heart.

> We had over and over again the picture of Christ as the hope of the world; Christ who could alone save India from racial hatred and strife: Christ in whom China would find the vindication for her ancient ethic, and redemption from opium and morphia, from materialism and greed: Christ in Whose service Africa and the backward peoples shall gain their perfect freedom: Christ Whose Spirit can accomplish the renewal and the perfecting of mankind: Christ in Whom for all the nations is revealed the Universality of God.[142]

The power to achieve all this rested in hearts and lives changed on the basis of personal faith in God through Christ. The task of evangelizing the world still remained, but the Christian nations could not be entrusted with it unless there was a radical return to faith in the living God.

Towards the end of 1922 Cairns was nominated moderator of the United Free Church, taking up the position in May 1923. On reading about the nomination in the *Scotsman* newspaper, T. M. Taylor of Edinburgh wrote to Cairns, saying that he was glad that the church as a whole has "recognized what some of its younger members have known for years, and has entrusted its leadership to the one man in all Scotland who is best fitted for the task. There will be many that I know, not only in our own land, but throughout the world, who will hail this news with delight though they may never have the boldness to write and tell you of it."[143]

141. Raven, "Impression of the Conference," xiii–xix.
142. Raven, "Impression of the Conference," xix.
143. T. M. Taylor to Cairns, 22 November 1922, Box 3/1 Cairns Papers.

The people of Burnmouth and Ayton, Cairns's first charges, presented him with his moderatorial robes,[144] and on the occasion of his installation, a letter arrived from Talbot, the bishop of Winchester, congratulating Cairns and declaring, "You are one of the best gifts of God at this time to the Christianity of these islands." He continued his praise saying that Cairns inspired the tone and influence of the counsels of the church, and asked for two copies of the moderatorial address as one would be sent to Pretoria.[145] With the distinction of the moderatorship, Cairns was also unanimously elected to the presidency of the United Free Church College in Aberdeen.[146] Just before embarking on his moderatorial year, Cairns went to America, where he gave the Deems Lectures in New York University and Lafayette College, published years later as *The Riddle of the World*. On his return, Alison, now aged twenty-one, became the "Moderator's Lady," accompanying her father as he carried out his duties.[147]

The moderatorial address, of which Talbot had spoken, was delivered in May 1923, and entitled "God the Hope of the World." With echoes of the *Army and Religion* report in his frequent mentions of the war, he described the world as a society so complex that war now meant suicide, and declared the need for a new world order based on association and cooperation rather than on self-interest and competition, and of the need for the church to lead the way. Cairns began with an appreciation of the "Church of our fathers and a long hereditary connection with that Evangelical tradition for which it stands," and above all the example of his father, which had drawn him into the ministry. He saw two urgent questions facing the church: How was it to solve its problems at home? What could it do to help forward the cause of God at a critical time in human history? These two questions had to be answered before the church tackled the task of world mission. Referring frequently to the experience of the war and what it had revealed about the church, he suggested three ways forward. First, he turned to the Home Mission, and to the fact that there were many, especially men, outside the fellowship of the church. Cairns attributed this more to misbelief than unbelief, and to the fact that people did not even know enough to ask the right questions about religion. He believed that people were indifferent to a defective picture of God, and that they criticized Christianity based on knowledge of the faith that was thirty to forty years out of date. There was

144. Alison to her father, 6 March 1923, Cairns Papers Acc. 6786/3, N.L.S. archive.

145. E. Talbot to Cairns, 24 May 1923, Box 3/6 Cairns Papers.

146. George Adam Smith to Cairns, 24 May 1923 sent congratulations on the appointment, Box 3/6 Cairns Papers.

147. Irvine, *Alison Cairns*, 38.

a need for conviction among Christians, and an ability to present a reasoned truth—the living faith of the educated Christianity of the day.[148] His
second theme concerned youth and the problem of Christian education,
which seemed to end with adolescence. Those who were at present in the
Sunday schools and day schools would be the ones making the important
decisions in the years ahead, and a problem with Christian education had
been recognized. They could not afford to wait years for the union of the
churches, but should go ahead and form a Christian Council, drawn from
the various denominations, to work for the Christian good of Scotland. The
council's job would be to get a clear picture of the situation, and suggest
ideas for improvement.[149]

The third and deepest problem facing the church was the need for an
enriching of the moral and spiritual life.[150] Early in his address Cairns had
quoted Hegel in his *Philosophy of Religion*, "A nation which has a false or bad
conception of God, has also a bad State, bad government and bad laws."[151]
Having stated that at the root of all society's problems was unbelief or misbelief—a defective view of Christianity, he declared that the solution was to
change Christendom's thought of God, and to nurture a real and living faith
in the Fatherhood of God and in the Brotherhood of Man that Jesus had
revealed. Only this would rid the world of the fear and self-interest among
the nations. God's spirit was at work in the world, empowering people to
become like Christ, and the New Testament offered victory in the world of
time as well as in eternity. Christians themselves had been infected by the
general loss of faith in society, so if the church was to meet the needs of the
world it needed to have more faith in God's power.

> As I read the Scriptures, the Spirit is given through Faith in
> the Truth. Every man who whole-heartedly receives the Truth
> receives the Spirit. The Truth, if I may use the expression, is
> electrically charged with the Spirit. The way, therefore, to such
> a moral change in the life of the peoples is to change Christen-
> dom's thought of God, to change its unbelief and misbelief into
> a real and living faith. Not otherwise is the way to a reawakening
> of the whole life of the Christian Church itself. We know how
> great is the need to-day for a rebirth of the life in the Church, if
> it is to be a true herald and prophet of God to the world in its
> hour of need. The Church can have that new life at any moment
> by reaching a truer thought of, and a deeper belief in God. There

148. Cairns, *God: The Hope of the World*, 5–10.
149. Cairns, *God: The Hope of the World*, 10–14.
150. Cairns, *God: The Hope of the World*, 14–23.
151. Cairns, *God: The Hope of the World*, 3.

is no other way. The root of all our weakness and failure is our unbelief and our misbelief in God.

Conclusion

For many years before the outbreak of the Great War, Cairns had been speaking out about the dangers of growing materialism and militarism. For him the churches had been infected with a materialism that had led to a weakening of faith and a loss of moral and spiritual power. The war provided an unprecedented opportunity to reflect on the state of the church, and attitudes to it, especially among the youth of the nation, and the inquiry documented a unique perspective on the church in the second decade of the twentieth century. The *Army and Religion* report revealed how out of touch the church was with many people, how it had failed to get across the message of the gospel, and pointed to its need to change. While still stressing the need for personal faith and morality, the report also focused attention on the social dimension of the gospel, particularly in regard to the search for peace. Cairns was a theologian who searched for practical ways to implement the Christian ideal of the kingdom of heaven on earth, finding such means first of all in the missionary movement, and later in the Student Christian Movement, the World Student Christian Federation, and the Young Men's Christian Association. These last three movements also gave him a platform for the dissemination of his own ideas, and he became a significant figure within them. There, he was supported and encouraged by like-minded people such as Mott and Oldham. Fundamental to all these connections was the church, which he continued to see as the main vehicle for delivery of the kingdom, with the movements in its vanguard. He was rewarded with the church's highest honor: his election as moderator. He continued to make and deepen his connections with other Christian denominations, especially the Church of England, and to carry on a number of significant lines of correspondence. He made an effort to persuade the churches of the importance of inter-denominationalism as a way of appreciating one another's differences and learning from them.

In his personal life he suffered the loss of his older brother John, but was able to share his grief with his close friend Neville Talbot. His extended family helped him care for Alison and David during his many and often prolonged periods away from Scotland. Thanks to their support, this was a highly productive time for Cairns, in terms of publication. The war had sharpened the social perspective of his theology, especially in relation to international peace, and it had made him aware of the great work of education that needed to be done among those who belonged to the church, so that they could understand and own its doctrines. Above all he believed that Christians needed an enlarged view of God, and a living faith in God's power to act in the world.

Chapter 6

Explorations in the Nature of the Kingdom, 1924–1946

IN HIS LAST TWO decades of life, Cairns remained very productive, continuing his involvement with the Student Christian Movement, the YMCA, and the World Student Christian Federation. He made a "world tour" in 1927, and published *The Faith That Rebels* in 1928 and *The Riddle of the World* in 1937, the year of his retirement from Aberdeen. He had played a large part in the religious and common life of the city, and according to Donald Baillie, was much esteemed there. He had continued to preach, and although he could not be described as an orator, he spoke "with a depth and grandeur of thought which made his preaching at its best unforgettable."[1] Throughout his career Cairns had received many academic distinctions, and in 1935, when the old United Free Church College united with the divinity faculty of the University of Aberdeen, following the reunion of the largest two Scottish Presbyterian churches in 1929, he was made professor of Christian dogmatics. Cairns had played his own part in the reunification of the churches in that he had served on the Union Committee for many years, getting to know many church leaders on both sides. He acknowledged that while the Presbyterian committee system in Scotland cost much in terms of time and money and labor, it was a useful way of enabling church members from all over Scotland to become acquainted with church business. Despite the "anomalies and defects" of the system, it worked reasonably well:

> The rotation rules put men on committees who have little or no sympathy with their aims. It gives obscurantist moderates the chance of administering missionary affairs, or rather of crabbing or neglecting them. And it puts undue influence in the

1. Baillie, in Cairns, *Autobiography*, 32.

hands of "committee wallahs." But on the whole it gets the work done, and is a very powerful agent in informing and unifying the Church. I am sure that it has given me a far fuller understanding of what a rich and wonderful thing the Christian Church is, ramifying, as it does deep into every department of human life, secular as well as sacred, international as well as national. It has body as well as soul. It is a real incarnation, however imperfect, of the Spirit of Christ.[2]

Travels to the Far East

Having confessed to Glover in 1915 that he wanted to live and work for the World Student Christian Federation, Cairns was not always able to accept the opportunities that presented themselves.[3] On behalf of the student movement he had traveled to speak at a number of conferences throughout Europe, but had had to turn down several requests from Mott to travel further afield. Baillie records that as early as 1913 Mott had asked Cairns to undertake a lecture tour of the Far East, but that Cairns had been advised against the trip on medical grounds.[4] While Mott had felt Cairns would bring a special "touch" to the cause, he wrote that, for the sake of Cairns's children, then nine and eleven, he had not "the heart or the conscience" to ask him to reconsider.[5] Again in 1915 Mott asked him to go to Japan; a request which Cairns seems to have turned down because he had increased duties at the college during the war.[6] Later, parental responsibility and his commitment to the college, which had been "knocked almost to pieces by the war," led him to turn down an opportunity to go to India with Glover.[7]

In his mid-sixties, he was finally able to respond positively to a request from Mott and the World Student Federation, and embarked on a tour which included a few weeks in America, and then about five months in China and Japan, which were coming increasingly under the influence of Western secularist philosophy. The instigators of the invitations came from the Chinese Student Movement through Rev. Dr. John Stewart of Moukden,

2. Cairns, *Autobiography*, 181.

3. Cairns to Glover, 12 April 1915, Glover Papers 5/2/13, St John's Library, Cambridge.

4. Baillie, in Cairns, *Autobiography*, 27.

5. Mott to Cairns, 14 December 1913, Box 3/4 Cairns Papers, Aberdeen.

6. Mott to Cairns, 25 March 1915, Yale and Cairns to Mott, 6 April 1915, Mott Papers, RG 45, 13/244, Yale.

7. Cairns to Glover 31 May 1915, Glover Papers 5/2/22.

and from the National Christian Council of Japan, through Anne Caroline Macdonald, who was involved in prison work there and was a former pupil of Cairns in Aberdeen.[8] Correspondence between Cairns and Mott revealed some initial hesitancy on Cairns's part due to the financial constraints involved in the continuing education of his family, with Alison in her last year at Girton College, Cambridge, and David in his first at Balliol College, Oxford. A generous offer of help from Mott made it possible for Cairns to accept, which he did with the proviso that he would go only if the church sent him, which meant that Mott had to approach the United Free College and its college and mission committees.[9] The demand for the proviso signified Cairns's commitment to strengthening the allegiance between the Student Christian Movement, the YMCA, and the churches, as had been advocated in the *Army and Religion* report.[10] The tour lasted from March to September in 1927, and Alison, who had by now had completed her time at Girton, was invited to go as his secretary. Her travel diary provides a vivid and sometimes humorous record of their many tourist activities, visiting palaces, temples, Buddhist shrines, and mosques. She also described some of his official engagements, visiting mission stations, and lecturing and preaching in universities.[11]

Around the turn of the century there had been around three thousand Protestant missionaries, sponsored by a large number of organizations and denominations, working in China and Japan.[12] The United Presbyterian Church had a long history of missionary engagement in the Far East. Reverend Dr. John Ross (1842–1915) had gone to Manchuria in 1872 and in conjunction with missionaries of the Irish Presbyterian Church, had developed mission posts there, offering educational and medical facilities as well as evangelization. Ross had had an open attitude to the culture and religion of China, believing that Christian teaching did not conflict with Confucianism, asserting the existence of a strand of monotheism in ancient Chinese religion, and denying that ancestral rites were idolatrous. In the Buddhist ascetics he perceived earnest seekers after truth.[13] In general, how-

8. Baillie, in Cairns, *Autobiography*, 28.

9. Cairns to Mott, 19 April 1925, Mott Papers.

10. *Army and Religion*, appendix 2, 209–12.

11. Alison Cairns, *Diary, 1927, of a Trip round the World*, Acc. 6826, Cairns Papers, National Library of Scotland. Other reports of the tour may be read in Baillie, in Cairns, *Autobiography*, 27–31, and Irvine, *Alison Cairns*, 44–48.

12. *Directory of Protestant Missionaries in China, Japan and Corea* [sic] *for the Year 1904*, accessed at http://images.library.yale.edu/divinitycontent/china/Directoryof-ProtestantMissionaries1904.pdf.

13. Mayfield Salisbury Parish Church, "Revd. Dr. John Ross." Ross returned to

ever, attitudes toward Christianity were hostile because of the intimidation of China by the Western powers in pursuit of their economic interests. From the 1830s the British government had placed pressure on China to open its ports to British trade, including trade in opium. When open warfare broke out over British policy between 1839 and 1842 and again between 1856 and 1860, China was forced to accept peace settlements that led to further concessions.[14] Popular Chinese resentment of the privileges conferred on foreign merchants, Chinese Christians, and foreign missionaries eventually expressed itself in the violence of the Boxer Rebellion of 1899–1900, when thousands of Chinese Christians and hundreds of foreign missionaries were massacred; this was followed by terrible reprisals by Western military forces on the Chinese population.[15] From then onward the nationalist movement grew in China, and with it the desire to rid the country of Western influences. This desire was inflamed by the allies' transference of Shantung from Germany to Japan at the Treaty of Versailles in 1919, and during the 1920s hostility to the West and to Christianity reached new heights.[16] A virulent propaganda campaign targeted Christianity and its perceived superstition and immoral practices. Ironically it was the infiltration of Western ideas that helped the Chinese nationalist cause. Using the findings of biblical criticism and the arguments of philosophers such as the atheist Bertrand Russell, the nationalists were able to paint Christianity as an anti-scientific movement that was a block to modernization and to the national aspiration for independence. Marxist-Leninist writings were influential in providing an ideological foundation for anti-imperialism, and many within the Chinese nationalist movement looked to Russia and the Bolshevik revolution for inspiration. When the World Student Christian Federation decided to hold its 1922 meeting in Shanghai, a group of students there reacted by forming the Anti-Christian Student Federation, whose opposition was based on the belief that Christianity and the church supported "tyrannical and cruel, unreasonable and inhumane" societies. This protest group later became known as the Great Federation of Anti-Religionists, when it developed into a movement to oppose all religions, including traditional indigenous religions such as Daoism, Buddhism, and Confucianism.[17]

Edinburgh from China in 1900 and became an elder at Mayfield United Free Church (today Mayfield Salisbury).

14. Brown, *Providence and Empire*, 143–46.

15. The horrific nature of this violent uprising is described in a paper by Pastor P. Kranz, "Chinese Martyrs," read to the Shanghai Missionary Association at their meeting in 1903.

16. Hall, "Western Question," 219–35.

17. Lutz, "Chinese Nationalism," 395–416.

This was the situation that Cairns encountered during his visit to China. Mott had made a Pacific Basin Tour in 1925–26, to take soundings for the International Missionary Conference for a world missions conference, to survey the work of the YMCA, and to meet national student groups and evangelize. He found the crisis facing the YMCA had intensified since his last visit in 1922, with student interest declining and sponsorship from businessmen dropping.[18] Cairns arrived during the latter stages of the Northern Expedition (1926–27), during which the nationalist party (the Kuomintang) was involved in armed struggle to unify the country. At one stage he wanted Alison to remain in the city of Moukden, rather than go with him into the outlying areas of Manchuria, but she was unwilling to let him go alone.[19] Another event made him nervous, but for a very different reason. Throughout his tour he sometimes lectured to non-Christian students. When asked about his apparent agitation before the first of these lectures, at which there were several hundred students, he replied that it was the first time in his life that he had addressed an entirely non-Christian audience, and that "the prospect of presenting the Gospel to those who did not know it was moving him deeply."[20] Drawing on his apologetics, he countered the two major Western influences of materialism and humanism with lectures on science and religion and on belief in a personal God. As far back as 1910, the report of Commission IV had recognized the influence of industrialization on China and Japan, and had expressed doubts that the traditional religions could survive in such a milieu. The report had concluded that it would be better for China and Japan to keep their traditional religions, rather than fall into materialism and atheism.[21] According to Baillie, it was in the Far East that Cairns came to realize that the future conflict for all religions would be with the forces of materialism and humanism, determining his subsequent apologetics. Realizing in a new way the long histories of these countries, Cairns now saw, that with the vast populations and growing sense of national identities in China and Japan, the Far East was likely to dominate world affairs in the future.[22]

18. Hopkins, *John R. Mott*, 647–49, cites Mott Papers, Yale (JRM III, 327–29, IV, 514–17).

19. Irvine, *Alison Cairns*, 46–47.

20. Cairns, *Autobiography*, 28–29.

21. Cairns, *Missionary Message*, 224–26.

22. Baillie, in Cairns, *Autobiography*, 30–31.

The Search for a New Christian Theology of the World

In the winter following their "world tour," Alison and her father lived at 139 Desswood Place, Aberdeen, and there, with her help, Cairns began to draw together his thoughts on a subject which he had been considering for about twenty years: that of miracles.[23] He dedicated the subsequent book, not to the memory of his wife, but simply "To H. W. C." as if she were still present. Baillie reported that Cairns had never lost the vivid sense that Helen was alive, "more alive than ever, and not far away; and he had never ceased to cherish the active expectation of a rich and happy reunion with her in the life beyond."[24] Cairns saw the subject of miracles as part of the greater argument about the Christian doctrine of the world.[25] He described how the idea of nature as a closed physical system had "an almost hypnotic influence on the great Victorians."[26] He had perceived the effects of the intellectual climate of the times as having weakened the idea of God, so that faith had become limited and the church's life one of "peculiar flatness and deadness."[27] He believed that except on the mission fields, which he saw as far removed from the great intellectual currents of the day, people had stopped expecting great things from God.[28] Referring to the phrase "Thy will be done" in the Lord's Prayer, he suggested that the church had turned what "was meant to be a battle-cry into a wailing litany," that signified its limited belief, and its conflation of the idea of the empirically inevitable with the will of God.[29] The pioneers of faith, going back to Jesus, had had a much richer conception of God, which allowed them to achieve great things, and Cairns's book was a call for a reappropriation of such faith. His argument, he declared, rested on the ground of Theism, which saw the universe as a purposive system directed toward the creation of free human souls who were made in God's image and capable of communion with God: "They are, like their Maker, free purposive agents, made to seek Truth, Beauty, and Goodness."[30] He doubted that autonomous human life could correspond with a determinist view of the world.

23. Irvine, *Alison Cairns*, 49.

24. Baillie, in Cairns, *Autobiography*, 25.

25. Cairns, *Faith That Rebels*, 100.

26. Cairns, *Faith That Rebels*, 136.

27. Cairns, *Faith That Rebels*, 157.

28. Cairns, *Faith That Rebels*, 157.

29. Cairns, *Faith That Rebels*, 195. Cairns credited this image of the "wailing litany" to Archbishop Temple.

30. Cairns, *Faith That Rebels*, 108.

Refusing to accept the Newtonian paradigm of the universe as a closed system of cause and effect, in which God was powerless to act on behalf of individuals, he developed his own theology of the world. Central to his thesis was the idea of the power of faith over the outward and inward world. The scientific view of the world had led many to abandon belief in miracles, and those who did believe in them saw little religious value in them.[31] Cairns saw that modern theology was unsure about, or denied the power of faith over the physical world, but, for him, this was not the message of Jesus in the gospels.[32] For Cairns, the subject touched on issues of profound importance, ideas about God and the world and about the nature of prayer, and it could not be ignored.[33] "No one would ever pray unless he thought it worthwhile to pray. To believe that it is worthwhile to pray, means faith in the ultimate nature of things."[34] He began by critiquing the traditionalist and modern approaches to miracle.

The traditionalist view, formed for the purpose of apologetics, saw the miracles of Jesus as narratives of historical events, signs of his divinity rather than part of his message. A distinction was drawn between God's answers to petitionary prayer and miracle. Both came through nature, but miracles involved interference with the course of nature. The early disciples also had the power to perform miracles, because of the exceptional circumstances of the time and the need to establish the church; but there now existed among the denominations, a variety of beliefs about whether or when miracles ceased to occur. While the traditionalist view had maintained faith in the historical character of the gospel events, and while it had allowed for the possibility of a living Providence and for the reality and power of prayer, for Cairns, it had major drawbacks. Most seriously, it failed to connect Jesus' faith in God with his actions. It failed to see that rather than performing miracles to prove that he had God's favor, Jesus performed them out of faith in God and out of love for humanity. He also disagreed with the ascription of the miracles to the divinity of Jesus, rather than to his perfect manhood, which allowed the Spirit to work through his faith. To those who said that the task of the early church was so difficult and dangerous that special power from God was needed, Cairns pointed to other extreme challenges that the church had faced.[35] He agreed with Harnack's view that miracles had ceased because the church had compromised with the world and its faith

31. Cairns, *Faith That Rebels*, 17–18.

32. Cairns, *Faith That Rebels*, 78.

33. Cairns, *Faith That Rebels*, 19.

34. Cairns, *Faith That Rebels*, 206.

35. Cairns, *Faith That Rebels*, 23–40.

had weakened, and he declared that history had shown that "wherever great spiritual personalities endowed with primitive energy of faith have arisen, faith has still been able to move mountains in the world of circumstances as well as in the world of the Spirit."[36]

The modernists, according to Cairns, in their attempt to find an accommodation with science, abandoned miracles as unhistorical.[37] They also dispensed with the idea that prayer could in any way affect the outward course of nature: God's interference was limited to the sphere of the inner life of the spirit, which was free. In other words, while God could not be expected to change the circumstances of the world, God could give spiritual help to individuals to help them triumph over adverse circumstances. Cairns expressed appreciation for what he termed the "Modernist compromise," in so far as it kept many people from abandoning Christianity altogether, but he objected to the rigid separation of the physical world, driven by natural forces, and the spiritual or psychical world, which might be swayed by the Divine Spirit. Pointing to new developments in psychology and psychiatry, which had raised the issue of the reciprocal relations of mind and body, he maintained that this undermined a "closed system" model of physical nature. In developing this argument, Cairns cited Professor James Denney of Glasgow (1856–1917), who had insisted that the natural and the spiritual were interpenetrative.

> Nature is not merely the stage of the moral life, but in some sense its soil. The moral life is not merely transacted in the face of nature: it is rooted in it, and grows up in profound and vital relations to it. The nature which is absolutely severed from the spiritual life—which does nothing but confront it in serene or scornful partiality—is not the real nature in which we live and move and have our being. It is one of the abstractions which physical science constructs for its own convenience . . . and our problem is not to acquiesce in the idea of the ethical neutrality of nature . . . but to see in it, in the last result, the manifestation, the organ, the ally of God. The universe is a system of things in which good can be planted, and in which it can bear fruit; it is also a system of things in which there is a ceaseless and unrelenting reaction against evil.[38]

36. Cairns, *Faith That Rebels*, 40.

37. Cairns, *Faith That Rebels*, 40–54.

38. Cairns, *Faith That Rebels*, 131–32. Cairns cites James Denney, *Christian Doctrine of Reconciliation*, 201–2.

Modernist theology had been formed in response to the authoritative status of scientific achievement, but Cairns argued that science itself was becoming less dogmatic in its statements, and more willing to recognize its own limitations. According to Cairns, the inductive method of working through classification and analysis in order to discover the laws of nature, had focused on similarities at the expense of difference. He suggested that the whole scientific process depended for its validity on the postulate of the uniformity of nature. However, this failed to take into account individuality and the difference it made in nature. Using a fishing metaphor, Cairns suggested that the inductive method was "a net to catch certain kinds of fish, and to let other fish through." He concluded, "Among these escaping fish that argument would compel us to put many of man's physical actions and achievements in the physical regions. They do not contravene the natural laws, they simply elude them."[39]

Another of Cairns's objections to modernist theories was that they read into the Bible rather than out of it, imposing their own ideas on the gospel narrative. By contrast, Cairns claimed that a proper theology should start with Scripture. Just as Jesus' teaching on love was vital for the understanding and treatment of humanity, so his teaching on faith must be seen as vital for understanding the nature and ways of God.[40] Cairns's aim was to discover the true interpretation of Jesus' teaching about the power of faith, therefore the core of the book was the exegetical section, focusing on the Synoptic Gospels. Quoting Ritschl's phrase, "The Old Testament is the lexicon of the New," Cairns emphasized the importance of the Jewish Scriptures in understanding the discourse used by Jesus.[41] He stated this hermeneutic principle, reassuring his readers that it was one used by all scholars. Among such were the English theologians William Sanday (1843–1920) and Francis Crawford Burkitt (1864–1935), and German theologians such as Johannes Weiss (1863–1914), and Albert Schweitzer (1875–1965). Cairns argued that Judaism did not accept sin and suffering as "part of the unchangeable nature of things": it believed that they were alien elements that had entered the world because of the unbelief and weakness of humanity, and would cease if people turned to God with their whole hearts. Regarding the Spirit of God, Judaism saw this as a Divine Potency, active in both nature and human life. The Spirit sustained all life and activity in the universe. Coexistent with these concepts was the idea of the future messianic kingdom, in which there would be deliverance from sin, but also from sorrow, disease and death.

39. Cairns, *Faith That Rebels*, 125.
40. Cairns, *Faith That Rebels*, 11.
41. Cairns, *Faith That Rebels*, 55–57.

The kingdom would come from God's grace, but could be prepared for by repentance, obedience and faith.[42]

Having described the Jewish world in which Jesus lived, Cairns proceeded to set out the view of the miracles taken by Jesus's contemporaries.[43] Cairns believed that the general view in the Synoptic Gospels was that the miracles were signs which showed that the kingdom had come "actually and potentially." Further, the miracles were manifestations of the kingdom— "fragments of heaven in the life of time."[44] However, Jesus had not given these signs simply for the sake of proving his divinity. The miracles were outcomes of his ideal or perfect faith in God and of his love for humanity. When Jesus saw need, compassion drove him to meet that need. Having complete faith in God as a loving Father, he was able to make God's will a reality in the world, because he was perfectly in tune with it. Responding to the rhetorical question, "Do we expect that the time is at hand when men will do all the things that Jesus did?" Cairns gave an emphatic "no," reasoning that there would always be too great a difference in the spirituality of individual Christians and that of Jesus, who had perfect faith. However, he continued, if what was meant by miracle was "something inexplicable in terms of physical nature I would say, 'Assuredly, yes.'"[45] In support of his argument that not everything could be explained in terms of physical law, he cited Lord Kelvin's opinion that from the point of view of science every free human action was a miracle in that it was inexplicable in scientific terms. The closing paragraph of the book sums up its message. "The malady of our time lies in its contracted thoughts of God. We think too narrowly and meanly of His Power, His Love, and His Freedom to help men. That is what the 'miracles' of Jesus and His teaching about Faith mean. That God is more near, more real and mighty, more full of love, and more ready to help every one of us than any one of us realizes, that is their undying message."[46]

In his introduction to the book, Cairns confessed that his work was incomplete, but he hoped it would encourage further thinking among biblical scholars and theologians. The book was regarded highly by the Student Christian Movement and received the kind of welcome that encouraged them to reissue it in the Torch Library Series, which was reserved for its outstanding publications. In this fifth edition, the publishers included, after the text, positive critical reviews from the *Guardian*, the *Times Literary*

42. Cairns, *Faith That Rebels*, 66–71.
43. Cairns, *Faith That Rebels*, 72–98.
44. Cairns, *Faith That Rebels*, 73.
45. Cairns, *Faith That Rebels*, 156.
46. Cairns, *Faith That Rebels*, 246.

Supplement, and the *Friend*. which seemed to suggest that Cairns had been successful in renewing the debate. The *Guardian* declared, "At last we have a book on miracles which really moves the problem out of the stalemate into which it had fallen. . . . This is a book of first-rate apologetic importance and value, which may mark a step forward in the treatment of this ancient issue. The tone of the discussion is candid, stimulating, reverent, and both thoughtful and thought-provoking."[47]

According to Donald Baillie, this book set out most clearly Cairns's distinctive theology and was the one which brought him most fame.[48] Professor Macintosh wrote to express his thanks because this "deeply Christian and intellectually most quickering book" had strengthened his faith.[49] On the other hand, there was a more ambivalent response by Charles Raven, Regius Professor of Divinity at Cambridge from 1932, who admired Cairns's "clear statement of the rival positions," but suggested that he had failed to do justice to the modernists by ignoring "their real concern for a satisfactory concept of God."[50] On a more positive note, Raven commented that Cairns had produced a "striking book," and had done well to insist that "it is as perfect man and by the quality of His life of prayer and faith that Jesus performed His works of power" but he felt that Cairns had weakened his argument by "an uncritical acceptance of all miracles on the ground that Jesus is unique and could do anything and everything."[51] Cairns refuted this criticism in his preface to the fifth edition of the book, but at the same time he objected to "the exclusion of any really significant sign on the sole ground that it is too remarkable to be credible."

Raven also criticized what he saw as the book's identification of evil with suffering, in that for him it did not get to the heart of the problem. Cairns had responded to the idea of nature as a neutral sphere (as held by Carlyle), or as an alien cosmic order (as described by Mill, Huxley and Russell), seeing it rather as a moral arena taking on the character of its creator, and one that was decisively on the side of the ideals of the kingdom. For Cairns, nature sided with those who staked their lives on "essential morality." Also, Cairns did not see suffering only as the result of individual sin, but as something that communities might endure because of "wrong doing and false thinking and intellectual sloth." Rebellion against the suffering of the

47. Cairns, *Faith That Rebels*. 289.
48. Baillie, in *Cairns, Autobiography*, 22–23.
49. Mackintosh to Cairns, 10 July 1928, Box 3/3 Cairns Papers.
50. Raven, *Jesus and the Gospel of Love*, 250.
51. Raven, *Jesus and the Gospel of Love*, 252, 257.

world included rebellion against social injustice, and this message featured strongly in the closing chapter of his book.

Although the book outlined a distinctive theology, it contained some ideas that had been set out by the American Social Gospel theologian Washington Gladden, as far back as 1899. Gladden too had described the biblical definition of the miracles of the New Testament as wonderful works or signs which indicated the presence of God, and he agreed with Augustine's teaching that miracles were not contrary to nature but to what we know of nature. Gladden saw miracles not as a violation of nature, but as its completion and perfection. Echoing the views of Lord Kelvin quoted by Cairns, Gladden also suggested that every free personality is a supernatural power, not under a fixed law, but rather with the power of thought, choice and love, and therefore, in a sense, a supernatural being. God had to have freedom to act in the world otherwise humankind possessed attributes nobler than their Creator. For Gladden, nature was the middle ground between humanity and God. "God here meets us, makes terms with us, gives us our lessons, and assigns us our tasks."[52]

The fact that Cairns's book went into five editions in as many years indicates that many were drawn to a work, which, although focused on the subject of miracle, was about the very nature of reality and how God and humanity might operate within it. For Cairns, prayer was about the response of faith to the ultimate nature of things—to the moral character of the created order. What might Christians expect from engaging in prayer? Could they expect anything? The timing of his publication coincided with discussions within the United Free Church between 1924–27, on the closely related topic of spiritual healing. At the 1924 general assembly, an elder from Paisley, Mr. James A. McDougal had supported an overture asking for a committee to examine the ministry of healing, which he said had been arousing public attention and discussion for a considerable time. As a bookseller, he had been aware of the increasing number of books on healing that were being published, particularly in relation to psychoanalysis, and there were many people who needed guidance on this whole area. The historian Ewen A. Cameron has recorded the scale of mortality in Scotland during the second decade of the twentieth century, due to losses on the battlefield, and to tragic accidents during mobilization and demobilization, in which hundreds of servicemen lost their lives; and to the postwar influenza epidemic thought to have resulted in the deaths of around thirty-four thousand people in Scotland.[53] As well as the psychological effects of loss on such a

---

52. Gladden, *How Much Is Left*, 64.

53. Cameron, *Impaled upon a Thistle*, 122.

scale, there were many who returned from the Great War suffering from shell shock and other nervous and mental disorders. McDougal drew attention to the Anglican Church's attempts to examine the concept of spiritual healing and to the attraction of the Christian Science Church for so many people. Topics such as the laying on of hands, healing at Lourdes, and so on, were giving rise to questions about the gift of healing and whether or not it could be recovered and exercised. Mr. John Hall of Edinburgh, in supporting the overture, advised that the time had come for careful investigation and clear guidance. When opposition was voiced, Cairns spoke up in favor, declaring that he would greatly deplore suppression of the overture. This question was troubling a great many people, and would have to be dealt with at some time. Following his call for the acceptance of the overture, Hall's motion passed with a large majority.[54] A committee of twenty-four was appointed with the capacity to consult experts in particular areas related to healing, and Cairns was among them. The process raised even more questions and the committee's findings, in 1927, were cautious and inconclusive, suggesting that continued study was needed by experts in the fields of medicine, psychology, philosophy, and theology.[55]

Cairns's *Faith That Rebels* had entered into a religious culture that was already asking difficult questions about the nature of reality. Science was revealing a universe in which matter was composed of energy, and people were being drawn to movements that did not rely on rational explanations. For instance, since the late nineteenth century there had been a growing interest in spiritualism, while Celtic spirituality, with its emphasis on the unity of the spiritual and physical, had been enjoying a revival of interest.[56] Baillie points out that although Cairns had reached his position through a long process of original and solitary thinking, at least two other European theologians were working independently on similar sets of ideas. Karl Heim (1874–1958), dogmatics professor at Tübingen was, around the same time, in dialogue with philosophy and science, developing his theory of nature, in which he challenged the static, mechanical and materialistic worldview that provided the predominant contemporary conception of reality. Central to this was his theory of time as both physical and eternal.[57] Donald Baillie described an essay entitled "Spiritual Healing" that Heim produced in 1930 as setting out a conception of miracle, "not as a reversion of the order of nature

54. Reith, "Overture anent Spiritual Healing," 160–64.

55. "Report on Church Life and Social Problems." *Proceedings and Debates of the General Assembly of the United Free Church, May 1927,* 22–27.

56. Brown, *Providence and Empire,* 281–84, and Oppenheim, *Other World.*

57. Heim's complex theory is described in Eerikainen, "Time and Polarity," and his *New Divine Order* was translated by Edgar Primrose Dickie.

but as the victory of God, in which men can share by faith, over the demonic forces of evil that oppose His kingdom."[58] Bishop Gustaf Aulen (1879–1977), professor of theology of the Lutheran Church in Sweden, published in 1930 his thesis on the atonement, arguing that the New Testament doctrine "conceives of God as waging war in Christ upon the elemental Powers of Evil and winning a victory in which men can share by faith." Cairns would certainly have approved Aulen's final statement. "For my own part, I am persuaded that no form of Christian teaching has any future before it except such as can keep steadily in view the reality of evil in the world, and go to meet the evil with a battle-song of triumph."[59]

It is interesting to note that Heim was involved in the World Student Christian Federation as traveling secretary for the German student movement, and Cairns did go to Sweden on behalf of the federation, so the three men may have met and have been aware of each other's work. Donald Baillie recorded that in respect of his thinking about the existence of suffering, pain and death, and about prayer and the idea of miracle, and in trying to understand Jesus' teaching about faith, Cairns was influenced by J. H. Oldham, A. G. Hogg, and Lily Dougall.[60] Oldham's influence has already been described. It was through him that Cairns was introduced not only to the Student Christian Movement, but also to the ideas of Christian Science and spiritual healing. In Dougall, novelist and writer of religious essays, Cairns discovered a fellow traveler whose work stimulated his own thinking on the subject of healing.[61] The final paragraph of *Faith That Rebels* echoed her belief.

Lily Dougall (1858–1923)

According to her biographer, Joanna Dean, Lily Dougall was one of the "New Women," a group of independent, well-educated, and assertive women who exercised a significant influence on British intellectual life from the later nineteenth century.[62] She was born in Montreal in 1858, but had in 1884 come to live with an aunt in Edinburgh.[63] In 1911 she moved to Cum-

58. Baillie, in *Cairns, Autobiography*, 27.

59. Aulen, *Christus Victor*, 176.

60. Baillie, in Cairns, *Autobiography*, 24.

61. Baillie, in Cairns, *Autobiography*, 170; Dean cites A. M. G. Stephenson, *Rise and Decline of English Modernism*, 59.

62. Dean, *Religious Experience*, 70.

63. Streeter's introduction and biographical note in Lily Dougall's posthumously published *God's Way with Man*, 11–23.

nor, near Oxford, where she became a prominent member of the Anglican modernist movement, contributing to the shaping of liberal spirituality in the early twentieth century.[64] Like Cairns, she became a popular mentor to the Student Christian Movement, publishing some books with them.[65]

Dougall's early evangelical faith had been located in the Holiness movement, which emphasized, not the conversion experience, but the subsequent need for the continual gift of the Holy Spirit in the Christian's life and the accompanying sense of the presence of God.[66] For Dougall, a reasoned faith must be accompanied by personal experience of God. The American Quaker, Rufus Jones, who collaborated with her on a volume on prayer in 1916, defined mysticism in broad terms as "the type of religion which puts the emphasis on immediate awareness of a relationship with God, a direct and intimate contact with the Divine Presence."[67] It was on these terms that Dougall shared the early twentieth century's enthusiasm for mysticism, which was promoted and popularized by figures such as Evelyn Underhill, Baron Von Hügel, and William Ralph (Dean) Inge. Influenced by both Jones and Inge, Dougall favored a practical mysticism, coming to see it as time spent in prayer and devotion, and not as a solitary pursuit of God.[68] She eschewed its extreme manifestations, encouraging others to withdraw only "temporarily from the things of sense in order to find God," for instance, by establishing the habit of daily prayer.[69] She insisted that personal experience of God must be sought within the Christian fellowship.[70] Dougall spent the last years of her life promoting a heightened spirituality in fellowships like the Student Christian Movement and the Guild of Health.

With the help of the Anglican New Testament scholar, Canon Burnett Hillman Streeter, and her friend Sophie Earp, Dougall turned her home at Cutt's End, Cumnor, into a center that focused on the search for solutions to the religious, moral and social issues of the day. Those who were invited to the conversations were from different denominations, and included ministers and theologians, but also leading figures in the spheres of art, history, philosophy, and psychology. Both Cairns and Oldham were

64. Dougall, *God's Way with Man*, 1–2. See also 280–85 for Dean's list of Dougall's published and unpublished works.

65. Dean, *Religious Experience*, 136, cites Tissington Tatlow, *Story of the Student Christian Movement of Great Britain and Ireland*, 435–36.

66. Dean, *Religious Experience*, 24–25.

67. Dean, *Religious Experience*, 129.

68. Dean, *Religious Experience*, 126–29.

69. Dean, *Religious Experience*, 129.

70. Dean, *Religious Experience*, 131–32.

among those who took part.[71] Another of Cairns's closest friends, Neville Talbot, also became a friend and associate of Dougall, and contributed to her group books.[72] Discussions were based on the assumption that there was no opposition between true religion, true art and true science, and were preceded by a time of prayerful fellowship. Papers were then read, and after the application of rigorous criticism to group discussions, the results of the deliberations were then embodied in a series of group books.[73] According to Streeter, although several people contributed ideas to the books, it was the atmosphere created by Dougall that produced their special character. The books were widely received in Britain, but also in America, Australia, and China. Streeter summed up Dougall's mature understanding of the central message of the gospel as focusing on four main ideas: first, that God was a Father—a wiser and kinder Father than any human father—who did not respond to humankind with wrath, and that sin, sickness, and calamity were not God's will; second, that God was like Christ, battling evil and sharing in the suffering of the world; third, that prayer was a natural response to God as Father—as well as retention of prayers of petition, she emphasized a quiet, receptive concentration of the heart and mind on the all pervading presence of God as a way of attaining spiritual power; fourth, that the life to come would be a continuation and enrichment of the highest life known on earth. While opposed to spiritualism or attempts at making contact with the dead, she believed that the souls of the righteous were never far away from their loved ones, and could assist and inspire them through personal contact, although not in the form of voices or visions.[74] According to Streeter, she believed that conventional Christianity thought too highly of human capacity while thinking of God on too small a scale, and she was profoundly aware of the limitations of language in the attempt to talk about God.[75]

It is unclear when Cairns and Dougall first met. The earliest evidence of a connection between them is recorded by Dean, who wrote that Cairns had read over parts of the manuscripts for two of Dougall's books before

71. Oldham and his wife, Mary, visited from 12 to 19 December 1916, and took part in the discussions that led to the publication of the group book on *Immortality*. See Dean, *Lily Dougall*, 257n87. One of Cairns's visits is recorded in Dougall's visitors' book, 8 September 1912—see Dean, *Lily Dougall*, 251n19—this was probably in relation to *Practice of Christianity* (1913), which Cairns read through prior to publication. A subsequent visit is described later in this thesis chapter.

72. Dean, *Lily Dougall*, 251n22.

73. The process or method of working is described in some detail by Harold Anson, "Lily Dougall 1858–1923," 201, cited in Dean, *Lily Dougall*, 147. It was the method that had been used to produce *Essays and Reviews* (1860).

74. Streeter, in Dougall, *God's Way with Man*, 20–22.

75. Dougall, *God's Way with Man*, 8.

publication: *Christus Futurus* (1907) and *The Practice of Christianity* (1913). Dougall had published her first article on health, "The Salvation of the Body by Faith," in the *Hibbert Journal* in 1907, round about the time Helen Cairns had been diagnosed with Bright's Disease. In her article Dougall declared that disease was not God's will and that God was ever ready to remove it through faith. The article was later incorporated into *Christus Futurus* with its central theme of spiritual healing. Both Dougall and Cairns had experienced long struggles with physical ill-health and psychological breakdown, and became interested in issues relating to healing. They had examined the claims of Christian Science and found something valuable there, although they had not been able to embrace them wholeheartedly. Dougall drew on the findings of psychology and neurology in her efforts to find a scientific explanation for spiritual healing. She became a member of the Society of Psychical Research which had been founded by Henry Sidgwick, professor of moral philosophy at Cambridge. It was a body of eminent academics, writers, and politicians who were interested in discovering if there were scientific explanations for phenomena otherwise perceived as supernatural.[76] Janet Oppenheim has described the society's motivation as a desire to find an empirical basis for faith. "Although repudiating orthodox Christianity, they longed to find some other basis for the ethical precepts they cherished and some reassurance that all human suffering was not utterly devoid of purpose. Implicitly they sought to use science to disclose the inadequacies of a materialist world view and to suggest how much of cosmic significance scientific materialism failed to explain."[77]

Fundamental to both Cairns and Dougall was the influence of F. D. Maurice and his concept of the kingdom of God, which was built on his controversial interpretation of the concept of eternity as something that could be experienced within time, and which influenced the sociological aspect of their theologies. The kingdom was not something to be worked toward, but recognized as being already present. It was an alternative reality that existed outside of time but was simultaneously being realized within time. It was both present and eternal and individuals had simply to recognize the existing true relationships with God and with each other, as revealed in the life of Jesus, to bring about the kingdom on earth. As well as being a spur to improve social conditions, this idea provided the basis for Cairns's and Dougall's approach to healing. The eternal kingdom was characterized by health and wholeness, as this was the will of a loving Creator. Faith in this reality, allowed individuals to appropriate healing in the earthly sphere.

76. Dean, *Religious Experience* 188.
77. Oppenheim, *Other World*, 52.

In 1913, Dougall had been asked to take on a leadership role in the Anglican Guild of Health, which had begun in 1904 as a response to the variety of healing movements. One of its founders, Conrad Noel, had felt that Christian Science and other movements outside the church had been driven to heresy because the church had neglected the ministry of healing. Dougall was regarded as one who could revitalize a declining membership. She became a key member, hosting in 1914 a conference at Cutt's End on "The Relation of Spiritual Health to Bodily Health." A subsequent meeting from 28 July to 4 August 1915 was attended by Cairns.[78] Just a few days after the meeting, Dougall wrote to him, describing an inner perception that she had experienced, of the dead urging their loved ones to begin the physical salvation of the world now. This had left her with the conviction that what they were doing at Cumnor was not enough. For Dougall, the ordinary Anglican had no conception of fellowship in prayer that was not formal. On the other hand, Christian Science had a sense of the presence of God, but did not appreciate the importance of fellowship. She was convinced that the two must be harmonized, and described her conviction, with its echoes of Maurice, "that just beyond our present grasp—not far off in time or in processes of thought—there is something much greater and deeper." She confessed that she had been disappointed by recent Guild of Health meetings at Cumnor, because they failed to meet the ideal mix of inward contemplation and spiritual fellowship. Expressing her frustrations about the healing movement, she wrote that Cairns could be of great help to the movement, which had come to be dominated by people who "skate gaily on the surface. They do not worship God with their reason; their God is not reasonable, yet they have a secret key which can open great riches of the mind of Christ if they know how to use it . . . those who are refinding [inward recollection and concentration of faith] in Christian Science and kindred movements think they can experience its full power without being 'of one accord in one place' with others."[79]

How much more deeply Cairns might have become involved with the Cumnor School is impossible to say, but the war intervened, and shortly after this he went off to France, and was involved in the producing the *Army and Religion* report, which was not ready for publication until 1919. There are no records of meetings at Cumnor between 1917 and 1925, so it is likely that they ceased for the duration of the war and beyond.[80] The conflict

78. Dean, *Religious Experience*, 160. Also 261n54, where it was observed that Cairns had signed the visitors' book.

79. Lily Dougall to D. S. Cairns, 7 August 1916, Box 3/5 Cairns Papers.

80. Dean, *Religious Experience*, 257n87.

brought into a new and sharper focus questions about suffering, death and immortality. Cairns, having finished his *Army and Religion* report, was able to return to many of the themes discussed by the Cumnor Group, wrestling with them over the years, presenting his ideas in his lectures in Aberdeen, and eventually publishing his thoughts in *The Faith That Rebels* in 1928.

Alfred George Hogg (1875–1954)

In *Not to Destroy but to Fulfil*, Eric J. Sharpe described the close relationship between A. G. Hogg and Cairns.[81] Hogg was the son of the missionary John Hogg, whom Cairns had met during his visit to Egypt. John Hogg, with his lively personality, breadth of interests and concentration on practical service, had made a significant impression on the young Cairns.[82] In 1886, only two years after Cairns's return from Egypt, John Hogg died and the family returned to Edinburgh, where they joined Morningside United Presbyterian Church. When Cairns spent six months at Morningside in 1892, Alfred G. Hogg was a member of Cairns's Bible class and, according to Baillie, the pair developed a "deep intellectual friendship."[83] Later, as a student passing through a crisis of faith, Hogg was helped by an extensive correspondence with his friend, and was able to continue his theological studies and then go out to India as a lay missionary with the United Free Church in 1903. The two men kept up their correspondence, which from 1908 onward included Hogg's reflections in response to Commission IV's questionnaire.

Hogg was among the missionaries who advocated a new approach to mission, but he was not satisfied with fulfillment theory. As the previous chapter has indicated, Hogg's struggle to form a theology of mission led him to put more emphasis on the discontinuity between Christianity and Hinduism. Focusing on the concepts of *karma* and redemption, he compared the underlying principles of each as they related to the order of things. According to Hogg, *karma* explained the universe in terms of "mechanical retribution in the moral and ethical spheres"; it was a "judicial system without a judge," in which the very nature of the universe was judicial, and the purpose of life was expiation or atonement in an effort to escape from *karma*. By contrast, Christianity was, for Hogg, "a religion of mercy and grace, not a judicial system." In thinking through a theological basis for the relation of Christianity to Hinduism, he touched on a subject that Cairns had been struggling with in relation to the science and religion

81. Sharpe, *Not to Destroy but to Fulfil*, 282–84.
82. Cairns, *Autobiography*, 96–101.
83. Baillie, in Cairns, *Autobiography*, 25, and Sharpe, *Not to Destroy*, 283.

debate: the so-called supernatural or miraculous element in religion. Referring to the difficulties and ambiguities related to these concepts, Hogg
focused on what he called the religious use of the terms, which referred to
"a kind of fact which no one can directly experience without an overpow-
ering religious emotion of awe and wonder."[84] In this sense he suggested
that what was wonderful was superior to the natural or commonplace, and
therefore supernatural; as opposed to the definition of the supernatural
as the opposite of the natural. Like Cairns, Hogg was influenced by the
Ritschlian school, and distinguished between "faith" and "beliefs." For
him, supernatural apprehensions that gave rise to faith were not limited to
Christianity, although he also believed that genuine supernatural experiences did not necessarily lead to enlightenment as they might awaken "only
solemn awe or even craven terror."[85] Presumably this was how he judged
the effects of Hinduism on its followers.

While many dismissed the idea of the miraculous or supernatural, influenced by the German theologian Julius Kaftan, Hogg wrote of the narrow
interpretation within Protestantism of the concept of redemption, seeing it
as redemption from sin and punishment, instead of in the wider context of
redemption from the tyranny of the present world order, with its suffering,
pain, and death. For Cairns and Hogg, the universe was not a closed system, but one in which people had access to divine power through faith. This
power was available for the advancement of the kingdom of God on earth.
Where Hinduism led people to try to escape karma, Christianity offered
redemption that begins in the world. Hogg wrote:

> It is because Christianity is a religion of redemption from this
> world that it can look dark facts honestly in the face and yet
> remain optimistic. Because it knows that the invincible God
> is actively their enemy, it can frankly recognize their actuality
> and their ugliness without loss of hope or courage. . . . In and
> upon the unredeemed or natural world it finds the supernatural
> already operative, a supernatural which is sufficiently akin to the
> natural to be able to lay hold of it with the wrestler's grip, and yet
> which, being at strife with the natural, is *contrary* to it, and being
> victorious, is manifestly *superior* to the natural.[86]

The influence of Cairns, particularly in *The Reasonableness of the
Christian Faith*, is evident throughout Hogg's *Redemption*: his use of the
phrase "look dark facts honestly in the face" echoed Cairns's plea to young

84. Hogg, *Redemption from This World*, 5.

85. Hogg, *Redemption from This World*, 7.

86. Hogg, *Redemption from This World*, 17–18.

doubters to "gaze steadily into the darkness" as they confronted the urgent problem of the existence of suffering and death in a world supposedly ruled by a loving Creator.[87] Cairns and Hogg publicly admitted their mutual influence. On the title page of *Christ's Message of the Kingdom* (1912), in which Hogg challenged the Newtonian worldview of the universe as a closed system, he quoted a passage from Cairns that encapsulates the core of both men's theology. "For the first time in history there appeared on earth One who absolutely trusted the Unseen, who had utter confidence that love was at the heart of all things, utter confidence also in the Absolute Power of that Absolute Love and in the liberty of that Love to help Him."[88]

In the preface to the same book, Hogg notes his indebtedness to Cairns as the major influence on him, declaring that "for initiation into this distinctive standpoint I am indebted to my friend, Professor D. S. Cairns; and, compared with this fundamental obligation, all others have been but incidents in the germination and growth of seeds which were planted by him three years ago during certain memorable but all too brief conversations."[89]

Later, Cairns would write of Hogg's influence on him with regard to his interpretation of miracle.[90] Central to both men was the idea that, with faith, nothing is impossible: they saw this claim as a vital element of Jesus' teaching. Foundational to that faith was the belief in the plasticity of the universe. Hogg described the redemption offered by Jesus as concerning the whole of life; it was not simply redemption from sin, but from all the imperfections of the present order, including disease and suffering. The kingdom of heaven was present and future, and as children of God, individuals were raised above the natural order. The fact that Jesus had exhibited perfect faith in God as Father was marvellous, therefore supernatural, and those who followed his example could avail themselves of the same power of faith. "Perhaps the simplest way of expressing what He teaches us to believe is to say that while to all men God is Fatherly, to His sons He is Father. To all men He gives as much as they make it possible for Him to give; but although He is willing to enable all to make His highest giving possible, not all accept the enablement. . . . He cannot be fully Father unless we have let Him make us truly sons."[91]

87. Cairns, *Reasonableness*, 17.

88. This has been quoted by Hogg and by Donald Baillie (*Autobiography*, 25), but neither give its source.

89. Hogg, *Christ's Message of the Kingdom*, x.

90. Cairns, *Faith That Rebels*, 56n1.

91. Hogg, *Christ's Message of the Kingdom*, 160–61.

Those who had faith could "draw with filial confidence upon the mountain-moving omnipotence of God."[92] In spite of its optimistic apprehension of Christianity, and its focus on faith and prayer as means of appropriating power in the struggle against evil and suffering, *Christ's Message of the Kingdom* was not universally well-received. According to Cairns, it awakened suspicion and alarm in some minds because of its broader interpretation of the atonement. Defending the book in a letter to Mott, Cairns emphasized the importance of its treatment of faith and prayer. He pointed out that Hogg's theory of the atonement was not meant to be complete, and that the church needed to have a theological discussion about the doctrine. However, he warned that theological discussions tended to focus on the abstract, and had little to say to the average person who tried to apply faith to life. While theologians debated the finer points of doctrine, most people were asking a much more profound question: they wanted to know about the ultimate nature of reality, and if it was intrinsically moral, as Christianity taught, and if God was alive and active in the world. For Cairns, such questions were at the heart of Hogg's work, and they were central to Cairns's own continuing spiritual quest, finding their fullest expression in his *Faith That Rebels*.

Believing that Hogg was trying to bring to light "a vital and neglected truth," Cairns declared that he himself had spent the past six or seven years trying to get at the actual historic facts, and had concluded that Hogg's views were in tune with Jesus' teaching on faith and prayer. The topic was so fundamental that Cairns recorded his intention to spend a large part of his life confronting the difficulties that it presented, and making faith easier for others.

Thoughts on Immortality

Another of Cairns's friends, J. H. Leckie, had been working for a long time on similar themes. When J. H. Leckie prepared to publish his Kerr Lectures of 1917–20, *The World to Come and Final Destiny*, Cairns was one of three men who read the manuscript versions and gave critical advice. Influenced by the apparent loss of faith in immortality occasioned by the First World War, Leckie chose the topic in the belief that ideas of the Divine character of God were integral to those relating to the final destiny of humankind. Leckie's conviction that the ultimate triumph of the kingdom was the goal of human history incorporated the idea of future probation (or the opportunity after death for gradual spiritual education and development in an

---

92. Hogg, *Christ's Message of the Kingdom*, 163.

intermediate state), and he declared that this view had emerged within later Protestant opinion, although it had never been developed as doctrine. He differentiated it from the Roman Catholic idea of retributive pain in purgatory, which, according to him, Protestants saw as "out of harmony with the spirit of the Gospel."[93] Regarding the nature of eternal life, two forms of belief had existed within the church. The most common was that which conceived of the life to come as an endless existence in time, but there was also the idea of eternal life as "a spiritual quality of being . . . a state of mind so elevated, so possessed with devout emotion, as to be independent of time, above the flux of temporal things."[94] Both interpretations, he insisted, were to be found in the New Testament.

The doctrine of probationary salvation appeared occasionally in Dougall's work, and was a concept that Cairns embraced and continued to hold throughout his life. In a letter to Lavinia Talbot he asserted, "As I said, I do believe in an intermediate state, in which, none the less, we have still to learn and grow, and may still have to strive and wait. We shall not have attained perfection. But I believe 'sin will have no more dominion over us' and that it is a far happier life than this, with far more of the Eternal life in it. Is there not a clear distinction between moral imperfection and sin?"[95]

In a subsequent letter to Talbot, he referred to a sermon preached over a hundred years ago by his great-uncle who conducted his own wife's funeral, expressing the hope that she had gone to a better life. The lack of confidence in God's love shocked Cairns, who wrote,

When one thinks of Scotland in those days there was only one tremendous alternative to Heaven, and that this life was to good Protestants the one period of "probation"—one cannot but feel that this was a sub-Christian faith . . .

The longer I live, the more value I put on God's sheer *Grace*, which I take simply to be what by our human standards we would call His extravagant goodness, the forthcomingness, initiative and persistence of His Love. It is our *sole* Hope.[96]

When Lavinia's sister-in-law died in 1921, Cairns wrote to comfort Talbot, admitting to the most helpful influence of F. D. Maurice on his views on life after death, and confessing, "I have for many years prayed for the

93. Leckie, *World to Come*, 307.
94. Leckie, *World to Come*, 317.
95. Cairns to Lavinia Talbot, 15 May 1940, in *Autobiography*, 203.
96. Cairns to Lavinia Talbot, 28 August 1940, in *Autobiography*, 204.

dead, for their happiness and advancement in the world of Light and Life."[97] This seemingly un-Presbyterian practice was treated by Professor H. R. Macintosh of New College, Edinburgh, in his work on immortality published early in the Great War, and his views may well have been influenced by his friendship with Cairns. Mackintosh pointed out that traditionally in Protestantism it was proclaimed as certain that the limits to God's love were fixed by the soul's attitude to God at death, and that it was considered impossible that Christ would be revealed to anyone who left this world without a conscious faith. However, he declared that hopes of future probation now prevailed widely.[98] He did not consider the issue of prayers for the dead to be a question of major importance. He doubted whether any Protestant writer of standing could be found to "maintain the possibility of abridging by earthly intercession the purifying pains of departed saints," but he recognized that there were many people who saw no reason to fix a point where they must cease praying for loved ones, citing Pascal's dictum that "the heart has its reasons which the mind cannot understand." Although some said such prayers were meaningless because no one knows how the departed may be living, others defended such prayer as implicitly contained in prayers for the whole church, which, they argued, included both the living and the dead.[99] Mackintosh put forward the arguments on both sides, but concluded that it was an issue for private and spiritual feeling.

> In any case, we may be sure men will decide it for themselves; and hearts over-burdened with grief, as they follow the dead into the world of light with unspeakable longing, will not inquire too closely, or too much care, what rules of prayer have been devized by men whose minds are cast in another mould. To the demand that they must set limits to intercession they will be apt to reply that they cannot break off the utterances of fond wishes at the grave. To them it seems merely natural that at will they should speak to the Father concerning those whom He has in His safe keeping.[100]

97. Cairns to Neville Talbot, September 1921, Cairns, *Autobiography*, 214.
98. Mackintosh, *Immortality and the Future*, 157.
99. Mackintosh, *Immortality and the Future*, 161.
100. Mackintosh, *Immortality and the Future*, 163.

A Mature Apologetics

Near the end of his life, as he tried to set out his reminiscences for his children, Cairns had looked back on the publication of his first work of apologetics, *Christianity in the Modern World* (1906). Considering at one stage its possible reissue, he declared that his statements on the kingdom of God, providence, and science would have to be revised in the light of new scientific knowledge, and in relation to the theory of realized eschatology. He would also include in it something from *The Faith That Rebels*. However, he would hold to the substance of the first book, although laying more emphasis on the kingdom as *gift* rather than as *task*. *Christianity in the Modern World* was not, in the event, reissued, but, in retrospect, Cairns felt that he had achieved these aims in his last book, *The Riddle of the World*, which was published in the year he retired from Aberdeen.[101] He dedicated his final work of apologetics to Alison, who had become his secretary, and to whom he credited much of its form and substance.

The book was aimed at "the educated men and women in all social classes who are interested in things of the spirit."[102] In it Cairns developed ideas contained in the Deems Lectures, which he had given in America in 1923, and which he further developed and delivered as the Baird Lectures in 1932. The Baird Trust had been set up in 1873 by the industrialist James Baird, with the aim of countering "the mitigations of spiritual destitution among the population of Scotland" and "to secure the [religious] upbringing of the young."[103] Naturalist philosophy based on eighteenth-century science had found in Deism its predominant religious expression, through which God might still be seen as Creator, but a Creator who did not interfere with the laws of nature that he had set in motion. Cairns understood how many people found no comfort in the idea of such a remote God, and who were attracted to humanist philosophies. His own experiences during the First World War had led Cairns to refocus on the mystery of the existence of evil. He had met so many men who, confronted with such violence and bloodshed, felt they could no longer believe in an almighty or loving God.[104] From then on he was intent on developing the Theodicy which found its most complete form in his last book. He was not a rapid thinker or worker, and needed someone with organizational skills to take him in hand.[105] The

101. Cairns, *Autobiography*, 176.
102. Cairns, *Riddle of the World*, v.
103. http://www.bairdtrust org.uk.
104. Cairns, *Riddle*, 240.
105. Baillie, in Cairns, *Autobiography*, 25.

extent of Alison's role in its publication is described by Irvine, who records that by 1936, four years after delivering the Baird Lectures, the work had still not been prepared for publication, and Alison had to keep urging him to complete it, and the only way she could achieve this was to come to grips herself with the material; which she did with so much success—in spite of her distaste for theology—that the lectures appeared in 1937, under the title *The Riddle of the World*.[106]

In *The Riddle of the World*, Cairns turned to the age-old question of the existence of suffering and death, which, in his eyes, all the scientific progress of the past century had not been able to address satisfactorily, but which he saw as a fundamental problem for all the world's philosophies and religions: "That which we think to be real invariably determines our views of what we believe to be good or right, and nerves us to struggle for its victory."[107] Cairns wanted to examine humanism as a coherent and satisfactory system of thought in its response to the riddle of the world.

He presented the humanist argument through the voices of John Stuart Mill (1806–73), Thomas Henry Huxley (1825–95), and Bertrand Russell (1872–970), all of whom he believed had rejected Theism, and who seemed to him to represent the spirit of the age. In their work, Cairns could see the poignancy of their distress in finding nature to be either indifferent or morally evil. Mill observed the indifference of nature in meting out suffering on good and bad alike.[108] Huxley, in his revolt against such indifference, declared that if society was to make ethical progress it must not imitate the cosmic process, but fight against it.[109] Russell urged his readers to accept the findings of science, which he regarded as nearly certain, that life had no intrinsic meaning. He warned that they must find a non-religious home for their ideals and aspirations, building "on the firm foundations of unyielding despair." Cairns quoted at length from Russell's "Free Man's Worship" in *Philosophical Essays*, of which the following short extract gives a flavor:

> A strange mystery it is that Nature, omnipotent but blind, in the revolutions of her secular hurrying through space, has brought forth a child, subject still to her power, but gifted with sight and knowledge of good, with the capacity of judging all the works of his unthinking mother. In spite of Death the mark and seal of the parental control, man is yet free, during his

106. Irvine, *Alison Cairns*, 62.

107. Cairns, *Riddle*, 23.

108. Cairns, *Riddle*, 14, cites Mill, *Three Essays—The Utility of Religion and Theism*, 28–31.

109. Cairns, *Riddle*, 14, cites Huxley in his Romanes Lecture "Evolution and Ethics."

brief years, to examine, to criticise, to know, and in imagination to create. To him alone in the world with which he is acquainted, this freedom belongs; and in this lies his superiority
to the resistless forces that control his outward life. . . . When
we have realised that Power is largely bad, that man with his
knowledge of good and evil is but a helpless atom in a world
which has no such knowledge, the choice is again presented
to us: Shall we worship force or shall we worship goodness?
Shall our God exist and be evil or shall he be recognised as the
creation of our own conscience?[110]

In critiquing the philosophers, Cairns admitted that if the scientific
account was correct then it was logical to dismiss Theism, but he detected a
flaw in their arguments. All three philosophers regarded nature as indifferent to suffering, but implied that humanity was nobler than nature. Cairns
pointed out that the two ideas were contradictory, stating, "You cannot have
an absolute standard of right and wrong emanating from a morally evil or
indifferent universe."[111] Cairns also set out the thoughts of some of the leading American humanist intellectuals, for example John Dewey (1859–1952),
Joseph Wood Krutch (1893–1970), and Walter Lippmann (1889–1974), for
whom, in Cairns's view, the basis of both Theism and Christianity had been
undermined by science, and according to whom science provided the only
trustworthy knowledge of the universe, and was the only pathway to Reality.[112] Cairns responded to the challenges presented by the proponents of
humanism: first, that science was the only pathway to reality; second, that
belief in God promotes quietism and apathy; and third, that the problem of
evil in the world is inimical to belief in God. In spite of disagreeing fundamentally with their arguments, Cairns had a high regard for these thinkers,
recording that "they show a wide range of culture, a genuine love of humanity and a high *morale*."[113] Elsewhere he described Krutch and Lippman as
facing the issues with "dignity and courage."[114] His respect for those with
whom he disagreed is also illustrated by the fact that he was prepared to
quote at length from them, thus providing his readers with an opportunity
to consider his opponents' ideas more fully for themselves.

In a chapter on science and religion, Cairns stated that humanism had
over-estimated the place and function of science. Suggesting that science was

110. Cairns, *Riddle*, 18, cites Russell, "The Free Man's Worship," in *Philosophical
Essays*.

111. Cairns, *Riddle*, 20.

112. Cairns, *Riddle*, 25.

113. Cairns, *Riddle*, 31.

114. Cairns, *Riddle*, 49.

not as impartial as had been widely believed in the Victorian period, he rehearsed some of the arguments he had made in *The Faith That Rebels*, about the limitations of science in terms of its methodology, referring frequently to his image of science as a net to catch certain kinds of fish and to let other fish through. He also pointed out that developments in quantum and relativity theories were changing the scientific outlook, making scientists less dogmatic in their pronouncements. He explained that quantum mechanics was having a "most disturbing effect not only upon the existing theories of wave motion, and the structure of the atom, but on the conception of the 'Laws of Nature' and the whole theory of mechanical determinism." The strict determinism that seemed to apply on the larger scale, did not seem to apply in the subatomic world. Where once there had been certainty, there now was probability. The laws of nature that were once considered determinant, were now thought to be of a secondary type, whose character was mainly statistical. In such a world there might be room for human and divine freedom. Cairns was here basing his opinions on the work of scientists such as the British astrophysicist Arthur Stanley Eddington (1882–1944), the development of whose work he was able to trace over a period of years, but Cairns also made clear that others like Albert Einstein (1879–1955), Ernest Rutherford (1871–1937), and Max Planck (1858–1947), the originator of quantum theory, suggested that if scientists knew all there was to know, then they would find strict mechanical determinism at the quantum level.[115]

Cairns's view that science could only give partial knowledge of the world, and his critique of its methods, was accompanied by a profound respect for its disinterested love of the truth, which he saw as a form of the love of God. Science and religion needed each other, and there need be no conflict between them. As he drew his argument to a close, he included a plea from the English historian and theologian John Robert Seeley (1834–95) that religion should seek the aid of science to help it think "more worthily of the glory of God."

> In too many Christians the idea of God has been degraded by childish and little-minded teaching; the Eternal, the Infinite and the All-embracing has been represented as the head of the clerical interest, as a sort of clergyman, as a sort of schoolmaster, as a sort of philanthropist. But the scientific man *knows* Him to be Eternal; in astronomy, in geology, he becomes familiar with the countless millenniums of His lifetime. The scientific man strains his mind actually to realise God's infinity. As far

115. Cairns, *Riddle*, 79–85.

off as the fixed stars he traces Him "distance inexpressible by numbers that have name"[116]

To the scientists Cairns suggested acceptance of other pathways to reality, including the beauty of the world, the history of religious faith, and the experience of moral conviction.[117] Focusing on the latter, Cairns wrote that science accused religion of anthropomorphism, but he noted that it too relied on concepts that originated in human nature. The concepts of substance, causality, and law came respectively from consciousness of self, human will, and experience of society. As far as naturalistic evolutionary theory was concerned, morality had its roots in conceptions of utility to the tribe in its struggle for existence, and values that were created by society. The debate raised questions about moral authority in terms of international relations, and for Cairns, acceptance of morality as a human construct did not bode well for the hopes of international peace, the pursuit of which he considered to be of primary importance.[118] "And if there is no immutable law or standard for nations other than those maintained because of their advantageousness in the struggle for group existence, what hope is there of their escaping from the grip of that black fear which is to-day launching them anew on the race for armaments, with what everybody of reason and goodwill knows will be the dire and inevitable consequence?"[119]

The religious interpretation of life saw morality as inherent in the natural order and instinct in the consciousness of individuals, revealing the universe "as a purposive system, creative of spiritual beings akin in nature to their Creator and Father."[120] Science could not measure such things, as they were of a completely different order to that of facts and events, however the two pathways did not have to produce conflict. On the one hand, science saw the world as a "vast system of Space-Time and Energy, operating according to uniform law" while for religion the world was a "creative process realising spiritual ends of absolute and enduring value, a system, therefore, full of purpose and meaning." Both were true. In fact, Cairns saw the thought form of science as complementary to a spiritual worldview. The "reign of law" was entirely in harmony with the love of God for humanity, and "in his devotion to the discovery of law the man of science is fulfilling not only a human service, but a divine vocation."[121] Thus far Cairns had defended the

116. Cairns, *Riddle*, cites J. R. Seeley, *Natural Religion*, 19–20.
117. Cairns, *Riddle*, 97–126.
118. Cairns, *Riddle*, 120–21.
119. Cairns, *Riddle*, 152–53.
120. Cairns, *Riddle*, 122–23.
121. Cairns, *Riddle*, 151.

idea of the world having spiritual foundations without recourse to Scripture or the tradition of the church, but by appropriating the arguments of natural theology, concluding that while theology discerned meaning and purpose, art discerned beauty and harmony and mathematical science discerned order. All contributed to the search for ultimate reality.

Cairns's conception of different pathways to reality seems very similar to the thinking of a number of modern scientists and philosophers who see the explanatory accounts of science and religion as noncompetitive but rather as belonging to different domains or "magesteria." For instance, Stephen Jay Gould has said that life is so complex that we need to think of these "non-overlapping magisterial" (NOMA) as different but intrinsically complementary—they have different conceptualities and types of description and deal with distinct questions that cannot be satisfactorily addressed by any one discipline, but the integration of their knowledge can bring wisdom.[122]

Cairns's views were in opposition to those of the German theologian Karl Barth (1886–1968), whose dialectical theology had been attracting interest in Scotland since the mid-1920s. Barth repudiated natural theology, confining revelation to Scripture. For him, sin had destroyed the image of God in humanity, thus preventing people from gaining any knowledge of God through nature or conscience. Scottish theologians were divided over Barth, with H. R. Mackintosh firmly in the Barthian camp. Those like Cairns who had been influenced by the liberal Protestant Ritschlian school, saw Barth's approach as untenable. While appreciating Barth's contribution to a fuller awareness of the uniqueness of the Bible message, and to the defence of the independence of the church against growing nationalism, Cairns saw dialectical theology's refusal to recognize the reasoning of natural theology as a backward approach. Cairns recognized that such general revelation fell short of the full revelation in Christ, but nonetheless natural theology produced real knowledge, and all truth was of God. He could not accept that throughout the long history of humankind, God had revealed nothing of the divine until the revelation that began with the Old Testament.[123] "There is at the very basis of the 'Dialectic Theology' a whole nest of unexamined presuppositions, which are all challenged to the roots by the aggressive Naturalism of to-day. I do not think, therefore, that this age of all ages is one

---

122. Fergusson, *Faith and Its Critics*, 43–44, cites Stephen Jay Gould, *Rocks of Ages: Science and Religion in the Fullness of Life*, 59 and 65.

123. Cairns, *Riddle*, 364–66.

in which Christians can refuse to give a reason for the faith that is in them, or can leave any skeleton chambers of thought unopened."[124]

Cairns spent a mere fifteen pages defending Christianity against the humanist accusation that belief in Providence led to quietism and apathy in the face of life's suffering and injustice.[125] His response was directed in particular to the work of the English biologist and eugenicist Julian Huxley (1887–1975) in *Religion Without Revelation* (1927). It seemed to Cairns that Huxley's education had been sadly lacking in terms of Christian history and biography, otherwise he would have been able to see that the opposite effect was true. In the lives of people like Lord Shaftesbury, Florence Nightingale, and General Booth, for instance, faith had sustained their courage and self-sacrifice in the fight against poverty and suffering.

In another long chapter on revelation Cairns gave some insight into his hermeneutics, the basis of which was the belief that the Bible revelation was unique in that the unity of theme found there was not to be discovered in the texts of any other religion. For Cairns, the real meaning of the Bible had been obscured by the doctrine of verbal inspiration, the development of which he saw as an extreme reaction of Protestantism to the Roman Catholic doctrine of the church, as both vied over the locus of authority. Criticism too had obscured the meaning of the Bible by reducing it to the status of one of the "Sacred Books of the East" (referring to the famous collection of texts produced under the general editorship of Professor Max Müller of Oxford University), and Jesus to another prophet, albeit the greatest of the prophets; and by reducing the gospel message to "the proclamation of the Fatherhood of God and the Brotherhood of man."[126] Unfortunately Cairns makes some rather sweeping negative statements about the sacred texts of the different religions, and in a way unacceptable to the modern reader, refers to "the jungle of the nature religions" and "the confused medley" of Hindu texts.[127] Reflecting on the variety of texts in the Bible, Cairns found that there was an "extraordinary unity beneath the difference, which surely implies direction and control and intelligence."[128] The documents themselves may be subject to error, but behind them was the history of special revelation to the Hebrews and to Jesus. Anticipating questions about the "capricious preference" of God for one nation, Cairns suggested that such selection was a vocation

124. Cairns, *Riddle*, 156.
125. Cairns, *Riddle*, 158–73.
126. Cairns, *Riddle*, 191–97.
127. Cairns, *Riddle*, 205–6.
128. Cairns, *Riddle*, 205.

to service, and that all nations had their vocations.[129] This begged the question of the uniqueness of the Christian revelation.

The longest section of the book was concerned with the Old Testament, which Cairns described as largely a theodicy, the vital center of which was faith in "the sovereignty of God, the righteousness and moral purity of God, and the grace of God."[130] This theodicy had developed out of the experience of exile and suffering, and provided the groundwork for theism and for Christian theology. Out of it had arisen six seminal convictions, which provided the elements of a solution to the riddle of the world: the linear conception of history as expressed in the idea of the kingdom of God denoted purpose in creation; the divine creation was of God whose nature is love and who is limited only by respect for the reality of human freedom; humankind's misuse of freedom resulted in sin or "missing the mark"; suffering and death were judgment and discipline brought on by human action and not by God's will that any should suffer; the vicarious law operated by which the righteous may suffer in consequence of the sins of others, but also suffer for the sake of others; and with a developing sense of the worth of the individual, faith projected into the future and conceived of the messianic age and the hope of immortality.[131] Such Old Testament convictions were reinterpreted, in the light of the Christian revelation, widening and deepening thoughts of God and universalizing the Covenant relationship.

In the concluding chapter Cairns described what he saw as "absolutely central" to Christian faith, based on his interpretation of the new revelation in the teaching and person of Jesus.[132] He warned those who described God as "wholly other" than man that this posed the danger of suggesting God was therefore "wholly" unknowable by man. For Cairns God was wholly other "in the sense that He is greater, mightier and better than we can conceive."[133] The filial consciousness of Jesus revealed fatherhood as God's essential nature: the defining character of the ruling unseen power was a loving and caring fatherhood in whose moral purposes individuals could trust. The analogy of fatherhood implied a kinship between God and humanity, the corollary of which was the sacredness of the individual and the brotherhood of man. Cairns saw this distillation of theology as one on which all Christians could agree, although there remained fundamental differences concerning ideas about the person of Jesus and the work of the Holy Spirit. For instance,

129. Cairns, *Riddle*, 206–7.
130. Cairns, *Riddle*, 230.
131. Cairns, *Riddle*, 239–305.
132. Cairns, *Riddle*, 312–62.
133. Cairns, *Riddle*, 326.

some Christians could go no further than accepting Jesus as the greatest of all the prophets, but for Cairns this reduced the substance of the faith through its limited conception of God and Jesus. Speaking of the great gulf between humankind and God, he did not see how it could be bridged except from God's side; by God taking the initiative: "That is the great Christian story of the grace of God incarnate in Jesus Christ, something coming from a depth in God beyond all normal human expectation of ordinary justice or even ordinary love."[134] And here he recalled the words of his teacher, Wilhelm Herrmann, "He that has not seen the grace of God as a wonder has never seen it at all." With regard to the work of the Holy Spirit, Cairns objected to the ideas of Schleiermacher and Ritschl who had reduced it to a body of knowledge of God given by Jesus and maintained in the church through Christian education and the example of ensuing generations.[135] He did accept that understanding of such knowledge might set people free, and in this was a work of the Spirit, but the biblical view of the Spirit as divine influence or power, was a much richer conception than one in which the Spirit was seen more as a "state of mind" or a state of consciousness. Rather, it was humanity filled with the Spirit that would continue the work of Jesus. How might it be appropriated? "Like God's Providence, rather, the Spirit is always there waiting for men to realise it. All the fluctuation in receptivity is in man, not necessarily only in the individual man, but in the social medium in which he lives as well as in himself, and man's supreme concern is to cease, and to persuade others to cease, from hindering the steady divine initiative of the Spirit of God."[136]

And quoting the words of Meister Eckhart, Cairns emphasized the pro-active character of God's love, active in Creation—a love that had initiated the possibility of communion with God. "Thou needst not seek Him here or there. He is not farther off than at the door of thine heart; there He stands lingering, awaiting whoever is ready to open the door and let Him in. Thou needst not call to Him afar. He waits much more impatiently than thou for thee to open to Him."[137]

The Riddle was, according to Baillie, thoroughly biblical in its thinking, especially in its use of the Old Testament, and in spite of having little time for Barth's theology of the Word, all Cairns's thinking was scripturally inspired. For Baillie it was impossible to read it without exclaiming:

134. Cairns, *Riddle*, 340–41.

135. Cairns, *Riddle*, 346–47.

136. Cairns, *Riddle*, 360.

137. Meister Eckhart, Sermon 4; quoted in *Heavenly Vision*, cited in Cairns, *Riddle*, 361.

"How that man knows the Bible and understands it!" The book crowns his life's work and reveals him above all as a man of faith.[138] Many years after its publication a tribute was conveyed to David Jr. by a reader who had passed his copy on to a minister struggling to maintain his faith in the days of the Second World War. Having read it and reread it, the book "had changed his whole outlook as a man and as a minister."[139] The Riddle was published in America in 1938, and drew a very favorable review by Edwin Henry Kellogg, professor of philosophy and religion at Skidmore College, New York. Kellogg recorded his opinion that all who taught Old Testament would, on behalf of their students, welcome the book with its "deeply sympathetic and finely toned exposition of the ever-growing soul of Old Testament faith" and recommended that it should become required reading throughout the college.

> No special philosophical backgrounds are presupposed for the reading. Yet those leading issues of a general philosophical character which are most relevant to religious faith, and specially to the challenges to Christian Theism in just our own day, are canvassed in a semi-popular and yet by no means superficial way, with clarity, persuasiveness, much beauty of thought and of expression, and, together with a depth and range of spiritual sympathy and insight, a thorough scientific and other competence.[140]

From this it may be concluded that Cairns was successful in his aim to appeal to the mass of educated lay people. The book was eloquent and contained frequent use of analogies drawn from everyday experience to elucidate some of the theological or scientific concepts. Although there is a certain amount of repetition in his publications, the ideas that are treated again and again benefit from his continuous reading in the sciences, poetry and novels, as well as in theology and biblical studies. A final quotation from the book reveals a characteristic approach in all his thinking, writing, and teaching, and portrays the humility of a theologian who knows well the limits of human thought and speech in the search for truth and reality. Having set out his case for his theodicy, he declared "that the answer still leaves mysteries unexplained we have no reason to deny, for, I repeat, it is unreasonable to expect that human beings so undeveloped and sinful as we are should have a complete solution. But we have light enough to be sure that a very great

138. Baillie, in Cairns, *Autobiography*, 32.

139. Principal Ralph Chalmers, Pine Hill Divinity Hall, Nova Scotia to David Cairns, 21 May 1968 in Cairns Papers Acc. 6786/2 National Library of Scotland.

140. Kellogg, review of *The Riddle of the World*, 147–48.

Wisdom and Power and Love is over all things, and to look forward with confident hope that the end will justify every step of the long road."[141]

Retirement and Move to Edinburgh

After the union of the Church of Scotland and the United Free Church in 1929, prospective ministers acquired their academic qualification in the Divinity Faculty at Aberdeen, and the two divinity halls merged to provide the practical aspects of training at Alford Place, in what now became known as Christ's College. The systems of the two churches for training ministers were different. The divinity professors of the Church of Scotland were subject to the discipline of the church and their salaries were partly paid by the church, but they were also professors in the university with the same responsibilities, rights and status of other university professors. In the United Free Church the professors were appointed and monitored, and had their stipends paid, solely by the church, so a balance of authority had to be worked out. There were tensions: in 1933, for example, the courts of St. Andrews and Glasgow Universities protested against certain aspects of the ordinance governing new theological chairs arising out of the union. In his role as principal of Christ's College, Cairns had to oversee the merger in Aberdeen. New chairs were proposed in 1933 and in 1935, near the end of his academic life, Cairns was appointed professor of Christian dogmatics.[142]

On this theme of union, there is strong indication that during the 1930s Cairns was involved with a group of Scottish clergy who entered into discussions on unity with the Anglican Church. By this time Cairns would have been known personally to many in the Anglican Church, through his work on Commission IV, the *Army Report*, and his work with the Student Movement. The First World War had revealed the negative effects that the disunity of the churches had on the men who responded to the questionnaires. In an effort to deal with this, the Lambeth Conference of 1920 had made an "Appeal to All Christian People," calling for the visible unity of the churches of the Anglican communion, the Orthodox churches and the "great, non-episcopal Communions, standing for rich elements of truth, liberty and life which might otherwise have been obscured or neglected."[143] The potential difficulty of achieving such an aim was seen in a further resolution in which the Lambeth Conference refused to coun-

---

141. Cairns, *Riddle*, 362.

142. Simpson, *Fusion of 1860*, 1–3, 220–37.

143. Resolution 9, Lambeth Conference 1920. Lambeth Conference official website www.anglicancommunion.org/media/127731/1920.pdf.

tenance the idea of general schemes of intercommunion or exchanges of pulpits.[144] However, by the time of the 1930 Lambeth Conference, the Reunion Committee was able to record signs of growing movement and unity.[145] A joint committee was set up, appointed by the Archbishop of Canterbury, a Scotsman, William Cosmo Gordon Lang (1864–1945) and representatives of the Church of Scotland. A letter from Lang to Cairns suggests that the latter was involved in the union discussions when Lang hosted a meeting of Scottish churchmen in 1933 and gave them communion in Lambeth Chapel.[146] This act preceded by a year the official recommendation that members of either communion should be welcomed in the other at the celebration of Communion.[147]

In 1937 Cairns retired and he and Alison went to live at 13 Mayfield Terrace in Edinburgh, near his sister, Jessie, and younger brother William, who had continued to live in the house his parents had moved to when they left Stichel. There had been much deliberation over the decision to leave Aberdeen, with Cairns experiencing doubts and changes of mind. However, at the beginning of 1937 Cairns required a minor operation, and although his condition was not serious, the illness clarified for him the need to retire that summer. Alison had taken on the burden of finding a suitable house and supervising the move. Both Cairns and Alison were to enjoy the next years in Mayfield Terrace, where they felt a new awareness of the family heritage, as Alison described to a friend. "My parent is pleased to think he looks on the backs of the houses of Spence Street, where his uncle John lived, and just round the corner from us is Arthur Lodge where Dr. John Brown's father lived and my grandmother, his niece, kept house for him when she was a girl."[148]

In reference to them he remarked to Alison, "These old people, they stood behind us like a *wall*."[149] Although he had moved far from the theological position of his parents and uncles, he never lost his respect for the authenticity of their faith, or the sense that God had spoken to him through them, that God had been "reaching after us in every dear one."[150]

144. Resolution 12 at 1920 Lambeth Conference.

145. Resolutions 31 and 43 at the Lambeth Conference 1930.

146. Lang to Cairns, 1933 Box 4/5 Cairns Papers.

147. Extract from the report of the joint committee appointed by the Archbishop of Canterbury and representatives of the Church of Scotland, February 1934, in *Relations between Anglican and Presbyterian Churches*, appendix 1, 33–36.

148. Irvine, *Alison Cairns*, 71, cites a letter from Alison, 1 August 1937.

149. Baillie, in Cairns, *Autobiography*, 33.

150. Cairns, *Autobiography*, 33.

Jessie died the year after his move, but William lived on until 1944 and the two men saw a lot of each other. They had always kept in touch, but Cairns regarded this time as a special pleasure of retirement. His daily routine involved work in the morning, followed by light reading and then an hour's letter or note writing in the afternoon. At four o'clock, he walked to the university club to read the papers and meet with friends, returning by tram for dinner at 7:15. After dinner and into the early hours of the morning, there was more light reading, work, and finally letter writing.[151]

Throughout his life Cairns carried on a voluminous correspondence. In a letter to his sister Jessie, during his probationary period, Cairns had written, "Correspondence is a necessary part of civilisation, and besides the pleasure of it, is truly an ethical discipline of the highest kind."[152] His private papers testify to his commitment to such a discipline, including letters to friends from United Presbyterian College days, Joseph Leckie and John Oman, both of whom he corresponded with until their deaths. He maintained a mentoring role for another United Presbyterian, Alfred G. Hogg of Madras Christian College, after his missionary father, John Hogg, died. With these and with others, Cairns discussed their theological thinking and welcomed feedback on his own work. For example, Cairns and Hugh Ross Mackintosh, leading interpreter of German theology and professor of divinity at New College from 1904–1936, also corresponded for nearly thirty years, commenting on each other's theological ideas and publications. Among others who wrote to him were people as diverse as Walter Rauschenbusch, the American Christian Socialist; Nathan Soderblom, archbishop of Uppsala; Mary Slessor, Scots missionary in Nigeria; the economist R. H. Tawney, and the German theologian Johannes Weiss.[153] As well as communicating with his contemporaries, Cairns corresponded with the new generation of theologians that included John Baillie and John Macmurray. It was the latter who wrote convincingly to Cairns that those coming back from the war would not be willing to go back to the way things had been in the church; and that students for the ministry would be looking for a new kind of theology which they themselves would develop.[154] In choosing correspondence to include in their father's *Autobiography*, David and Alison selected only a small number from the hundreds of letters available. Their selection reveals a side of Cairns not normally seen in his published works, and allows the more unconventional (for a Presbyterian)

---

151. Cairns, *Autobiography*, 32–34.

152. Cairns to Jessie Cairns, 12 June 1893, Box 1/5 Cairns Papers, Aberdeen.

153. Weiss to Cairns, 1921, Box 3 Cairns Papers.

154. Macmurray to Cairns, 1919, Box 3 Cairns Papers.

aspects of his theology to show, for instance his views on the after life. Most of the published letters were between him and family friend, Lavinia Talbot, revealing the depth of relationship he had with this family. Over a period of thirty years he discussed with Lavinia not only questions of faith, but explained the differences between the Anglican Church to which she belonged and Presbyterianism. In this latter task his sense of humor broke through the usually serious nature of his letters to her. Explaining that he had been "half poisoned" by Assembly meetings that week, he wondered if she knew what a moderator was, and went on to say, "It is significant of our national truculence that we should use such a name for our highest office-bearer for the year. But it is as good as *Primus* anyway, which now has acquired a secondary meaning."[155]

His sense of humor also infused his later correspondence with Sir Herbert Grierson, Emeritus Professor of Rhetoric and English Literature at the University of Edinburgh. Beginning one of his letters with a comment on the improved legibility of Grierson's handwriting, Cairns responded that he would make a "like laudable effort, and so choose a larger page." However, the significance of his letters to Grierson lies in the fact that, amid their discussion of differences between Catholicism and Protestantism, they form a concise summary of Cairns's theology, what he described as his "pretty bold cosmic hypothesis." True to his Ritschlian roots, he stated that when he spoke of God, he meant "the God and Father of our Lord Jesus Christ," and continued,

> Explicated I find that means, that I think of Him—
>
> a. As One who is in supreme control (Sovereign).
>
> b. As One who is always incomparably better than the very best we can think of Him, and finally
>
> c. That He is no simply static goodness, but that He is gracious. That is to say that He is always better to every one of us than any of us ever deserves, is always seeking communion with every one of His children, that is is always seeking a deeper intimacy of trust and affection with every human being. That again is to say that He is in His Sovereignty and Wisdom seeking to make one family out of this sinful world.[156]

For Cairns, the main problem with his hypothesis was that it seemed "too good to be true," but he believed that such a conception of God was

---

155. Cairns to Lavinia Talbot, May 1920, in *Autobiography*, 187.

156. Cairns to Grierson, 13 August 1943, in *Autobiography*, 209.

fundamental, and that all the Christian doctrines must be judged in light of this. "Anything in 'doctrine' that conflicts with this is **wrong**. That to me is an axiom and a touchstone."[157]

In his last years, Cairns continued to write and publish occasional papers and articles. He also continued to preach occasionally. He maintained an active interest in church and world affairs, and in the League of Nations Union in its search for peace in the world. This union had been founded on 13 October 1918, with the aim of winning public support for the League of Nations, and became one of Britain's most influential peace organizations. At the height of its influence it won the support of eleven million people who signed up to its 1935 Peace Ballot, urging peaceful resolutions to international problems. After this, however, its influence waned as the Second World War approached, although its work was not entirely lost and the organization merged with the United Nations Association of Great Britain after 1945.[158]

Cairns involved himself in another movement that has continued to the present day: he became one of the earliest sponsors of the Iona Community founded by George MacLeod in 1938. Cairns's son, David, had already gone to work with MacLeod in his Govan parish in Glasgow, first as a volunteer and then as assistant minister. During the war, MacLeod had seen at first hand the alienation of the working classes from the churches, and this was reinforced for him in Govan. He was determined to find a way to make the gospel real in the parish situation. His solution was to provide opportunities for student ministers to spend time working and worshipping with craftsmen as together they rebuilt the domestic quarters of the historic Iona Abbey, thereby coming to a better understanding of each other. In George MacLeod, Cairns found a figure with whom he had much in common, despite the more than thirty-year age difference. Both had experienced the weight of family expectation within an ecclesiastical dynasty. Both had been affected profoundly by their experiences in the First World War, and both saw the need for a new approach to the training of ministers, that would provide them with solidarity as they tried to incarnate faith in a world of skepticism and materialism. The fellowship of the men at the front had been of vital importance, but such a sense of fellowship was missing in the churches at home, a fact remarked on by the men themselves and recorded by Cairns in the *Army Report*.[159] Both Cairns and MacLeod were ecumenical in outlook, and had a high theology

---

157. Cairns, *Autobiography*, 209.

158. *League of Nations Union Collected Records, 1915–45, Collection: CDG-B Great Britain*, www.swarthmore.edu/library/peace/CDGB/leagueofnationsunion.htm.

159. Cairns, *Army and Religion*, 205.

of the church, but one that incorporated a social vision, with prayer as the basis for action, and neither recognized a dichotomy between the sacred and the secular. Both saw peacemaking and the search for cooperation as *the* vital issues of the time, and both wanted to see a recovery of the healing ministry of the church. They had found in the scientific discoveries of the day a fillip to their own belief in the unity of the material and the spiritual, expressed in the following way by MacLeod.

> Just when the Church of today has confined itself to the "spiritual" more exclusively than at any time in its history, at that very moment the world of matter has been transformed.
>
> For decades, the Church has gone up the spiritual road, and science had taken over "the world that matters." But now, suddenly in our generation, science gives spiritual significance to matter. Einstein summarises it by declaring, "There is no such thing as dead matter; the ultimate constituents of the atom are light/energy."[160]

Unlike Cairns, MacLeod, perhaps partly due to his privileged background, had the confidence and ability to instigate a practical movement that incorporated the social vision that the church had often spoken of, but neglected, as it busied itself with preparation for reunion in 1929. MacLeod expressed his frustration with the general situation: "I think I shall go mad if the Student Christian Movement produces another book on *Christianity and Communism, Christ or Chaos, Deliverance or Doom*. Everything that can, need, or ever will be said has now been said, a hundred times over, about the superiority of Christianity in theory. We have enough theories to last a generation. The modern world knows quite well what our theory is, what they are interested in is whether we are prepared to show the vaguest signs of putting them into practice."[161]

Although not an organizer himself, Cairns always wanted to know how the things that he believed in might become a practical reality. After reading MacLeod's plans, Cairns agreed to back the project by becoming one of the community's first sponsors,[162] in which role he became a member of the committee of eighteen, who advised on "all the details of polity and practice."[163] Their first meeting, described as the "First Meeting of the Iona

---

160. Ferguson, *Daily Readings*, 67, cites MacLeod in *Mobilisation for Survival*.

161. Ferguson, *George MacLeod*, 140, cites MacLeod, *Speaking the Truth in Love*, 55.

162. Cairns to G. F. MacLeod, 12 and 14 February 1938 in Acc. 9084 MacLeod of Fuinary and Iona Community Papers, Sponsors' File (294), National Library of Scotland.

163. From the founding document of the Iona Community, reprinted in the *Coracle* 36, March 1960, 9.

Experiment" was held at 63 Northumberland Street, Edinburgh on 7 April 1938.[164] Among those in attendance with Cairns were Professor John Baillie, Charles Warr of St. Giles Cathedral, and Dr. John White of Glasgow. Within the Church of Scotland there was much suspicion about the new community, and in an effort to forestall any problems MacLeod had approached some of those who were in sympathy with his aims, but who were "unimpeachable in the eyes of the Church of Scotland establishment."[165] Cairns was one of those who were invited to address conferences of students and ministers on the island of Iona, and in doing so displayed his faith in the youth of the church, and his concern for any who had intellectual difficulties in matters of faith. In return the young people responded positively to him. Baillie attributed this to Cairns's ability to listen and learn from the young. He records that on one of his visits to the Iona in 1943, at the age of eighty-one, one of the younger men commented, "You know, he was the man with the youngest and most flexible mind in the room."[166]

In 1938, Cairns and Alison went on a cruise to Greece and the Holy Land, where in the latter they saw at first hand the plight of the Arabs, and felt the implacable tension between Arabs and Jews. In spite of this, they enjoyed the visit, with Alison recounting to a friend that she had never seen her father enjoy anything so much: "I wish you could have seen him skipping up and down the walls of Jerusalem."[167] Both were moved by the scenes that had long been familiar in their imaginations. On one occasion Cairns stopped the car to spend a long time looking out over the Sea of Galilee before remarking, "It was here he lived and taught for most of his three years." In response Alison wrote, "And I thought of F. [Father] and his long life, 75 years, following and teaching the truths of that life of 2000 years ago, and here at the end of it he had come to the place where it had actually happened, an old man."[168] The trip was of such consequence for Alison that she recorded her own conversion to the Christian faith as a result of it.

World War II

In the year after the Hellenic cruise, the Second World War broke out, and Edinburgh experienced blackout and air raid warnings. By 1942, Alison had become organizer of Food Advice for Southeast Scotland and David was already

164. MacLeod, Sponsors' file (294).
165. Muir, Outside the Safe Place, 25, cites her interview with Rev. George Wilkie.
166. Baillie, in Cairns, Autobiography, 19.
167. Irvine, Alison Cairns, 73.
168. Irvine, Alison Cairns, 74.

a chaplain with the Scots Guards, serving in Aldershot and later in France after its invasion by Germany. Cairns had begun to write autobiographical memoirs, and he was also studying the political ideas of the Federal Union, which had been founded in 1938 and advocated the establishment of a federal Europe after the war. In a letter to Mott in 1941, Cairns wrote about the general feeling in Scotland concerning the war, and his tone suggests that he was in agreement with it, and that he saw the Allies as engaged in a just cause. He wrote just a few days after the capitulation of Greece to the Axis powers, and at a time when Libya was under their control. Winston Churchill was prime minister of Great Britain. "At present all our thoughts turn to Greece and Libya. There is no difference of opinion among us. I have never known the nation so solid or more resolute, nor has any Prime Minister since Gladstone had the same ascendancy. We have a valley of the shadow before us, but please God, we shall come through it."[169]

While it appears that Cairns felt the Allies to be engaged in a justifiable cause, he had already set out his views about war in *The Riddle of the World*.[170] For him, war was not an inevitable part of being human, but the result of sinfulness—pride, deceit, and self-interest—by which humankind strayed from the Divine order. War had the capacity to show people the horrific consequences of choosing to depart from this order, urging them to find a basis for international relations that would lead to peace. As far as 1930s Germany was concerned, Cairns saw what he termed Hitler's "racial mysticism" as a threat to the churches—"a threatened national apostasy from Christian faith."[171] Not everyone in the Church of Scotland believed that the Nazi reorganization of the Protestant Church in Germany threatened its independence. S. J. Brown records that some were in favor of the pro-Nazi Christian movement, for instance David McQueen, minister in Paisley. When, at the general assembly of 1934, the church's Continental Committee expressed its support for the Confessing Church, McQueen suggested instead closer relations with the state-supported German Evangelical Church. The convener of the committee, Professor William Curtis, along with Cairns, reiterated calls for solidarity with the Confessing Church.[172]

In retirement Cairns remained interested in the theological debates of the day, for instance, according to Donald Baillie, he made a habit of attending the Gifford Lectures. When the American theologian Reinhold Niebuhr came to Edinburgh between 1938–40, to give the lectures in New

---

169. Cairns to Mott, 28 April 1941, Mott Papers RG 45, Box 13/245, Yale.

170. Cairns, *Riddle*, 290–94.

171. Cairns, *Riddle*, 365.

172. Brown, "Social Ideal," 22–23.

College, Cairns went to hear him. The two men formed a friendship, which they continued by correspondence, even though, as Donald Baillie wrote, Cairns "hardly agreed with his theology."[173] Baillie does not reveal on which points the men disagreed, but Niebuhr, according to Kenneth Scott Latourette, had adopted the neoorthodoxy of which Barth was the chief spokesman, and which Cairns could never accept.[174] This theology emphasized the sinfulness and depravity of individuals, and the gulf between God and humankind, which could be bridged only through the Word of God in the Bible.[175] While disagreeing with the theology, Cairns was able to understand how it could develop in reaction to the situation in Germany.[176] Niebuhr also had a particular approach to the problem of international relations, and saw as crucial the distinction between individual and collective morality. For him there was a danger in the religious idealism which had declared individual morality the norm for social and political action, and he saw all large-scale social cooperation as requiring some kind of coercion because of the variety of interests of the groups involved.[177] He therefore described social justice as being of a lower order than individual justice, and described the Christian goal of self-giving love as "a moral ideal scarcely possible for the individual and certainly not relevant to the morality of self-regarding nations."[178] Cairns, on the other hand, took the view that although international relations were an "abominable" outlaws market, the life of "the great nations might have been a supremely noble thing instead."[179]

Donald Smith described the attitude of the Church of Scotland when war did eventually break out in 1939. He recorded that the "holy crusading spirit" that had attended the early days of the First World War had gone, and was replaced by "a sober consciousness of the demonic power and mystery of war," and of the fact that it was an evil that was always contrary to the will of God.[180] Feeling that a terrible judgment had come upon it, the church set up in 1940 the Commission for the Interpretation of God's Will in the Present Crisis, which produced a report in each following year of the war, dealing with every aspect of church life, including social and industrial life. Cairns

173. Cairns, *Autobiography*, 35–35.

174. Cairns, *Autobiography*, 121.

175. Latourette, *Advance through Storm*, 26.

176. Cairns, *Riddle*, 364–66.

177. Boerma, "State as Juggler."

178. Macquarrie, *Principles of Christian Theology*, 461, cites Reinhold Niebuhr, *Man's Nature and His Communities*, 42.

179. Cairns, *Reasonableness*, 210.

180. Smith, *Passive Obedience and Prophetic Protest*, 373.

had continued to be busy with church affairs, and was invited to be a member of what came to be known as the Baillie Commission (after its convener the theologian John Baillie).[181] The reports opened the way for a new approach by the church to the social problems of the day. The historian William Storrar recorded that in the late 1930s the Church of Scotland was "dangerously out of tune not only with many social realities within Scottish society but also with some of the grace notes in its own Reformed tradition."[182] S. J. Brown has described the social ideal of the church during the 1930s as one defined by Dr. John White of the Barony, who led a campaign to transform Scotland into a Christian commonwealth, with a conservative social vision based on social programs conducted in the parishes. The project was embodied in the Forward Movement and in Church Extension schemes. The emphasis was on evangelizing: the roots of the social problems of the day being considered to lie in the immoral practices of the people rather than in any failings in the political or economic structures. This outlook combined with racist attitudes to the Irish population in Scotland failed to win the working classes back to the churches.[183] In 1944, with the publication of the Baillie Commission Report, a new direction was taken and endorsed by the general assembly of the Church of Scotland. According to Storrar, it helped shape the postwar church and society by emphasizing the importance of healthy relationships in politics and economics, limits to individual freedoms that threatened community, and justice in the production and distribution of wealth. Its critical social theology was adopted as the official church policy, and its effects were felt into the last two decades of the twentieth century.[184] This social theology was in line with the one that Cairns had advocated for much of his adult life. It emerged through the next generation of younger ministers, all well known to him, such as Archie Craig, George MacLeod, and Joe Oldham, all involved in the ecumenical movement. While it needed their energy to find expression at the level of the general assembly, there is no doubt that there were some in the church who had kept alive the idea of the social dimension of the gospel, creating a foundation for its wider adoption, and Cairns must be numbered among these few who contributed to what

181. The membership of the commission is listed in the appendix of the SCM's 1946 publication of the main findings of the reports of 1942–45 inclusive, *God's Will for Church and Nation*. SCM had made what they described as "a very brief and provisional Report of 1941," but they did not include it in this volume.

182. Storrar, "Liberating the Kirk," in Morton, *God's Will in a Time of Crisis*, 60.

183. Brown, "Social Ideal," 14–31.

184. Storrar, "Liberating the Kirk," 62–63.

Donald Smith described as "the long development and reawakening of social criticism in the Scottish Church."[185]

As far as Cairns's individual contribution to the Baillie Commission is concerned, his personal papers include letters containing ongoing discussions between him and a number of other senior churchmen about the 1945 report on evangelism, and a galley proof of an early draft of the report showing deletions and comments by Cairns on every one of its sixteen pages.[186] Professor W. R. Forrester of St. Andrews, Nevile Davidson (both members of the commission), and Principal Alec Martin, had shared with Cairns concerns about some aspects of the report. In a letter from Cairns to Robert Mackintosh, secretary of the Home Board, it appears that the men were part of a delegation whose remit was to comment on the report, and the letter revealed some of their concerns.[187] The men were anxious to show their admiration for John Baillie, and Cairns began by asserting the value of the report, and the fact that he had learned a lot from it. He also pointed out that he knew from personal experience the difficulty of writing a report, and for this reason had been reluctant to join the delegation. (The fact that he and Baillie knew each other well, having corresponded for years about theology and critiquing each other's books, might have added to his sense of reluctance.) Having taken up the task, however, he had many suggestions to make. Overall he believed that the report was "too depressing," and that its analytic sections were too long in proportion to the rest. It needed to be much shorter, and a summons. The main criticism centered round the discussion of evangelism, in which the report was interpreted by the delegation as disparaging the older form of evangelization as too individualistic and dependent for effect on emotionalism. It seemed to suggest that a new form of social evangelism was necessary to replace the old, if the church was to appeal to postwar society. Having been deeply influenced by Drummond, Cairns pointed out that while some older style evangelization may have been narrow, there were others like Wesley, Moody and Drummond whose theologies had enlivened the social conscience. The delegation was concerned with what appeared to be a sharp antithesis between the idea of personal and social evangelism. For Cairns, the last word belonged to Ritschl with his twin foci: the gift of individual reconciliation with God, and the ethical task of working to bring in the kingdom of God. The personal and social could not be separated.

185. Smith, *Passive Obedience and Prophetic Protest*, 374.

186. MS3384/Box 1/2 (1930–45) Cairns Papers.

187. Cairns to Robert Mackintosh, 10 June 1945, in above.

Nineteen forty-four also brought the death of Cairns's brother William. At the age of eighty-one, Cairns was still going to Iona to give lectures to the student ministers, but in early 1946 he became ill and had an operation for cancer. At the end of June he was confined to bed, and was supported by his son and daughter during the next month. David Smith Cairns died on 27 July 1946. On that day the staff of the Student Christian Movement were meeting in Annandale, their headquarters in Golder's Green, London. When news of Cairns's passing was brought to them, they all stood up immediately and one of the older members led the group in a prayer of thanksgiving for his life.[188] Before the end, he had spoken calmly to Alison and David about his approaching death and funeral service, urging, "Thanksgiving. A long life and good friends. Don't read the passage about the flower fading—we know all about that. Grace, that is to be the note."

Conclusion

A fitting epigraph for this period of Cairns's life might be taken from a letter he wrote to Mott in 1928. After declaring his gratitude for Mott's friendship, he wrote: "I like Benjamin Jowett's saying that a man's final stadium of labors ought to be his best, when he pulls himself together, surveys his experience and what it has taught him, and commits himself to God once more for the fulfilment of his vocation."[189]

Cairns drew together his work of twenty years in *The Faith That Rebels*, exploring the concept of miracle, and questioning the scientific theory of the world as a closed system. Drawing on his reading in the emerging sciences of psychiatry and psychology, and encouraged by the fact that science itself was becoming less dogmatic in its claims, the book provided a stimulus for the discussion of miracles that chimed with the culture of the day, which was already questioning the nature of reality. Central to the book was the idea of the power of faith over the outer and inner worlds. His second book of the period, *The Riddle of the World*, developed ideas that he had worked on throughout his life, and in a more focused way in the nineteen twenties and thirties for the Deems and Baird lectures. The First World War had led him to refocus on the fundamental mystery of the existence of evil, and he tried to articulate a theodicy that would speak to the men and women who, like himself, had suffered doubts about Christian faith. He presented Christianity as the ultimate response to the problem of suffering in the world, and

188. This incident was reported to me in a personal e-mail 4 December 2013, from Rev. Robin Boyd of Edinburgh, who was a member of staff at the time.

189. Cairns to Mott, 7 November 1928, Mott papers, RG 45, 13/44, Yale.

engaged with science and humanism to show the reasonableness of faith. His theology was strongly biblical, but dialogical, engaging sympathetically with the ideas of prominent thinkers of the day who had rejected belief in God. Central to his epistemology was the idea that there are many pathways to reality. Although Cairns later tried to systematize his theology, including an examination of the person and work of Christ and of the Holy Spirit, his apologetics was characterized by his longing for the unity of the church.[190] To this end he presented a distilled theology of the kingdom of God, which he believed all Christians could accept in spite of other fundamental differences: it focused on the Fatherhood of God, the brotherhood of man and the sacredness of the individual.

After much worry about his health in his younger years, Cairns was hale enough to travel extensively in his sixties and seventies, accompanied by Alison, on whom he had become more dependent. There was no expectation on his part that she would perform this role, but as was typical for many well-educated women of her day, a stimulating career was hard to find. It is doubtful if Cairns would have managed to publish his later books without her assistance. David's career path had been assumed from an early age, and he followed his father into the ministry, and after the war, took up the first chair of Practical Theology in the University of Aberdeen. Until his very last years, Cairns was regarded as an elder statesman of the Church of Scotland, playing his part in its reunification and making a contribution to the work of the Baillie Commission. At the same time he continued a variety of wider ecumenical activity through the student movement, and committed himself to work for peace at the international level. Identification with the smaller Cumnor Group had contributed to the development of his thoughts on suffering, death and immortality, and on the ministry of healing. As the group searched for solutions to the religious, moral, and social problems of the day, its practical mysticism located it firmly within the church, and it stressed the need for prayerful fellowship, and emphasized the importance of personal experience of God rather than the passive acceptance of religious beliefs. Similarly, the nascent Iona Community proclaimed a social gospel, with action located in and directed by a life of worship and prayer.

190. Cairns, *System of Christian Doctrine*.

Conclusion

DAVID SMITH CAIRNS WAS one of Scotland's leading theologians, internationally renowned and respected for his apologetics, which for many breathed new life into the Christian religion. Perhaps ironically for this life-long abstainer, his only visible public memorial is outside one of Aberdeen's popular drinking places: now known as the College Bar in Alford Place. On the exterior of the building, which once housed the United Free Church College, there are plaques relating to two of its former academics. One is dedicated to the memory of the Semitic scholar William Robertson Smith, whose path-breaking work in the higher criticism and cultural anthropology had contributed significantly to the air of intellectual freedom enjoyed by Cairns; and the other to Cairns himself, remembered on the council's website as a theologian and pioneer of the ecumenical movement. Ecumenism was certainly a defining characteristic of Cairns, and it was in the ecumenical spirit, combined with a rigorous search for truth, that he made his distinctive contributions in three major areas during the first four decades of the twentieth century: the science-religion debate; the search for a new paradigm for mission; and the response to the events of the First World War.

The Formation of Cairns as a Theologian

An ecumenical disposition was one of several factors that shaped Cairns's perspective as he grew up in the United Presbyterian Church in the Borders. His religious tradition was imbued with a democratic spirit that expressed itself in a strong sense of justice. Abuses in the system of church patronage within the established Church of Scotland had highlighted the existence of class privilege and promoted perceptions of oppression. His denomination's adherence to the voluntary principle was based on the idea that the church must be independent from state control in its spiritual functions. Its idea of religious freedom embraced the importance of individual conscience in religious affiliation, and its idea of social justice extended into the realm of civic society. The ecumenical spirit of the eighteenth-century Relief Church was communicated to the United Presbyterian Church at its formation in 1847, providing the new denomination with a catholicity that allowed it to welcome those who were perceived by others as unorthodox. Indeed, from its beginning, the United Presbyterian Church disavowed intolerance. Added to these qualities were a high regard for scholarship and an energetic missionary spirit. Such were the values that formed the backdrop to Cairns's formation as a theologian and a person. They were enshrined in his family life, and found expression in the example of his father's warm relationship with the established church minister George Gunn; and in his desire to see women's influence extended in the church. Such values were also seen in his mother's commitment to the missionary cause, and in her embracing of the Broad Church divines, who questioned not only the prevailing doctrines of atonement and predestination, but also the social injustices of the day. Generations of his family had played their part in the liberalization of the church, including an easing of adherence to the Westminster Confession of Faith. An independence of mind, based on the concept of spiritual freedom, and grounded in respect for the individual conscience, was the inheritance of Cairns's childhood, and it later allowed him to move away from his father's rigid Calvinism, while maintaining a deep respect for his father's piety. This attitude of respect was a keynote in his apologetics, leading him to adopt a dialectical style, which allowed a fair hearing for the opinions of those with whom he might disagree. Coupled with the rigorous application of scholarship in the search for truth, and a passionate and eloquent style, Cairns's writings had great appeal, especially among the young.

The Science-Religion Debate: Cairns as Apologist

In 1962, the University of Aberdeen celebrated the centenary of the birth of David Smith Cairns, inviting Dr. Archie Craig, then moderator of the general assembly, to deliver a lecture to mark the occasion. Craig described the former principal of Christ's College as "a towering figure in the intellectual and spiritual life of his day, a theologian whose legacy of thought is still a lively force."[1] He admitted that he found it difficult to decide on the chief contribution of Cairns to the life and thought of his day because he had assimilated and appropriated so much of Cairns's thinking himself. However, he went on to describe Cairns's apologetics and the impact of his theology at a time when scientific determinism seemed to rule out the Christian conception of the world as governed by Providence. According to Craig, through his apologetics "David Cairns helped to release a multitude of people, especially young people, from a delusion [scientific determinism] which threatened to enslave their minds."[2]

In Cairns's early years and youth, late nineteenth-century developments in archaeology, psychology, anthropology, comparative religion, history, biblical criticism, and science, particularly as applied to evolutionary theory, had combined to challenge the teleological interpretation of the universe, resulting in widespread skepticism about religion. For many, the higher criticism appeared to undermine belief in divine revelation and the authority of the Bible. The ideas of a beneficent God and a purposive world seemed to contradict the scientific view; and the church had lost many people who could no longer accept its claims. Cairns was aware of the loss that had occurred, particularly in the 1870s and 1880s, when a number of able students, including his close friend Thomas Kirkup, had left the theological halls of the United Presbyterian Church and Free Church, in part because of a narrow vision that was reflected in a series of heresy trials. These trials continued into the beginning of the new century, and the acquittal of the prominent biblical scholar, George Adam Smith, in 1902. Cairns did not escape the intellectual turmoil of these years, and while a student in Edinburgh, he experienced a profound spiritual crisis, when it seemed to him that the very foundations of his Christian faith had collapsed. So powerful was this personal crisis of faith that he dedicated the rest of his life to finding an apologetics that would help others in a similar position.

In the scholarship of American theologian, Newman Smyth, and the Scottish naturalist and evangelist, Henry Drummond, Cairns found Christian thinkers who embraced the zeitgeist and its spirit of inquiry. Their openness to new ideas contrasted starkly with the conservatism of many in the Scottish Presbyterian churches. Smyth called on science and religion to work together to interpret the world, while Drummond embraced both science and the new biblical criticism, and in his preaching tried to offer young people a "reasonable" faith. Under their influence, Cairns worked to develop a new foundation for his faith. Some attempts by early modern thinkers to

1. Craig, foreword to Cairns, *System of Christian Doctrine*, vii.
2. Cairns, *System of Christian Doctrine*, xiv–xvii.

reconcile scientific and religious claims had led to a Deist theology, which recognized God as Creator, but one who chose not to interfere in human affairs. Cairns saw this as having a disempowering and deadening effect on the life of the church, and challenged the assumption that scientific rationalism provided the only intellectually legitimate means of exploring the world, although at the same time, like Drummond, he welcomed the new scientific discoveries as further demonstrations of the glory of God. He believed that the scientific stress on the measurable and demonstrable had permeated the culture, limiting discourse about reality to physical experience. Against the prevailing scientific approach, he asserted belief in the efficacy of the unseen world. For Cairns, the religious sense was the conviction of the reality and power of this unseen world; it was "the immediate consciousness of God." The vital question for him was not whether God exists, but concerned the nature of God. From Jesus' teaching about God as father, Cairns concluded that love was at the heart of all things, and that in that absolute love God had the power and freedom to act on behalf of individuals as humanity struggled against sin and suffering in the world. The idea of such an interventionist God was central to his theology. His self-imposed task was to discover a way to harmonize belief in providential purpose with the scientific concept of nature as an impersonal system of law.

In his first book of apologetics, *Christianity in the Modern World: Studies in the Theology of the Kingdom of God* of 1906, Cairns examined the modern threats to Christian belief: the scientific view of the world as a closed system; the challenges from philosophy, particularly from Kant; and the findings of the higher criticism. For Cairns, these threats were in truth part of God's plan for human development, part of the coming to life of a new and nobler world. For instance, the higher criticism had forced the church to reexamine the life of Jesus, and had brought his life and teaching into focus in a way that had been absent for centuries. Rather than condemning those who expressed religious doubt, Cairns sympathized with their struggle, citing the examples of such "honest doubters" as Thomas Carlyle, Matthew Arnold, and Mary Ann Evans [George Eliot]. Cairns combined a complete confidence in the reality of the unseen world with a belief in progress in this world and a positive engagement with science.

During the next thirty years, as professor of dogmatics and apologetics in the United Free Church College in Aberdeen, he produced three major books: *The Reasonableness of the Christian Faith* (1918), *The Faith That Rebels* (1928), and *The Riddle of the World* (1937). In these works, Cairns continued his dialogue with science; and despite what he perceived as the limitations of the scientific method, he respected the scientist's disinterested love of truth as a form of the love of God. In the early decades of the twentieth century, as science revealed a universe in which matter was composed of energy, and in which strict determinism did not seem to operate at the subatomic level, Cairns found in the new quantum and relativity theories fresh grounds for belief in human and divine freedom.

Finding a New Paradigm for Mission: Edinburgh 1910

Since the middle of the nineteenth century there had been a vibrant mission-centered movement in the British universities. The academic integrity of the movement had included openness to science and to biblical criticism. For Cairns, the student missionary movement was a way to turn the vision for a global Christianity into reality. However, he also became aware of the growing discontent among young people about a missionary movement that emphasized conversion and personal sanctity at the expense of the struggle for social and political justice in Africa, Asia, and South America. Cairns was wrestling with such ideas when he published *Christianity in the Modern World* in 1906. In it he set out a practical program for the churches, stating that their first priority was world evangelization based on the missionary activity that had already spread globally. But he pointed to the need for accompanying this with social change; for developing an environment in line with the ideals of the kingdom of God, and in which there was no economic exploitation of the subjects of mission, thus making it easier to nurture new converts.

Cairns's missionary commitments found expression in his contributions to the World Missionary Conference held in Edinburgh in 1910. For Cairns, the struggle to extend the boundaries of the kingdom was part of the struggle against evil and suffering, so much in his mind because of his wife's illness. If the goal of world evangelism was to be achieved, the churches needed a vital faith in a God who was active in the world. He believed that the theology of the church had become effete. Its vision of God had been contracted, leading to a contraction in missionary vision and expectation. The church needed to recover a living faith expressed in a living theology. Just as he had reacted to scientific theory, philosophy, and biblical criticism, seeing them as part of the divine activity in history and an opportunity for growth in faith, so Cairns approached the challenge of the world religions. For him, a better understanding of the world's living religions might help the church recover some of its own undervalued riches.

In chairing Commission IV of the Conference, Cairns departed from the traditional missionary approach, in which the different world religions were seen as lacking any divine inspiration. Rather, the questions which Cairns devised for Commission IV assumed a fulfillment theology, which sought "points of contact" or similarities among the religions. With his emphasis on providence in history, his rejection of predestination, and his refusal to see the church as synonymous with the kingdom, it was logical that Cairns would recognize the possibility of divine activity among the different world religions. In any case, the fulfillment approach had been gaining ground in Scotland since the middle of the nineteenth century, while Cairns's favorite English theologian, F. D. Maurice, had argued that the living religions of the world showed some great truths and that Christians could learn from them.[3] The responses from the missionaries involved in Commission IV had revealed an attitude of understanding, respect, and empathy for the different world religions. The fulfillment approach adopted at the conference was not original to Cairns, but the acceptance of his report contributed significantly to a new basis for the relationship between Western churches and the other religions, and a distancing of the church from an imperialist, civilizing agenda. Cairns also paved the way forward in practical terms, particularly in regard to training missionaries to operate within the new paradigm of empathy and understanding for the different faith traditions.

The First World War and Its Impact on the Churches

The upheavals of the First World War gave Cairns's apologetics yet another focus and provided an opportunity to reflect on the churches' failure to engage the hearts and minds of a large section of the population, particularly the young men—a subject which had vexed the ecclesiastical establishment for some years. In 1916 the United Free Church gave Cairns leave to work for three years on an ecumenical project funded by the Young Men's Christian Association, which inquired into the effects of the war on the religious life of the nation, and in particular on the fighting men. When the committee to oversee the project was set up, Cairns and Edward S. Talbot, the high Anglican bishop of Winchester, were chosen as co-conveners, but the task of drafting the report was delegated to Cairns. As the driving force of the inquiry, Cairns was convinced that much could be learned that would help the church reflect on its past performance and plan a more effective mission in the postwar world. When the men were questioned, it became clear that the main causes for their disengagement from the churches were their denominational divisions, their failure to

3. Maurice, *Religions of the World*, 3–55.

meet the social and physical needs of working people, and the perceived selfishness and materialism of church members. It was also clear that the men lacked much understanding of Christianity, raising concern about the quality of the religious teaching they had received.

From the publication of his first book, Cairns's apologetics had had a strong social dimension, influenced by the Ritschlian theology with its twin emphases on personal experience and social ethics. Cairns had spoken out against forms of capitalist economics that pursued profit through the exploitation of the poor. The findings of *The Army and Religion* inquiry suggested that the churches' perceived collusion with an unjust economic system was a major factor in keeping people away, and the report concluded that the church had a social mission, which it had been neglecting. It had been complacent about social evils, and now must remedy the situation by taking action to improve the social environment, for example in striving for better working-class housing, and wages, and the provision of leisure facilities for the young. As well as this social witness, *The Army and Religion* report saw the need to engage in the two major tasks of evangelism and education. It seemed that the churches' methods of teaching had been unsuitable, and that its own life had been cold and unattractive. Cairns defined certain points of contact in relation to the men, including their willingness to sacrifice their lives for their fellow soldiers or a certain primal religiosity, which the churches might use in reviving Christian influence and building a better society in the postwar period. The report was unique in attempting to express the theological beliefs of the laity, and especially the working classes. The evidence of the inquiry showed that the men blamed the church for not having done more to prevent the war, and the *Army and Religion* report therefore made an emphatic commitment to the cause of international peace. At the conclusion of the report Cairns returned to the central theme of his theology: the need for a greater vision of God in society, based on a reexamination of Jesus' teachings.

The Army and Religion report of the inquiry was published in 1919. While the general exhaustion of the population and the economic slump sidelined much of its social agenda, its findings revitalized the search for unity, and one achievement came in Scotland in 1929 when the United Free Church and the Church of Scotland reunited. Cairns kept the social witness alive in his last two publications, *The Faith That Rebels* (1928) and *The Riddle of the World* (1937), and in his work with the Student Christian Movement. In doing so, he provided one of the voices that helped the Scottish Presbyterian Church to maintain its social witness until the later 1930s and 1940s, when leaders like John Baillie and George MacLeod found a way to implement more of its vision. He continued to address the themes contained in *The Army and Religion* report. For instance, in response to the idea that the men had rejected an outworn idea of Christianity, Cairns and a group of mainly Anglican clergy published in 1923 a book of sermons intended to make clear some of the teachings of Christianity: *Religion and Life: The Foundations of Personal Religion*. After the war, Cairns also explored theodicy, and this formed a central theme in *The Faith That Rebels*. His own experience with doubt had led to long years of soul-searching and wrestling with Christian beliefs to make them his own. He embraced contemporary challenges in the light of both the teachings of Jesus and contemporary scholarship. His long and genuine intellectual struggle lent an authenticity and originality to his theology, and allowed him to describe the doubts, fears and aspirations of his society with a clarity and compassion that helped many in the churches to respond positively to the challenging environment of the first half of the twentieth century. These words of his lifelong friend John Oman seem particularly apposite in any discussion of Cairns and his work:

> Every age needs the work of the prophet to teach it to discover, in every advance in thought, in every change of the expression of thought, God's presence and man's gain. And not least is he needed in an age when the change of thought has been great and the change of expression greater still, in an age when we call God Environment and the permanence of human worth the Survival of the Fittest. Even with the change of name he might have no quarrel, if only men would understand what is involved, and follow it out to the end with heart and soul.[4]

In a variety of ways, but particularly through his apologetics, in his contribution to the 1910 Missionary Conference, and in his involvement in the *Army and Religion* inquiry and report, Cairns provided such a prophetic voice.

---

4. Oman, *Vision and Authority*, 79.

Backmatter

This biography provides an exploration of the formative influences, development, and impact of the theology of David Smith Cairns, Scottish minister, academic, and writer, during the high point of British imperial expansion, and at a time of social tension caused by industrialization. It describes and evaluates his role in the church's efforts to face major challenges relating to its relationships to the different world religions, its response to the First World War, and its attitude to the scientific disciplines that called into question some of its long-standing perceptions and suppositions. An eminent figure, born into the United Presbyterian Church and rooted in the Church in Scotland, Cairns operated ecumenically and internationally. His apologetics challenged the prevailing assumptions of the day: that science provided the only intellectually legitimate means of exploring the world, and that scientific determinism ruled out the Christian conception of the world as governed by Providence. A major feature of his theology was the presentation of Christianity as a "reasonable" faith, and throughout his life he maintained a particular concern for young people, having endured his own crisis of faith when a student in Edinburgh. He enjoyed a decades-long involvement with the World Student Christian Federation, based on a mutually enriching relationship with one of its leading figures, the renowned American evangelist John Raleigh Mott.

Author Biography

Dr. Marlene Finlayson is a graduate of the University of Edinburgh, member of the Iona Community, Church of Scotland elder, and board member of Interfaith Scotland. She left a career in teaching young children to pursue some of the theological and spiritual questions that have engaged and absorbed her attention over the years. This book is a product of that continuing search that every generation of Christians must make for itself.

Acknowledgments and Thanks

Use of the following archives: University of Aberdeen Historic Collections, Special Libraries and Archives, King's College: Papers of David Smith Cairns, and Oral History Archive.

University of Edinburgh, New College Library Special Collection: Cairns papers and J. H. Oldham papers: and Centre for the Study of World Christianity, papers relating to the World Missionary Conference 1910, including questionnaire responses.

John R. Mott Papers, Yale Divinity School Library.

National Library of Scotland, Cairns Papers and MacLeod of Fuinary and Iona Community papers.

St. John's Library, Cambridge, the papers of Terrot Reavely Glover and of Lyn Newman.

Bodleian Library, the Lily Dougall Papers, Temporary Box 2.

National Records of Scotland, Historical Search Room: Records of the General Assembly Reports on the Schemes of the Church of Scotland, 1914–19.

Archives of St. Colm's College—Original College Archive (OCA Boxes I and III).

Staff at New College library, Edinburgh; Martha Smalley and Joan Duffy, Yale Divinity School library.

I am particularly grateful for the sustained help of staff at the Wolfson Reading Room, University of Aberdeen, to Martin Cameron, Librarian at Highland Theological College, and to Martha Smalley and Joan Duffy in Yale Divinity School Library.

Thanks to the following who shared resources, knowledge, and experience, and gave pointers or encouragement along the way: Rev. Duncan Finlayson; Ms. Moyra McCallum; Rev. Robin Boyd; Ms. June Brown of Stichill; Juline Baird and Rachel Hosker, archives at Hawick Hub; Susan Elliot at Ednam Primary School; Rev. John Fulton, General Secretary of the United Free Church of Scotland; Dr. Rose Drew, University of Glasgow.

Dr. Doug Gay, University of Glasgow, for introducing me to David Smith Cairns.

Lis Macdougall, granddaughter of D. S. Cairns, for her hospitality in Aberdeen.

The Spalding Trust and the Hope Trust for generous financial assistance.

Special thanks to Professor Stewart J. Brown, University of Edinburgh, and to Duncan Finlayson for his support throughout.

Bibliography

Ariarajah, S. Wesley. *Hindus and Christians: A Century of Protestant Ecumenical Thought.* Amsterdam: Rodopi, 1991.

Aulen, Gustaf. *Christus Victor: An Historical Study of the Three Main Types of the Idea of the Atonement.* Translated by A. G. Herbert. Eugene, OR: Wipf and Stock, 2003.

Baillie Commission. *God's Will for Church and Nation.* Report to the General Assembly of the Church of Scotland. London: SCM, 1946.

———. *God's Will in a Time of Crisis: The Baillie Commission in the Church of Scotland.* Edinburgh: CTPI, 1994.

Barclay, William. Review of *Alison Cairns and Her Family*, by Lyn Irvine. *Expository Times* 78 (1967) 288.

Barr, James. *The Scottish Church Question.* London: Nisbet, 1920.

Bebbington, David W. *Evangelicalism in Modern Britain: A History from the 1730s to the 1980s.* London: Unwin Hyman, 1989.

Berger, Peter. *The Social Reality of Religion.* London: Penguin, 1969.

Bevans, Stephen. *John Oman and His Doctrine of God.* Cambridge: Cambridge University Press, 1992.

Black, Aileen. *Gilfillan of Dundee, 1813–1878.* Dundee: Ashgate, 2006.

Black, J. Sutherland, and George Chrystal. *The Life and Letters of William Robertson Smith.* London: Fb&c, 1912.

Booth, Gordon K. "William Robertson Smith." Unpublished thesis, University of Aberdeen, 1999.

Boucher, David, and Andrew Vincent. *British Idealism: A Guide for the Perplexed.* London: Continuum, 2011.

Boyd, Robin. *The Witness of the Student Christian Movement.* London: SPCK, 2007.

Brown, Callum G. *Death of Christian Britain.* London: Routledge, 2001.

———. *Religion and Society in Scotland since 1707.* Edinburgh: Edinburgh University Press, 1997.

Brown, S. J. "Martyr of Khartoum: General Gordon, the Mahdi and Christian Britain." In *Religious Writings and War: Les Discours Religieux et la Guerre*, edited by G. Teulié, 247–71. Montpellier: Université Paul Valéry, 2006.

———. *Providence and Empire: Religion, Politics and Society in the United Kingdom, 1815–1914.* London: Pearson, 2008.

————. "Social Ideal of the Church of Scotland in the 1930s." In Morton, *God's Will in a Time of Crisis*, 14–31.

————. "Solemn Purification by Fire: Responses to the Great War in the Scottish Presbyterian Churches, 1914–19." *Journal of Ecclesiastical History* 45 (1994) 1–23.

Brown, S. J., and George Newlands. *Scottish Christianity in the Modern World: Essays for A. C. Cheyne*. Edinburgh: T. & T. Clark, 2000.

Brown, Stewart J. "Revivals (British Isles)." In *Encyclopedia of the Reformed Faith*, edited by Donald McKim and David F. Wright, 325–27. Edinburgh: Saint Andrew, 1992.

Brown, Thomas. *Annals of the Disruption; With Extracts from the Narratives of Ministers Who Left the Scottish Establishment in 1843*. Edinburgh: Macniven & Wallace, 1893.

Browning, Vivienne. *My Browning Family Album*. London: Springwood, 1979.

Bruce, A. B. *Apologetics; or, Christianity Defensively Stated*. Edinburgh: Scribner, 1895.

Burleigh, J. H. S. *A Church History of Scotland*. London: Oxford University Press, 1960.

Burt, C. "Obituary of Dr. William Brown." *British Journal of Psychology*, statistical section, 5 (1952) 137–38.

Bury, J. P. T. "International Relations, 1900–12." In *The New Cambridge Modern History*, vol. 12, *The Era of Violence 1898–1945*, 300–328. Cambridge: Cadillac, 1960.

Cairns, David. "John Cairns 1818–1892." In *Fathers of the Kirk: Some Leaders of the Church in Scotland from the Reformation to the Reunion*, edited by Ronald Selby Wright, 204–13. London: Wentworth, 1960.

Cairns, David Smith. Address given in Claremont Church, Glasgow, Sunday, 15 October 1922. Printed for private circulation by MacLehose, Jackson Publishers to the University of Glasgow. MS 3384/5, Box 1, D. S. Cairns Papers.

————. *Answer to Bernhardi*. Papers for War Time 12. Oxford: Oxford University Press, 1914.

————. *Army and Religion: An Inquiry and Its Bearing upon the Religious Life of the Nation*. Memphis: Association, 2010.

————. *Autobiography*. London: Student Christian Movement, 1950.

————. *Call of God in the Present Crisis*. New York: International Committee of Young Men's Christian Association, 1917.

————. *Christianity and Macht-Politik*. New York: Doran, 1918. Digitised by Google from an original in the University of Michigan, and read at Hathi Trust Library site at https://catalog.hathitrust.org/Record/000403781.

————. "Christianity and Public Life." In *The Contemporary Review* 79 (1901) 195–211.

————. *Christianity in the Modern World: Studies in the Theology of the Kingdom*. London: Hodder and Stoughton, 1906.

————. *Faith That Rebels: A Re-examination of the Miracles of Jesus*. Based on the Russell Lectures at Auburn Theological Seminary. London: Student Christian Movement, 1928.

————. *God: The Hope of the World*. General Assembly moderatorial address, 1923. Edinburgh: MacNiven & Wallace, 1923.

————. "Instability of Theism: II." *Expository Times* 57 (1945) 66–68. http://journals.sagepub.com/doi/abs/10.1177/001452464505700304.

————. *Life and Times of Alexander Robertson MacEwen*. London: Hodder and Stoughton, 1925.

————, ed. *Missionary Message in Relation to Non-Christian Religions*. Edinburgh: World Missionary Conference, 1910.

———. *Reasonableness of the Christian Faith*. London: Hodder and Stoughton, 1918; Kessinger, 2010.

———. *Riddle of the World*. London: Student Christian Movement, 1937.

———. "Science and Providence." *Contemporary Review* 78 (1900) 358–65.

———. "Some Thoughts on the Atonement. I." *Expository Times* 52 (1940) 16–20. http://ext.sagepub.com Accessed 23.2.2010.

———. *System of Christian Doctrine*. Edinburgh: St. Andrew Press, 1979.

———. "Things Most Certainly Believed." *Expository Times* 46 (1935) 345–48.

———. "Victory in this World." *International Review of Missions* 31 (1942) 145–62.

———. *Vocation of Scotland in View of Her Religious Heritage*. London: SCM, 1911.

Cairns, D. S., and W. R. Inge. *Religion and Life: The Foundations of Personal Religion*. New York: Blackwell, 1923. Digitalized version, LaVergne, TN: Kessinger Rare Reprints, 2010.

Cairns, David H. "Memories of Lochton and Foulden." 1987. Unpublished family memoir, in the keeping of Lis Macdougall, granddaughter of Cairns.

Cairns, John. *Principal Cairns*. Edinburgh, 1903. eBook available at http://www.gutenberg.org/files/11113/11113-h/11113-h.htm. Originally no. 40 in the original Famous Scots series published 1896–1905.

Cameron, Ewen A. *Impaled upon a Thistle: Scotland since 1880*. Edinburgh: Edinburgh University Press, 2010.

Campbell, A. J. *Two Centuries of the Church of Scotland, 1707–1929*. Paisley: Gardner, 1930.

Campbell, Iain D. *Fixing the Indemnity: The Life and Work of George Adam Smith*. Eugene, OR: Wipf and Stock, 2004.

Campbell, Ian. "The Church in Scotland 1840–1940: An Overview." *Quodlibet Journal* 1 (1999) 8.

Campbell, John McLeod. *The Nature of the Atonement*. Cambridge: MacMillan, 1856.

Carlaw, Margaret, and Derek Ogston. *Stichill Parish: Past and Present*. Stichill: Baillieknowe, 2009.

Carswell, Donald. *Brother Scots*. London: Trieste, 1927.

Cheyne, A. C. *Studies in Scottish Church History*. Edinburgh: T. & T. Clark, 1999.

———. *Transforming of the Kirk: Victorian Scotland's Religious Revolution*. Edinburgh: Saint Andrew Press, 1983.

Clements, Keith. *Faith on the Frontier: A Life of J. H. Oldham*. Edinburgh: T. & T. Clark, 1999.

———. *Moot Papers: Faith, Freedom and Society 1938–1944*. London: Bloomsbury, 2010.

Clements, R. E. "The Study of the Old Testament." In *Nineteenth Religious Thought in the West*, edited by Ninian Smart et al., 3:109–41. Cambridge: Cambridge University Press, 1985.

Compton, J. M. "The Education of a Ruling Caste: The Indian Civil Service in the Era of Competitive Examination." *English Historical Review* 83 (1968) 262–84.

Cox, James L. "The Development of A. G. Hogg's Theology in Relation to Non-Christian Faith: Its Significance for the Tambaram Meeting of the International Missionary Council, 1938." Unpublished PhD thesis, University of Aberdeen, 1977.

Cracknell, Kenneth. *Justice, Courtesy and Love: Theologians and Missionaries Encountering World Religions 1846–1914*. London: Epworth, 1995.

Cusack, Carole M. *Invented Religions, Imagination, Fiction and Faith*. Farnham: Ashgate, 2010.

Darlow, T. H. *William Robertson Nicoll: Life and Letters*. London: Hodder and Stoughton, 1925.

D'Costa, Gavin. *Christianity and World Religions: Disputed Questions in the Theology of Religions*. Oxford: Oxford University Press, 2009.

Dean, Joanna. *Religious Experience and the New Woman: The Life of Lily Dougall*. Bloomington: Indiana University Press, 2007.

Denney, James. *The Christian Doctrine of Reconciliation*. London: Hodder and Stoughton, 1918.

Directory of Protestant Missionaries in China, Japan and Corea [sic]: *For the Year 1904*. Printed and published at the Daily Press Office, Hong Kong, 1904. http://images. library.yale.edu/divinitycontent/china/DirectoryofProtestantMissionaries1904. pdf.

Dodd, Charles H. *The Parables of the Kingdom*. New York: Eerdmans, 1938.

Donnelly, Jason. "Johann Wilhelm Herrmann 1846–1922." Edited by Derek Michaud. 2000. Available at the *Boston Collaborative Encyclopedia of Western Theology*, edited by Wesley Wildman. http://people.bu.edu/wwildman/bce/herrmann.htm.

Dorrien, Gary. *The Making of American Liberal Theology 1805–1900: Imagining Progressive Religion*. Louisville: Westminster John Knox, 2001.

Dougall, Lily. *God's Way with Man: An Exploration of the Method of the Divine Working Suggested by the Facts of History and Science*. London: Macmillan, 1924.

Dougall, Lily, and Burnett Hillman Streeter. *God and the Struggle for Existence*. New York: BiblioBazaar, 2009.

Drummond, A. L., and J. Bulloch. *Church in Late Victorian Scotland, 1874–1900*. Edinburgh: Saint Andrew Press, 1978.

———. *Church in Victorian Scotland, 1843–1874*. Edinburgh: Saint Andrew Press, 1975.

———. *Scottish Church, 1688–1843*. Edinburgh: Saint Andrew Press, 1973.

Drummond, Henry. *Ascent of Man*. London: Hodder and Stoughton, 1904.

———. *Greatest Thing in the World*. London: Barbour, 1880.

———. *Natural Law in the Spiritual World*. London: Hodder and Stoughton, 1883.

Dundee Courier. "If You Want to Impress the Hun—Hit Him." Editorial, 29 May 1917.

———. "U. F. Church and War Reprisals." Editorial, 28 May 1917.

Dunn, Douglas. *Robert Browning*. Oxford: Oxford University Press, 2003.

Dunstan, Vivienne S. "Stichill and Hume." Genuki, at http://www.genuki.org.uk/big/ sct/ROX/Stichill/.

Eddy, Mary Baker. *Christian Healing and the People's Idea of God*. Boston: Stewart, 1908.

———. *Science and Health with Key to the Scriptures*. Boston: Applewood, 1875.

Eddy, Sherwood. "Life in a Base Camp." Chapter 5 in *With Our Soldiers in France*. New York: Association, 1917. Available at http://net.lib.byu.edu/estu/wwi/memoir/ Eddy/Eddy2.htm#ch5.

Eerikainen, Atso. "Time and Polarity: The Dimensional Thinking of Karl Heim." Unpublished thesis, University of Helsinki, 2000.

Erskine, Thomas. *The Brazen Serpent*. 1831.

Ferguson, Ron. *Daily Readings with George MacLeod*. Glasgow: Wild Goose, 1991.

———. *George MacLeod: Founder of the Iona Community*. London: Collins, 1990.

Fergusson, D., ed. *Christ, Church and Society: Essays on John Baillie and Donald Baillie.* Edinburgh: Bloomsbury Academic, 1993.

———. *Faith and Its Critics.* Oxford: Oxford University Press, 2009.

Finlayson, Duncan. "Aspects of the Life and Influence of Thomas Erskine of Linlathen 1788–1870." In *Scottish Church History Society Records,* edited by James Kirk, 31–45. Vol. 20, pt. 1. Edinburgh: Scottish Church History Society, 1978.

Fleming, J. R. *The History of the Church in Scotland.* Vol. 1, *1843–1874.* Edinburgh: T. & T. Clark, 1933.

———. *The History of the Church in Scotland.* Vol. 2, *1875–1929.* Edinburgh: T. & T. Clark, 1933.

Flint, Robert. *Christ's Kingdom upon Earth.* Edinburgh: Blackwood, 1865. Accessed at https://archive.org/details/christskingdomupooflin.

———. *Theism.* Baird Lectures, 1876. Edinburgh: T. & T. Clark, 1877.

Forrester, Duncan B. "Baillie, Donald Macpherson (1887–1954)." In *Oxford Dictionary of National Biography,* edited by Brian Harrison. Oxford: Oxford University Press, 2004. http://www.oxforddnb.com/view/article/41014.

Fotheringham, James. *Studies in the Mind and Art of Robert Browning.* Cornell: Hansebooks, 1898. Accessed as eBook at http://www.onread.com/reader/357774.

Fraser, W. Hamish, and Clive H. Lee, eds. *Aberdeen 1800–2000: A New History.* East Linton: Tuckwell, 2000.

Freud, Sigmund. *New Introductory Lectures on Psycho-analysis.* Vienna: Norton, 1933.

Gairdner, W. H. T. *Edinburgh 1910: Account and Interpretation of the World Missionary Conference.* Edinburgh: Oliphant, Anderson, and Ferrier, 1910. Available at https://archive.org/details/edinburgh1910ana00gairuoft/page/n7.

Galbraith, Douglas. "Annie Hunter Small." Paper delivered to the Edinburgh Ecumenical Group, November 11, 2010.

Gammie, Alexander. *The Aberdeen Young Men's Christian Association: Its Origin and History; A Jubilee Retrospect.* Printed at the Aberdeen Daily Journal Office, 1908. Available at the Aberdeen YMCA website, http://www.aberdeenymca.org.uk/jubileeretrospect-first5oyears.pdf.

General Assembly of the United Free Church. "Report on Church Life and Social Problems." *Proceedings and Debates of the General Assembly of the United Free Church, May 1927.* Edinburgh: Edinburgh University Press, 1927.

Gill, S. D. *Dictionary of Scottish Church History and Theology.* Edinburgh: InterVarsity, 1993.

Gladden, Washington. *How Much Is Left of the Old Doctrines?* London: Houghton Mifflin, 1899.

Gowing, Peter G. "The Ecumenical Dreams and Deeds of Newman Smyth." Pdf available at www.biblicalstudies.org.uk/pdf/ijt/13-3_081.pdf.

Grant, Frederick C. *The Gospel of the Kingdom.* New York: Macmillan, 1940.

Hall, D. G. E. "The Western Question in Asia and North Africa, 1900–45: South-East Asia and the Far East." In *The New Cambridge Modern History: The Era of Violence 1898–1945,* edited by David Thomson, 12:219–35. Cambridge: Cambridge University Press, 1960.

Hamilton, Ian. *The Erosion of Calvinist Orthodoxy: Seceders and Subscription in Scottish Presbyterianism.* Edinburgh: Rutherford, 1990.

Hanna, William, ed. *The Letters of Thomas Erskine of Linlathen.* Edinburgh: Douglas, 1877.

Harkness, Georgia. *Understanding the Kingdom of God*. Nashville: Abingdon, 2005.

Harrison, Frederic. *The Choice of Books*. New York: Macmillan, 1886. Accessed at http://www.archive.org/details/choicebooks01harrgoog.

Hedges, Paul. *Preparation and Fulfilment: A History and Study of Fulfilment Theology in Modern British Thought in the Indian Context*. Bern: Lang, 2001.

Heim, Karl. *The New Divine Order*. Translated by E. P. Dickie. London: Student Christian Movement, 1930.

Henderson, G. D. *The Scots Confession, 1560 (Confessio Scoticana) and Negative Confession, 1591 (Confessio Negativa) with Introduction*. Edinburgh: Saint Andrew Press, 1937.

Henderson, Henry F. *The Religious Controversies of Scotland*. Edinburgh: T. & T. Clark, 1905.

Higham, Florence. *Frederick Denison Maurice*. London: Macmillan, 1947.

Hocking, W. E. *Re-thinking Missions*. New York: Biblio Bazaar, 1932.

Hogg, Alfred George. *Christ's Message of the Kingdom*. Edinburgh: T. & T. Clark, 1912.

———. *Karma and Redemption: An Essay toward the Interpretation of Hinduism and the Re-statement of Christianity*. Edinburgh: Christian Literature Society, 1909.

———. *Redemption from This World or the Supernatural in Christianity*. Edinburgh: Fb&c, 1922.

Holmes, Richard. *The Western Front*. London: Ebury, 1999.

Hopkins, C. Howard. *John R. Mott: A Biography*. Grand Rapids: Eerdmans, 1979.

Howson, Peter. *Muddling Through: The Organisation of British Army Chaplaincy in World War I*. Solihull: Helion, 2013.

Irvine, Lyn. *Alison Cairns and Her Family*. Edinburgh: SCM, 1967.

Ives, Keith A. *Voice of Nonconformity: William Robertson Nicoll and the British Weekly*. Cambridge: Lutterworth, 2011.

James, William. *The Varieties of Religious Experience*. London: Longmans, Green, 1935.

Jones, Henry. *Browning as a Philosophical and Religious Teacher*. Glasgow: Macmillan, 1892. Paperback edition accessed at www.simonandschuster.co.uk/books/Browning-as-a-Philosophical-and-Religious-Teacher/Henry-Jones/9781627936293/browse_inside.

———. "Robert Browning and Elizabeth Barrett Browning." In *The Cambridge History of English and American Literature*, edited by Ward & Trent et al, vol. 13, ch. 3. New York: Putnam, 1907–21; Bartleby.com, 2000.

Karkkainen, Veli-Matti. *An Introduction to the Theology of Religions*. Downers Grove: InterVarsity, 2003.

Kellogg, Edwin Henry. Review of *The Riddle of the World*, by D. S. Cairns. *Journal of American Academy of Religion* 6 (1938) 147–48. Accessed at https://academic.oup.com/jaar/article-abstract/VI/III/147/695475?redirectedFrom=fulltext.

Kirkup, Thomas. *An Inquiry into Socialism*. London: Longmans, Green, 1907. 3rd ed. available at openlibrary.org/books/OL6994614M/An_inquiry_into_socialism.

Klein, Franz. "Supernaturalism and Historical Study: An Account of the Resurrection of Jesus Christ from the Dead." *Quodlibet Journal* 7 (2005) 1–11.

Kraemer, Hendrik. *The Christian Message in a Non-Christian World*. London: Centre for Contemporary Christianity, 1938.

Kranz, P. "Chinese Martyrs." Shanghai Missionary Association meeting 1903. Accessed at dspace.library.cornell.edu/bitstream/1813/29869/1/z188_05_0759.pdf.

Landels, Thomas Durley. *William Landels: A Memoir*. London: Fb&c, 1900. Digitalized version available from the Roberts Library, University of Toronto, http://www. archive.org/details/williamlandelsoolanduoft.

Landels, William. *The Gospel in Various Aspects: A Book for the Anxious*. London: Nisbet, 1856. Read in digitalized version published by Kessinger Legacy Reprints, 2009. Catalogue available at www.kessinger.net.

Latourette, Kenneth Scott. *Advance through Storm, A.D. 1914 and After*. Vol. 7 of *A History of the Expansion of Christianity*. London: Eyre and Spottiswoode, 1945.

League of Nations Union Collected Records, 1915–45. Collection: CDG-B Great Britain. https://www.swarthmore.edu/library/peace/CDGB/leagueofnationsunion.htm.

Leckie, J. H. *Secession Memories: The United Presbyterian Church Contribution to the Scottish Church*. Edinburgh: T. & T. Clark, 1926.

———. *World to Come and Final Destiny*. Edinburgh: Biblio Bazaar, 1922.

Lee, James W., and Robert E. Bain. *Photographic Views of Bible Lands*. New York: Greshem, 1894.

Lewis, Samuel. *A Topographical Dictionary of Scotland*. 1846. Accessed at http://www. british-history.ac.uk/topographical-dict/scotland/489-500.

Lutz, Jessie G. "Chinese Nationalism and the Anti-Christian Campaigns of the 1920s." *Modern Asian Studies* 10 (1976_ 395–416. http://www.jstor.org/stable/311913.

Macdonald, Lesley Orr. *A Unique and Glorious Mission: Women and Presbyterianism in Scotland, 1830–1930*. Edinburgh: Donald, 2000.

MacEwen, A. R. *The Life and Letters of John Cairns*. London: Hodder and Stoughton, 1898.

Mackelvie, W. *Annals and Statistics of the United Presbyterian Church*. Edinburgh: Fb&c, 1873.

Mackenzie, R. *John Brown of Haddington*. London: Fb&c, 1918. References are to the 1st paperback ed., 1964.

Mackintosh, Hugh Ross. *Immortality and the Future: The Christian Doctrine of Eternal Life*. London: Hodder and Stoughton, 1915.

———. *Types of Modern Theology*. 2nd ed. London: Scribner, 1937.

Maclean, N., and , J. R. P. Sclater. *God and the Soldier*. London: BiblioBazaar, 1917.

Macleod, Donald. *Memoir of Norman McLeod*. Vols. 1 and 2. London: Virtue, 1876.

MacLeod, James Lachlan. "'The Mighty Hand of God': The Free Presbyterian Church of Scotland and the Great War." *Bridges* 12 (2007) 19–41. http://www.puritans.net/ news/FPCSinWW1.pdf.

Macquarrie, John. *Jesus Christ in Modern Thought*. London: SCM, 1993.

———. *Principles of Christian Theology*. London: SCM, 1966.

Maurice, Frederick Denison. *Religions of the World and Their Relations to Christianity*. London, 1847. Accessed at https://archive.org/details/thereligionsofthoomauruoft.

———. *Theological Essays*. Boston: Gould and Lincoln, 1854.

Mayfield Salisbury Parish Church, Edinburgh. "Revd. Dr. John Ross." http://www. mayfieldsalisbury.org/index.php/extensions-7/revd-dr-john-ross.

McGrath, Alister E. *A Life of John Calvin: A Study in the Shaping of Western Culture*. Oxford: Wiley, 1990.

McKay, Johnston R. "The Kingdom of God and the Presbyterian Churches: Social Theology and Action c. 1880–c. 1914." Unpublished PhD thesis, University of Edinburgh, 2007.

M'Kerrow, J. *History of the Secession Church*. Edinburgh: Fullarton, 1848.

McKimmon, Eric George. "John Oman, Orkney's Theologian: A Contextual Study of John Oman's Theology with Reference to Personal Freedom as the Unifying Principle." Unpublished thesis, University of Edinburgh, 2012.

Miles, Sara Joan. "Charles Darwin and Asa Gray Discuss Teleology and Design." *Perspectives on Science and Christian Faith* 53 (2001) 196–201.

Mill, John Stuart. *Principles of Political Economy and Some of the Applications to Social Philosophy.* London: Appleton, 1848.

Miller, Lydia. *Passages in the Life of an English Heiress; or, Recollections of Disruption Times in Scotland.* London: Simpkin, Marshall, 1847.

Milroy, Adam. "The Doctrine of the Church of Scotland." In *The Church of Scotland, Past and Present: Its History, Its Relation to the Law and the State, Its Doctrine, Ritual, Discipline, and Patrimony,* edited by Robert Herbert Story, 131–302. London, 1890.

Morgan, Herbert, ed. *Christ and Human Need.* Addresses delivered at a conference on international and missionary questions, Glasgow, 1921. London: Student Christian Movement, 1921.

Morison, James. *The Extent of the Propitiation.* London: Paternoster Row, 1842. Google eBook version accessed at https://books.google.sn/books?id=eEe6xGtxv JAC&printsec.

Morton, Andrew, ed. *God's Will in a Time of Crisis: A Colloquium Celebrating the 50th Anniversary of the Baillie Commission.* Edinburgh: University of Edinburgh, 1994.

Mott, John R. *The Decisive Hour of Christian Missions.* London: Young People's Missionary Movement, 1910.

Muir, Anne. *Outside the Safe Place: An Oral History of the Early Years of the Iona Community.* Glasgow: Wild Goose, 2011.

Muir, Pearson McAdam. *The Church of Scotland: A Sketch of Its History.* 2nd ed. Edinburgh: Black, 1900.

Needham, N. R. "David Smith Cairns." In *A Dictionary of Scottish Church History and Theology,* edited by N. Cameron, 117. Edinburgh: T. & T. Clark, 1993.

Nicoll, William Robertson. "Henry Drummond: A Memorial Sketch." Preface to Drummond's posthumous volume, *The Ideal Life.* London, 1897.

Niebuhr, Reinhold. *Moral Man and Immoral Society.* New York: Scribner, 1932.

———. *The Nature and Destiny of Man.* From Niebuhr's Gifford Lectures, Edinburgh, 1941–43. 2 vols. New York: Scribner, 1943.

Niven, T. B. W. *The Church from the Revolution to the Present Time.* Vol. 4 in *The Church of Scotland Past and Present.* 5 vols. Edited by Robert Herbert Story. London: Paternoster Row, 1890.

Oldham, Joseph Houldsworth. *Christianity and the Race Problem.* London: Fb&c, 1924.

———. *Devotional Diary.* London: Association, 1926.

———. *Real Life Is Meeting.* London: Association, 1942.

———. *World and the Gospel.* London: Association, 1916.

Oldham, Joseph Houldsworth, and W. A. Visser 't Hooft. *The Church and Its Function in Society.* London: Allen and Unwin, 1937.

Oman, John. *Vision and Authority.* London: Fb&c, 1902. References are to the 2nd ed., 1928.

O'Neill, J. C. "The Study of the New Testament." In *Nineteenth-Century Religious Thought in the West,* edited by Ninian Smart et al., 3:143–78. Cambridge: Cambridge University Press, 1985.

Oppenheim, Janet. *The Other World: Spiritualism and Psychical Research in England, 1850–1914.* Cambridge: Cambridge University Press, 1985.

Orr, James. *Ritschlianism: Expository and Critical Essays.* London: Hodder and Stoughton, 1903.

Philip, T. V. *Edinburgh to Salvador: 20th Century Ecumenical Missiology.* Delhi: ISPCK, 1999.

Philp, Robert Kemp. *Index Scholasticus: Sons and Daughters; A Guide to Parents in the Choice of Educational Institutions, Preparatory to Professional or Other Occupation of Their Children.* London, 1872 Downloaded from http://www.archive.org/stream/cu31924101205643.

Popkin, Richard H., ed. *David Hume: Dialogues concerning Natural Religion.* 2nd ed., with "Of the Immortality of the Soul," "Of Suicide," and "Of Miracles." Indianapolis: Hackett, 1998.

Ramachandra, Vinoth. "The Missionary Message in Relation to the Non-Christian Religions: The Edinburgh 1910 Commission IV Report and Beyond." Paper prepared for the centenary celebration of the 1910 conference.

Rankin, James. *A Handbook of the Church of Scotland.* Edinburgh: Blackwood, 1888.

Rauschenbusch, Walter. *Christianity and the Social Order.* New York: SCM, 1912.

———. *Theology for the Social Gospel.* New York: Macmillan, 1917.

Raven, Charles E. "An Impression of the Conference." In *Christ and Human Need: Being Addresses Delivered at a Conference on International and Missionary Questions, Glasgow, 4–9 January 1921.* London: Fb&c, 1921.

———. *Jesus and the Gospel of Love.* London: Hodder and Stoughton, 1931.

Reardon, Bernard M. G. *From Coleridge to Gore: A Century of Religious Thought in Britain.* London: Longman, 1971.

Reith, George M., ed. "Overture anent Spiritual Healing." *Proceedings and Debates of the General Assembly of the United Free Church, May 1924.* Edinburgh: Harper, 1924.

Representatives of the Church of England, the Church of Scotland, the Episcopal Church in Scotland, the Presbyterian Church of England. "Relations Between Anglican and Presbyterian Churches, Being a Joint Report." Edinburgh: Saint Andrew, 1957.

Reznick, Jeffrey S. *Healing the Nation: Soldiers and the Culture of Caregiving in Britain during the Great War.* Manchester: Manchester University Press, 2004.

Riesen, Richard A. *Criticism and Faith in Late Victorian Scotland: A. B. Davidson, William Robertson Smith and George Adam Smith.* Lanham, MD: University Press of America, 1985.

Ritschl, Albrecht. *The Christian Doctrine of Justification and Reconciliation.* Translated by H. R. Mackintosh and A. B. Macaulay. 2nd ed. Edinburgh: T. & T. Clark, 1902. Accessed at https://archive.org/details/christiandoctriooedgoog/page/n8.

Robbins, Keith. *England, Ireland, Scotland, and Wales: The Christian Church 1900–2000.* Oxford: Oxford University Press, 2008.

Robertson, J. A. "Tribute to Cairns." *Aberdeen University Review* 25 (1937–38) 70–72.

Ross, Kenneth R. "Edinburgh 1910: Scottish Roots and Contemporary Challenges." *Theology in Scotland* 17 (2010) 5–21.

Rowdon, "Edinburgh 1910, Evangelicals and the Ecumenical Movement." *Vox Evangelica* 5 (1967) 49–71.

Schweitzer, Albert. *Mystery of the Kingdom of God: The Secret of Jesus' Messiahship and Passion.* Translated by Walter Lowrie. New York: Dodd, Mead, 1950.

———. *Quest of the Historical Jesus*. London: Black, 1910.

Scottish Church and University Almanac 1917. Edinburgh: Edinburgh University Press, 1917.

Sefton, Henry. "Christ's College." *Divinity Alumni Association University of Aberdeen Newsletter* 22 (Winter 2000/2001).

Senatus. "Tribute." *Aberdeen University Review* 25 (1937–38) 70–72.

Sharpe, Eric J. *Not to Destroy but to Fulfil: The Contribution of J. N. Farquhar to Protestant Missionary Thought in India before 1914*. Lund: Gleerup, 1965.

Sharpe, Eric J. *Faith Meets Faith: Some Christian Attitudes to Hinduism in the 19th and 20th Centuries*. London: SCM, 1977.

———. *Theology of A. G. Hogg*. Madras: Christian Institute for the Study of Religion and Society, 1971.

Simpson, W. Douglas. *The Fusion of 1860: A Record of the Centenary Celebrations and a History of the University of Aberdeen, 1860–1960*. Edinburgh: University of Edinburgh Press, 1963.

Small, Annie H. *Buddhism*. New ed. Delhi: Dent, 1997.

———. *Islam*. London: Dent, 1905.

———. *Missionary College Hymns*. Edinburgh: Funk and Wagnalls, 1912.

———. *Yeshudas: A Bond Servant of Jesus*. Edinburgh: Macniven and Wallace, 1907.

Small, Robert. *History of the Congregations of the United Presbyterian Church from 1733 to 1900*. 2 vols. Edinburgh: Riverside, 1904.

Smith, D. C. *Passive Obedience and Prophetic Protest: Social Criticism in the Scottish Church, 1830–1945*. New York: T. & T. Clark, 1987.

Smith, George Adam. *Life of Henry Drummond*. London: McClure, Phillips, 1899.

Smout, T. C. *A Century of the Scottish People*. London: Collins, 1986.

Smyth, Newman. *Old Faiths in a New Light*. New York: Scribner, 1879.

———. *Religious Feeling*. London: Ward, Lock, 1877.

———. *Through Science to Faith*. London: Scribner, 1902.

Snape, Michael, ed. *Back Parts of War: The Y.M.C.A. Memoirs and Letters of Barclay Baron, 1915–19*. Woodbridge: Boydell, 2009.

———. *God and the British Soldier: Religion and the British Army in the First and Second World Wars*. London: Routledge, 2005.

Somervell, D. C. *A Short History of Our Religion*. London: Macmillan, 1922.

Stahlin, Leonhard. *Kant, Lotze, and Ritschl: A Critical Examination*. Translated by D. W. Simon. Edinburgh: T. & T. Clark, 1889. Accessed at https://archive.org/details/kantlotzeandritsoostahuoft.

Stalker, James. "The Preacher as Patriot." Lecture 3 of *The Preacher and His Models*. Yale Lectures on Preaching, April 25, 1891. http://articles.ochristian.com/article18001.shtml.

Stanley, Brian. *The Bible and the Flag: Protestant Missions and British Imperialism in the Nineteenth and Twentieth Centuries*. Leicester: Apollos, 1990.

———. "Discerning the Future of World Christianity: Vision and Blindness at the World Missionary Conference, Edinburgh 1910." Seminar paper delivered in New College, under the auspices of the Religion and Society Edinburgh Network, November 2010.

———. *World Missionary Conference: Edinburgh 1910*. Grand Rapids: Eerdmans, 2009.

Statistical Account of Scotland, Stichell and Hume, County of Roxburgh (1791–99). Vol. 3, 290, accessed at www.bordersfhs.org.uk/stitchill.asp.

Stewart, A. Morris. *The Origins of the United Free Church: A Sketch of Scottish Presbytery.* Edinburgh: Oliphant, Anderson and Ferrier, 1901.

Stewart, Marjorie. *Training in Mission, St. Colm's College.* Edinburgh: Richardson, 1972.

Story, Robert Herbert, ed. *The Church of Scotland, Past and Present: Its History, Its Relation to the Law and the State, Its Doctrine, Ritual, Discipline, and Patrimony.* 5 vols. London: Clark, 1890.

Stubbs, Charles W. *Christ of English Poetry.* London: Dent, 1906.

———. Review of *The Poetry of Robert Browning,* by Stopford A. Brooke. Hibbert Journal 1 (1902–3) 363–73.

Sutherland, Elizabeth. *Lydia, Wife of Hugh Miller of Cromarty.* East Linton: Tuckwell, 2002.

Tatlow, Tissington. *The Story of the Student Christian Movement of Great Britain and Ireland.* London: SCM, 1933.

Taylor, Charles. *A Secular Age.* Cambridge: Harvard University Press, 2007.

Templeton, Elizabeth. *God's February: A Life of Archie Craig, 1888–1985.* London: BCCI, 1991.

Thacker, Justin, and Susannah Clark. "A Historical and Theological Exploration of the 1910 Disaffiliation of the Cambridge Inter-Collegiate Christian Union from the Student Christian Movement." Downloaded from http://www.eauk.org/efb/downloads.cfm.

Thomson, Andrew. *The United Presbyterian Fathers.* Part 1, *A Historical Sketch of the Origin of the Secession Church.* Edinburgh: Fullerton, 1848.

Thomson, J. A. *The System of Animate Nature.* Gifford Lectures, University of St. Andrews, 1915–16. New York: Holt, 1920. Accessed at https://www.giffordlectures.org/lectures/system-animate-nature.

Truffer, Beat P. *The History of the Matterhorn: First Ascents, Projects and Adventures.* Translated by Mirjam Steinmann. Zermatt, Switzerland: Aroleit-Verlag 2001.

Turner, Paul, ed. *Browning Men and Women.* Oxford: Routledge, 1972.

United Presbyterian Church. Record of the Presbyterial proceedings at Berwick, January 19, 1864. *United Presbyterian Magazine,* n.s., 7 (1864?) 82–84. Digitized version downloaded from http://books.google.co.uk/books?id.

"The University of Glasgow Story." http://www.universitystory.gla.ac.uk/ww1-background.

Van Lin, Jan. *Shaking the Fundamentals: Religious Plurality and the Ecumenical Movement.* Amsterdam: Rodopi, 2002.

Vidler, Alec R. *Church in an Age of Revolution.* New ed. London: Penguin, 1971.

———. *Theology of F. D. Maurice.* London: Penguin, 1948.

Wallace, William. *Kant.* Edinburgh: Saint Andrew, 1882.

Ward, Adolphus William, et al. *The Cambridge History of English and American Literature: An Encyclopedia in Eighteen Volumes.* New York: Putnam, 1907–1921; Bartleby.com, 2000. www.bartleby.com/cambridge/.

Watt, Hugh. "Ebenezer Erskine, 1680–1754." In *Fathers of the Kirk: Some Leaders of the Church in Scotland from the Reformation to the Reunion.* Edited by R. S. Wright. London: Oxford University Press, 1960.

Weiss, Johannes. *Proclamation of the Kingdom of God.* Edited and translated by R. H. Hiers and D. L. Holland. Minneapolis: Scholars, 1971.

Western Daily Press. "The Beginning of Reprisals." Editorial. 27 December 1917.

Whitelaw, Thomas. "The Church's Home Work in the Training and Maintenance of a Gospel Ministry." In *Memorial of the Jubilee Synod of the United Presbyterian Church*. Edinburgh: Publications Office, College Buildings, 1897.

Williams, Ioan M. *Robert Browning*. London: Arco, 1967.

Wilson, Fred. "John Stuart Mill (1806–73)." In *Stanford Encyclopedia of Philosophy*, edited by Edward N. Zalta. Spring 2009 ed. Accessed at https://stanford.library.sydney.edu.au/archives/spr2009/entries/mill.

Withrow, W. H. *Religious Progress in the Century*. Nineteenth Century Series. London: Athenaem, 1902.

Yates, Timothy. "A Case of Thorough Preparation: David Smith Cairns, Commission IV and the Missionaries' Returns, 2007." http://www.edinburgh2010.org/ko/resources/related-studies.html.

———. *Christian Mission in the 20th Century*. Cambridge: Cambridge University Press, 1996.

Young, G. M. *Victorian England: Portrait of an Age*. London: Oxford University Press, 1936.

www.ingramcontent.com/pod-product-compliance
Lightning Source LLC
Chambersburg PA
CBHW060331100426
42812CB00003B/954